Affirmative Counseling and Psychological Practice With Transgender and Gender Nonconforming Clients

Perspectives on Sexual Orientation and Diversity
Maria Lucia Miville, Series Editor

Affirmative Counseling and Psychological Practice With Transgender and Gender Nonconforming Clients

Edited by
Anneliese A. Singh and lore m. dickey

American Psychological Association • Washington, DC

Published by
American Psychological Association
750 First Street, NE
Washington, DC 20002
www.apa.org

To order
APA Order Department
P.O. Box 92984
Washington, DC 20090-2984
Tel: (800) 374-2721; Direct: (202) 336-5510
Fax: (202) 336-5502; TDD/TTY: (202) 336-6123
Online: www.apa.org/pubs/books
E-mail: order@apa.org

In the U.K., Europe, Africa, and the Middle East, copies may be ordered from
American Psychological Association
3 Henrietta Street
Covent Garden, London
WC2E 8LU England

Typeset in Meridien by Circle Graphics, Inc., Columbia, MD

Printer: United Book Press, Baltimore, MD
Cover Designer: Mercury Publishing Services, Rockville, MD

Library of Congress Cataloging-in-Publication Data

Names: Singh, Anneliese A., editor. | dickey, lore m., 1961- editor.
Title: Affirmative counseling and psychological practice with transgender and
  gender nonconforming clients / edited by Anneliese A. Singh and lore m. dickey.
Description: Washington, DC : American Psychological Association, [2017] |
  Series: Contemporary perspectives on lesbian, gay, bisexual, and
  transgender psychology | Includes bibliographical references and index.
Identifiers: LCCN 2016005076 | ISBN 9781433823008 | ISBN 1433823004
Subjects: LCSH: Transgender people—Mental health. | Transgender
  people—Counseling of. | Psychiatry, Transcultural. | Cross-cultural counseling.
Classification: LCC RC451.4.G39 A335 2017 | DDC 616.890086/7—dc23 LC record available at
http://lccn.loc.gov/2016005076

British Library Cataloguing-in-Publication Data
A CIP record is available from the British Library.

Printed in the United States of America
First Edition

http://dx.doi.org/10.1037/14957-000

Anneliese dedicates her work in this book to all the fierce trans activists of color who have given their lives—in often unsung ways—to the trans liberation movement, to Jeanine and Jenna who left this earth too soon, and to her beloved Lauren who fills her with more love and light than she ever could have imagined.
Sat siri akal!

lore dedicates his work to the people who have traveled with him on his gender journey. This includes the people who have participated in his research, his mentors, and the trusted advisors who have assisted him in difficult moments. Finally, he dedicates this book to the memory of the trans people who are no longer with us. The list is too long.

Contents

Contributors

Gabriel Arkles, JD, is an associate teaching professor at Northeastern University School of Law in Boston, Massachusetts. His work focuses on issues of race, gender, and disability in the law. While in practice at the Sylvia Rivera Law Project from 2004 to 2010 he represented trans and gender nonconforming clients in name change, public benefit, immigration, and prisoners' rights cases.

Kyle L. Bower, doctoral student, is in the Department of Human Development and Family Sciences at The University of Georgia in Athens. Kyle's work with marginalized older adult populations is guided by a feminist gerontological lens. Specifically, she explores caregiving experiences within the LGBT community and among low-income families.

Theodore R. Burnes, PhD, is an associate professor at Antioch University in Los Angeles, California, where he directs the specialization in LGBT psychology for the master of arts program in clinical psychology. Dr. Burnes is also the director of continuing education at the Los Angeles Gender Center, a group therapy practice and nonprofit wellness center that serves transgender; gender diverse; and TGNC individuals, communities, and systemic change agents.

Linda F. Campbell, PhD, is a professor and director of the training clinic in the Counseling Psychology program at the University of Georgia in Athens. Dr. Campbell's major area of publication and teaching is ethics and professional development and ethics in telepsychology. She is a member of the State Board of Examiners in Georgia and is currently a member of the American Psychological Association Board of Directors.

Sand C. Chang, PhD, is a Chinese American, genderqueer psychologist and gender therapist at the Multi-Specialty

Transitions Department at Kaiser Permanente and in independent practice in Oakland, California. Dr. Chang served on the American Psychological Association (APA) Task Force writing *Guidelines for Psychological Practice With Transgender and Gender Nonconforming People* and was the chair of the APA Committee on Sexual Orientation and Gender Diversity. Dr. Chang specializes in eye movement desensitization and reprocessing, trauma, addictions, eating disorders, gender, and sexuality.

Jessie R. Cohen, LCSW, is a clinical supervisor on the management team at A Better Way, Inc., in Oakland, California, serving children and families primarily in foster and adoption care. She is a gender therapist in private practice and a contract supervisor for Rainbow Community Center in Concord, California. Ms. Cohen serves on the Steering Committee of the Gender Spectrum Conference and is a founding member of the UCSF, Child and Adolescent Gender Center, Mind The Gap group.

Kelly Ducheny, PsyD, is a licensed psychologist and senior director of behavioral health services at Howard Brown Health in Chicago, Illinois. Dr. Ducheny served on the American Psychological Association Task Force that wrote *Guidelines for Psychological Practice With Transgender and Gender Nonconforming People* and is the principle investigator on a grant exploring retention of transgender women of color in HIV care.

Laura Edwards-Leeper, PhD, is an associate professor in the School of Professional Psychology at Pacific University in Hillsboro, Oregon. She previously worked at Boston Children's Hospital/Harvard Medical School, where she developed an affirmative protocol for assessing readiness in TGNC adolescents seeking medical interventions. She served on the American Psychological Association Task Force that wrote *Guidelines for Psychological Practice With Transgender and Gender Nonconforming People* and served on the panel that assisted the Substance Abuse and Mental Health Services Administration to develop the consensus statement *Ending Conversion Therapy: Supporting and Affirming LGBTQ Youth.*

Mel Ferrara, doctoral student, works in gender and women's studies and is a University Fellow at the University of Arizona in Tucson. Their research interests include trans and intersex studies, body politics, and medical ethics/comparative health care models. They cofounded the Muhlenberg College Trans Advocacy Coalition which connects scholarship to activism.

Michael L. Hendricks, PhD, ABPP, is a clinical psychologist in private practice at the Washington Psychological Center, P.C., in Washington, DC. He is a fellow of the American Psychological Association (APA) and a past president of APA's Division 44 (the Society for the Psychological Study of Lesbian, Gay, Bisexual, and Transgender Issues). Dr. Hendricks served on the APA Task Force that developed the *Guidelines for Psychological Practice With Transgender and Gender Nonconforming People.* He is the lead author on the seminal paper on a minority stress model for transgender individuals and was recently awarded an American Psychological Association Presidential Citation for his work.

Ruben A. Hopwood, MDiv, PhD, is the coordinator of the Transgender Health Program of Fenway Health and a psychology fellow at the Danielsen Institute of Boston University in Boston, Massachusetts. He received his doctoral degree in counseling psychology and religion from Boston University and his master's of divinity degree from Saint Paul School of Theology, Kansas City, Missouri. His research has focused on gender-sensitive clinical work, and religion and spirituality and transgender people, with particular focus on trans men.

Sel J. Hwahng, PhD, is an adjunct associate professor at City University of New York–Hunter College and, recently, a coinvestigator at Mount Sinai Beth Israel in New York. Dr. Hwahng has published over 30 articles and book chapters in peer-reviewed journals and edited volumes and has received grants, awards, and fellowships from the National Institute on Drug Abuse, the National Institutes of Health, and the American Public Health Association, Association for Women in Psychology, and the International AIDS Society. Dr. Hwahng is program chair of the LGBT Caucus of the American Public Health Association and is on the Center for LGBTQ Studies Board of Directors.

Colton L. Keo-Meier, PhD, is a clinical psychologist and an assistant professor in the Menninger Department of Psychiatry and Behavioral Services of Baylor College of Medicine, an adjunct professor at Southern Methodist University, and a lecturer at the University of Houston in Houston, Texas. He is pursuing an MD at the University of Texas Medical Branch in Galveston. His research explores the impact of testosterone on the mental health and sexuality of trans masculine adults and the experiences of TGNC children.

Parrish L. Paul, PhD, is in private practice in Nashville, Tennessee. He has worked extensively with issues of sexual identity and gender diversity, along with focusing on provision of clinical supervision and training throughout his career. He is a past cochair of the American Psychological Association Committee on LGBT Concerns.

Mick Rehrig, LCSW, is an Atlanta-based independently licensed clinical social worker who collaborates with, affirms, and supports LGBQ and transgender/gender nonconforming/questioning youth, adults, and their families and partners. He also works with people who identify as members of intersecting communities, including communities of color, open/poly relationships, LGBTQ identification, and/or involvement in the kink community.

Katherine Richmond, PhD, is an associate professor of psychology at Muhlenberg College in Allentown, Pennsylvania, and has published in the area of gender ideology, transgender and intersex mental health, insidious trauma, masculinity, sexual assault, feminist theory and methods, and intersectionality. Dr. Richmond maintains a private practice specializing in trauma and mental health concerns related to gender.

Kinton Rossman, MEd, is currently a resident in the LGBTQ Health Track at Northwestern Feinberg School of Medicine in Chicago, Illinois. They are completing their doctorate in counseling psychology at the University of Louisville in Louisville, Kentucky. Their research has focused on risk and protective factors for LGBTQ youth, nonbinary/genderfluid individuals and gender privilege and oppression in trans populations. Kinton is highly committed to increasing medical and mental health access to care for the trans community and has conducted outreach with trans individuals and providers on trans health issues.

Stacie Fishell Rowan, PhD, is a psychologist at the University of Oregon in Eugene and is a member of the University of Oregon's Transgender Care Team. She received her doctoral degree is in counseling psychology from the University of Wisconsin–Madison. Dr. Rowan's practice, advocacy, and research have focused on supervision and training, LGBTQI/queer identities, trauma, and substance use.

Jae Sevelius, PhD, is a licensed clinical psychologist and assistant professor at the Division of Prevention Sciences and the Center of Excellence for Transgender Health at the University of California, San Francisco. Dr. Sevelius's research leverages data to develop gender affirming programs and interventions to promote holistic health and wellness among transgender people.

Bali White, MA, is a research fellow and Intramural Research Training awardee in the National Institutes of Health's Office of Behavioral and Social Sciences in Bethesda, Maryland. She received her undergraduate and master's degrees from Columbia University in New York. Her research and activist work around transgender advocacy, LGB and youth has been influential in the field of public health.

Tarynn M. Witten, PhD, LCSW, FGSA, is a professor of biological complexity at the Virginia Commonwealth University, Center for the Study of Biological Complexity in Richmond. She is also a professor of physics and an adjunct professor of women's and gender studies. Her LGBT-related research, practice, and worldwide lecture advocacy center on aging in the TGNC and the intersex/DSD community. She has over 50 publications related to gender-identity issues in the elderly. Dr. Witten serves on the editorial boards of a number of LGBT-related scientific journals and received the 2009 Burnside-Watstein Award for LGBT Community Service.

Preface

As we edited *Affirmative Counseling and Psychological Practice With Transgender and Gender Nonconforming Clients*, we reflected on the history of counseling and psychological practice with transgender and gender nonconforming (TGNC) people, the origins of this particular text, and the people who have supported us in our professional and personal lives. With regard to the history of our profession, we have long acknowledged the uncomfortable role that we sit in as mental health professionals (MHPs) working with TGNC clients.

Historically, the mental health profession has not always been a source of support or advocacy for TGNC clients. As current MHPs working with TGNC clients, we feel strongly that we must acknowledge the history our profession has had in pathologizing TGNC identities, in addition to the extensive gatekeeping TGNC clients have faced when accessing health care. Further, as TGNC training research shows, TGNC people still face the need to educate their MHPs on how to best serve their needs. There is a great need to have information on how to engage in affirmative TGNC counseling that does not place additional barriers to access to care. TGNC activists and advocates have lobbied mental health professions for decades to provide more comprehensive and affirming health care for TGNC people. Without the efforts of these people (including TGNC youth, elders, and people of color), we strongly believe that the mental health profession would not be at the stage it is now. Therefore, as we have sought to help define what TGNC-affirmative counseling is throughout the lifespan, it was imperative for us to select chapter authors who are at the front lines of defining TGNC-affirmative counseling. It is our greatest hope that this text will contribute to the needed training for MHPs working with TGNC people and communities, and that MHPs acknowledge and integrate the essential role of advocacy into their counseling practice with TGNC clients.

Several pivotal events led to the compilation of this book. First, our decade-long friendship developed over a shared passion and commitment to challenge societal transnegativity and excessive gatekeeping with regard to TGNC mental health care in our field. To say that we have shared values in this regard is an understatement. We push one another to consider how we can be better and more affirmative practitioners with TGNC people, and we have honest and authentic conversations about our strengths and growing edges. In 2011, we were both nominated and eventually appointed to serve as coleaders of the American Psychological Association (APA) Task Force on Psychological Practice Guidelines With Transgender and Gender Nonconforming People. In leading this 10-person task force to develop TGNC guidelines that were consensus-based and grounded in the empirical research, we noticed many strengths and challenges in describing TGNC-affirmative counseling. For instance, the guidelines document is necessarily short by its nature, and we were not able to describe in detail the important role of advocacy as much as we would have liked. Therefore, as we neared the completion of the guidelines, we knew that we wanted to generate a work that would expound on what TGNC-affirmative counseling really looks like in practice with diverse TGNC clients. We also acknowledge that as we worked on this text, the field of TGNC counseling continued to evolve in exciting and innovative ways. We attempted to integrate a range of identities and experiences, and there are TGNC communities that we did not cover (e.g., disability, immigrant) that deserve further attention. We look forward to, and especially support, the ways that TGNC-affirmative counseling develops work in these areas, identifies ways to remove obstacles from the lives of TGNC clients, and increases access to both mental and physical health care.

As we edited this book, many people supported us professionally and personally along the road. We would like to thank the work of our APA Task Force members, as their tireless efforts on the guidelines were an inspiration to identify ways to apply the guidelines to everyday counseling practice. Members of the task force (in alphabetical order) include Walter O. Bockting, Sand C. Chang, Kelly Ducheny, Laura Edwards-Leeper, Randall D. Ehrbar, Max F. Fuhrmann, Michael L. Hendricks, and Ellen Magalhaes. We would especially like to thank Kelly Ducheny and Sand Chang, who both served on a smaller writing group with us that helped polish and refine the work of the task force. There are several APA members who also supported the APA Task Force work along the way: Louise Douce, Linda Forrest, Doug Haldeman, Terry Gock, Kris Hancock, and Armand Cerbone. We would like to give special thanks to Ron Schlittler and Clinton Anderson of the APA Office for LGBT Concerns. Division 44 has served as the lead governance group with the APA Committee for Sexual Orientation and Gender Diversity (CSOGD). Both Division 44 and CSOGD have been a source of financial and technical support. We also have developed a beloved community of scholars, who are now dear friends, who share our commitment to TGNC empowerment and liberation in counseling (in no particular order): Theodore R. Burnes, Dan Walinsky, Amney Harper, Seth Pardo, Konjit Page, Stephanie Budge, Colt Keo-Meier, Lauren Mizock, Ruben Hopwood, Stacey Prince, Damon Constantinides, and Kate Richmond. Finally, we would like to give our heartfelt thanks to our chapter authors (in alphabetical order): Gabriel Arkles, Kyle Bower, Theodore R. Burnes, Linda Campbell, Sand C. Chang, Jessie R. Cohen, Kelly Ducheny, Laura Edwards-Leeper, Mel Ferrara, Michael L. Hendricks, Sel J. Hwahng, Colt Keo-Meier, Parrish Paul, Mick D. Rehrig, Kate Richmond, Kinton Rossman, Stacie Rowan, Jae Sevelius, Bali White, and Tarynn Witten. Each of these authors contributed work and generously tackled revisions to make this text a strong primer on TGNC-affirmative counseling across the lifespan. We cannot thank them enough.

Affirmative Counseling and Psychological Practice With Transgender and Gender Nonconforming Clients

Anneliese A. Singh and lore m. dickey

Introduction

n counseling and psychological practice, mental health providers (MHPs) have traditionally used a gatekeeping approach (Singh & Burnes, 2010) with transgender and gender nonconforming (TGNC) clients. In this gatekeeping approach, TGNC people are asked to educate their MHPs and fit a certain definition of being TGNC; thus, they feel afraid to access counseling services to support their gender journeys if they do not fit into this strict definition (see Chapter 2 for further discussion of gatekeeping). The following sample dialogue between a client and a counselor demonstrates why the gatekeeping approach can be problematic:

> *Counselor:* When did you first know you were trans?
>
> *Client:* Well, I don't identify as trans. I am nonbinary.
>
> *Counselor:* What does that mean?
>
> *Client:* You don't know?

http://dx.doi.org/10.1037/14957-001
Affirmative Counseling and Psychological Practice With Transgender and Gender Nonconforming Clients, A. A. Singh and l. m. dickey (Editors)

> *Counselor:* Could you educate me a little?
>
> *Client:* I really wish I didn't have to.
>
> *Counselor:* Do you want to transition?
>
> *Client:* I think I am in the wrong place.

TGNC-affirmative counseling and psychological practice seeks to move beyond this gatekeeping approach by partnering and collaborating with TGNC clients so that they are in charge of their own mental health, as well as to set goals and aspirations that are client driven. Flexibility, resource building, consultation, and MHP advocacy are important roles within TGNC-affirmative practice.

As we shared in the Preface, we intentionally edited this book with the focus of advancing the field of affirmative counseling and psychological practice with TGNC people. We define *TGNC-affirmative counseling and psychological practice* as counseling that is culturally relevant and responsive to TGNC clients and their multiple social identities, addresses the influence of social inequities on the lives of TGNC clients, enhances TGNC client resilience and coping, advocates to reduce systemic barriers to TGNC mental and physical health, and leverages TGNC client strengths. In short, TGNC-affirmative counseling and psychological practice privileges the client's autonomy. Psychological practice spans not only the fields of counseling and psychology but also social work, marriage and family therapy, psychiatry, nursing, and other helping profession disciplines. When MHPs adopt TGNC-affirming approaches, there is the unique opportunity to transform mental health care for TGNC clients overall.

In this Introduction to the book, we discuss the important terms and definitions used in TGNC-affirming counseling and the major professional documents guiding TGNC-affirming mental health practice. In addition, we describe the theoretical frameworks counselors may use to develop TGNC-affirming practice and the common risk and protective factors TGNC clients experience.

Key Terms and Definitions in TGNC-Affirming Counseling

There are several key terms that will be used throughout this book that require a common definition. We acknowledge that terminology within the TGNC community continues to evolve, and the terms used here are bound in time. However, these terms represent the current thinking as it relates to work with TGNC people.

Sex and gender are often confused or conflated to mean the same thing. *Sex* relates to biological determinates. Specifically, it is concerned with chromosomes, genitalia, and secondary sex characteristics (Hock, 2012). In western societies, sex is typically thought of as being either female or male and is assigned to a newborn at birth. On the other hand, *gender* is a socially constructed term that originates with assumptions that people make about a person's sex. Following these assumptions are various rules about how a person should perform their gender (Butler, 1990). The terms *femininity* and *masculinity* are examples of how gender may be performed. When working with TGNC people, it is important to note that some TGNC people do not subscribe to the *gender binary*. Rather, they believe that gender falls on a spectrum and that a person might identify along that spectrum instead of at polar opposites. Some people who identify as gender nonconforming use the term *genderqueer*. This term can be an individual term and a collective term for people who do not ascribe to the gender binary and may use gender neutral, third-person pronouns, such as *they/them*.

Gender identity is a term that is used to describe a person's felt sense of themselves in terms of their gender. This is a psychological experience for a person and it can change over time, especially for TGNC people. *Gender expression* is the way in which a person performs their gender identity. Gender expression might include the style and manner of dress, the type of haircut worn, and the pronouns they use to describe themselves.

Within the TGNC community there are a variety of terms a person might use to describe their gender identity. In one study (Grant et al., 2011), over 500 respondents used different terms to describe their gender. Common terms might include *trans man* or *trans woman* and *female-to-male* or *male-to-female*. Another common term is *cross-dresser*. This refers to people who dress in clothing or express their gender in ways that society deems inconsistent with the sex they were assigned at birth. The terms that TGNC people use to describe their gender identity can be quite varied and influenced by culture and context. MHPs are cautioned not to make assumptions about the labels that people use to describe themselves; including those who do not use labels at all. A variety of terms have been used to describe TGNC youth. These include *gender diverse, gender expansive,* and *gender creative* (Angello, 2013; Ehrensaft, 2011). It is important to keep in mind that these terms are usually proposed first by adults. Though some youth may feel that they fit well as a self-descriptor, this may not always be the case. More recently, some TGNC people have begun using the terms *assigned female at birth* or *assigned male at birth*. These terms are used in place of other references to how sex was assigned at birth and can help to address any confusion a person might have about a TGNC person's history in an affirmative manner.

One area that can often be a challenge for TGNC people is the use of pronouns by others. It is very common for people to make assumptions about which pronouns to use with a person based on the perception of that person's sex or gender. Many times the assumptions made prove to be inaccurate and thus can be troubling for TGNC people. Repeated use of incorrect pronouns is considered to be a microaggression (Nadal, 2013). If an MHP is unsure of the correct pronoun to use with a client, simply ask, "What pronoun(s) do you use?" In this way, the TGNC client is empowered to use pronouns that are consistent with their identity. A word of caution: Please avoid asking for a client's *preferred* name or pronoun. This question can be perceived as being disrespectful by many TGNC people. The meaning behind asking for a *preferred* pronoun carries the message to the receiver that if it is convenient the sender will remember to use the stated pronoun or name.

Until recently, MHPs often struggled to find a good term to describe people who do not have a TGNC history. *Cisgender* has begun to be used to describe such people (Serano, 2007). *Cis* is a Latin term that can be translated to mean "the same as." Cisgender then means that a person sex (as assigned at birth) is consistent with their gender. *Cisgenderism* is the privileging of the gender binary and the expectation that people will perform their gender in a manner that is consistent with their sex. *Cisgender privilege* relates to the ability of many people to live their lives without questions, discrimination, or harassment because their gender and sex are perceived to be in alignment (Serano, 2007).

As previously mentioned, TGNC people with multiple identities will often use terms that are more reflective of their cultural identity. TGNC people of color are at much greater risk of violence, oppression, and discrimination than are TGNC White people (Grant et al., 2011). Regardless of the multiple identities a person embraces (race, ethnicity, age, ability status, religion, immigration status), those who are perceived to be from minority communities are at greater risk of adverse treatment and are more likely to have co-occurring mental and physical health concerns. Hendricks and Testa (2012) discussed at some length the effects of minority stress on transgender people.

TGNC people often face discrimination and oppression related to their TGNC identity. *Transphobia* is similar to homophobia in that it relates to negative reactions that people have toward TGNC people related to their gender identity. *Transprejudice* relates to the discrimination that TGNC people face as a result of their gender identity.

Major Documents Guiding TGNC-Affirming Counseling

Practice with TGNC people has evolved significantly over the past 50 years (American Psychological Association [APA], 2015). Where once a TGNC person had great difficulty finding providers (medical and mental health) who had received training or had experience in working with TGNC people, today there are interdisciplinary health centers in major cities who specialize in TGNC care (e.g., Howard Brown in Chicago, Illinois, and Whitman Walker in Washington, DC). In these large cities TGNC people are more likely to be able to access care in a setting that is respectful and up-to-date. This may not be the case for TGNC people who live in rural settings or in conservative areas of the United States. Providers in some parts of the country may not be aware of the movement to TGNC-affirmative care (Walinsky & Whitcomb, 2010). Historically, TGNC people have often found themselves in a place where they were called on to educate their provider (Pickering & Leinbaugh, 2006). This places the TGNC person in an untenable position. A number of documents have been developed to help assist providers in providing competent care. In this section we briefly describe the history of clinical practice with TGNC clients by highlighting the different guidelines and standards of care that exist. These documents can be quite useful for MHPs as they develop their understanding of culturally competent clinical practice.

Before describing the practice documents, it is important to remind readers of the ethical mandates that address work with clients. Every mental health and physical health association has a code of ethics (e.g., American Counseling Association [ACA], American Psychological Association). Common across these codes is the mandate to do no harm, to practice within the scope of one's training, and to privilege the autonomy of clients (ACA, 2014; APA, 2010). Chapter 4 of this volume addresses ethical concerns. Maintaining an ethical practice is paramount in the assurance of culturally competent care.

WORLD PROFESSIONAL ASSOCIATION FOR TRANSGENDER HEALTH

The World Professional Association for Transgender Health first published the "Standards of Care for the Health of Transsexual, Transgender, and Gender-Nonconforming People" (SOC) in 1979. Now in the seventh version, these standards address medical, psychological, and social aspects of work with TGNC individuals. Early versions of the SOC were quite prescriptive in regard to appropriate clinical treatment and, more specifically, the correct history a person must present to be eligible for transition-related care. One assumption that was made in these early days was that people who identified as TGNC all wanted to make a medical transition (hormones and surgery). Although this is true for many people, it is not so for all TGNC people. In fact, if a person expressed a lack of interest in a full medical transition they were deemed to be a poor candidate for transition. The current version of the SOC clarifies that there is no one way to transition. There is also a strong statement about the SOC being flexible and that the needs of TGNC people should be taken on a case-by-case basis rather than assuming a "one-size-fits-all" approach. MHPs are encouraged to be aware of the recommendations made in the SOC including the tasks related to assessment, referral, and psychotherapy, and readers are referred to the SOC glossary of terms (Coleman et al., 2012).

AMERICAN COUNSELING ASSOCIATION

In 2010, the ACA published a document titled "Competencies for Counseling With Transgender Clients." This document was the first of its kind from an MHP professional association. The document addressed work with TGNC clients across the domains of human growth and development, social and cultural foundations, helping relationships, group work, professional orientation, career and lifestyle development, appraisal, and research. These competencies were written from a feminist, multicultural, social justice perspective.

AMERICAN PSYCHIATRIC ASSOCIATION

The American Psychiatric Association published a report on the treatment of gender identity disorder (Byne et al., 2012). This report predates the *Diagnostic and Statistical Manual of Mental Disorders, Fifth Edition*, and should be used with some caution because the diagnostic criteria changed for gender dysphoria (American Psychiatric Association, 2013). The report recommends treatment approaches for children, adolescents, and adults who are "gender variant" (Byne et al., 2012, p. 1) and individuals with disorders of sex development. A review of the literature on these topics is included.

WORLD HEALTH ORGANIZATION

The World Health Organization (WHO) is responsible for developing the *International Classification of Diseases* (*ICD*). The *ICD* is used by providers throughout the world to appropriately code a diagnosis of a medical or mental health condition. The United States recently adopted the use of *ICD–10*. TGNC people may be diagnosed with gender identity disorder (F64.1) by providers who use the *ICD–10* (WHO, 2016). The WHO is in the process of developing the *ICD–11*, and it is not yet clear whether they will retain gender identity disorder or if they will change the name and diagnostic criteria.

AMERICAN PSYCHOLOGICAL ASSOCIATION

The APA developed the *Guidelines for Psychological Practice With Transgender and Gender Nonconforming Clients* in 2015. The guidelines are organized in the domains of foundational knowledge and awareness; stigma, discrimination, and barriers to care; lifespan development; assessment, therapy, and intervention; and research, education, and training. Readers are also provided with an extensive glossary of terms (APA, 2015). The guidelines are grounded in existing, extensive empirical work with TGNC clients and are informed by TGNC advocates and TGNC-affirming MHPs.

MEDICAL SOCIETIES

The Endocrine Society (Hembree et al., 2009) and the American College of Obstetricians and Gynecologists (2015) are among the associations of medical providers who have published treatment protocols for TGNC patients. These protocols are specific to the focus of care and may be useful for MHPs who are working with collaboration with medical providers. MHPs are encouraged to stay abreast of additional such resources that may become available.

Organizations like the National Association for Social Workers and the American Association for Marriage and Family Therapists do not yet have publications similar to those described in this section. School psychologists are referred to the Safe and Supportive Schools project which was developed as a joint project between the National Association of School Psychologists and the APA (2014). MHPs should be aware of the professional documents guiding work with TGNC people, especially as these documents evolve to inform TGNC-affirming practice.

Theoretical Frameworks for TGNC-Affirming Care

When developing TGNC-affirming counseling and psychological practice, counselors should ensure that their assessments, interventions, and advocacy are grounded in TGNC-affirming theories. Although there are currently no specific TGNC-affirming theories of counseling practice, there are theoretical perspectives that counselors may use in their work with TGNC clients such as (a) the minority stress model (Meyer, 1995, 2003), (b) trauma counseling principles (Briere & Scott, 2012), (c) strengths-based and resilience approaches (ACA, 2010; APA, 2015), and (d) multiculturalism and social justice advocacy approaches (Sue, Arredondo, & McDavis, 1992; Ratts et al., 2015).

The minority stress model (Meyer, 1995) was initially developed to describe the stressors that lesbian, gay, and bisexual (LGB) people face in society due to homophobia and heterosexist bias, and the model was recently applied to TGNC people (Hendricks & Testa, 2012). Meyer (2003) described minority stress as being additive stress, such that it is stress that is experienced over and above the everyday stress average people have, which is consistently present. For instance, TGNC people often experience constant fear that they may be harmed because of their gender identity and gender expression. Minority stress is also socially based and is related to institutional structures and anti-TGNC values, such as TGNC people not having access to protections and rights in society. Meyer discussed that there are processes of minority stress that include environmental or external events of discrimination and anticipation or expectation of these societal events of discrimination, which lead to people internalizing negative societal attitudes and prejudices about their sexual orientation and gender identity as well as concealment of their sexual orientation or gender identity. Each of the processes of minority stress influence TGNC mental health (Hendricks & Testa, 2012) and should be assessed at the counseling intake and throughout the counseling process.

Although the minority stress model provides important areas for MHPs to explore related to assessment and the counseling process with TGNC people, specific trauma counseling principles (see Chapter 9) are also helpful for MHPs to use because of the high rates of trauma TGNC people and communities experience (Richmond, Burnes, & Carroll, 2012). There are a variety of trauma theories that MHPs can use, and important components include the validation and support that trauma survivors need in healing from trauma, as well as the identification of trauma symptoms and the influence of these symptoms on the overall well-being of clients (Briere & Scott, 2012).

Just as TGNC clients experience minority stress and trauma in society, TGNC people may also experience resilience as they navigate anti-TGNC bias; therefore, TGNC-affirming counseling practice should use strengths-based approaches to enhance resilience (ACA, 2010; APA, 2015). Strengths-based approaches examine the competencies and coping resources that clients have that help them reduce stress in their lives (Budge, Adelson, & Howard, 2013). Masten (2001) defined *resilience* as the ability individuals have to "bounce back" from adverse events in their lives. For example, research with TGNC people of color suggested that developing racial and ethnic pride alongside pride in their gender identity and being connected to religious and spiritual approaches are sources of individual resilience (Singh, Hays, & Watson, 2011; Singh & McKleroy, 2011). In addition, resilience can be a community or collective experience. For example, TGNC people of color having connections to a TGNC activist community of color helped facilitate access to necessary financial and legal resources (see Chapter 2; Singh, 2013; Singh, Meng, & Hansen, 2013).

Multiculturalism has been a hallmark of counseling practice for over 2 decades, and multicultural counseling is therefore an integral part of TGNC-affirming counseling practice (Ratts, 2011). When first developed, multicultural counseling competencies asserted the importance of counselors understanding that cultural backgrounds (e.g., race/ethnicity, class, religion/spiritual beliefs) have important influences on mental health and overall well-being (Sue et al., 1992). These multicultural counseling competencies also noted the importance of counselors having the awareness, knowledge, and skills to be able to work with various cultural groups. For instance, related to TGNC-affirming practice, counselors should actively develop awareness about how their own attitudes about their own gender identity, gender training, and gender journey influence their beliefs and attitudes about TGNC people and their counseling needs. In terms of knowledge and skills, counselors should consistently seek professional development and training on TGNC client concerns, as well as develop and be aware of interventions that are effective and affirming with TGNC clients. The multicultural counseling competencies were recently revised to integrate social justice with a new dimension of competence termed action added to help guide counselor advocacy (Ratts et al., 2015). The role of advocacy is a critical aspect of TGNC-affirming counseling practice (see Chapter 12) and may be guided by the ACA Advocacy Competencies (Lewis, Arnold, House, & Toporek, 2003). The ACA Advocacy Competencies guide counselors to work with clients on specific advocacy skills that can be applied to work with TGNC people, such as self-advocacy skills with TGNC youth, or on behalf of clients such as removing systemic barriers TGNC people face such as bathroom access. In addition to the theories that support the development of TGNC-affirming counseling practice, counselors should have strong knowledge and skills related to consultation. Consultation approaches and scenarios in TGNC-affirming practice are discussed in Chapter 3.

Protective and Risk Factors Influencing TGNC Mental Health

There are significant risk and protective factors that influence the lives of TGNC people on a daily basis. It is important for MHPs to have a good working knowledge of the ways these factors impact a TGNC person in the areas of mental and physical health, health disparities, and resilience so these areas can be addressed.

MENTAL AND PHYSICAL HEALTH OUTCOMES

TGNC people are at increased risk for mental and physical health concerns. Research has consistently shown that TGNC people, especially TGNC women, are at elevated risk for HIV infection (Nuttbrock et al., 2009). Other physical health risks include the challenges associated with not accessing preventative health care. Many TGNC people are concerned about the manner in which they will be treated by administrative staff and providers, which can result in a person choosing to not access regular health care (Grant et al., 2011). Mollon (2009) accurately described the challenges that many LGB and TGNC people face when attempting to access care from a new provider. This included the use of intake forms that are not representative of people's lived experiences (e.g., a lack of culturally responsive questions about gender identity and sexual orientation) to hostile treatment after coming out to a provider. As a result of the discrimination, bullying, and harassment that some TGNC people face, this population showed higher rates of co-occurring mental health issues, nonsuicidal self-injury, and suicidal ideation (Clements-Nolle, Marx, & Katz, 2006; dickey, Reisner, & Juntunen, 2015; Grant et al., 2011; Matarazzo et al., 2014). Given the challenges that TGNC people face in realizing their gender identity, it is critical that MHPs work with their clients to address the myriad concerns that might adversely influence a TGNC person's well-being.

OTHER HEALTH DISPARITIES

TGNC people represent one group of people who are at risk for tobacco-related illnesses (Fagan et al., 2004). As a result, there are a number of health related concerns that TGNC people may be susceptible to, including cancers. Reisner, White, Bradford, and Mimiaga (2014) compared the health disparities of TGNC and cisgender patients at a community health center. Although they found no differences in risk for HIV, substance abuse, and smoking-related illnesses, it is important to keep in mind that the cisgender participants were LGB individuals, who were also at elevated risk for these health concerns. In this same study, TGNC participants "disproportionately reported social stressors" (Reisner et al., 2014, p. 177). Over time, social stressors have been shown to adversely affect a person's physical and mental health (Mays, Cochran, & Barnes, 2007).

RESILIENCE

In recent years, researchers have begun to explore the ways in which TGNC people exhibit resilience in their lives. Resilience is a psychological construct that includes the ways in which a person has learned to manage the day-to-day challenges they may face (Harvey, 2007;

Jew, Green, & Kroger, 1999). Singh, Hays, and Watson (2011) identified several common themes with regard to resilience "(a) evolving a
self-generated definition of self, (b) embracing self-worth, (c) awareness of oppression, (d) connection with a supportive community, and
(e) cultivating hope for the future" (p. 23). This last point, cultivating
hope for the future, can be a focus of clinical work with clients that is
often overlooked. Bockting, Miner, Swinburne Romine, Hamilton, and
Coleman (2013) also explored resilience in TGNC people. They found
that facilitating peer support was an important aspect of developing
resilience. Additionally, over time, older TGNC people were less likely
to experience felt stigma. This was attributed to the length of time that
a person was out to others about their TGNC identity.

POLICY LANDSCAPE

The number and kinds of policies that are TGNC-affirmative have grown
considerably in the past 10 years. This is due, in part, to the work of
the National Center for Transgender Equality (2015), the Sylvia Rivera
Law Project, the Transgender Law Center, and others. Federal policy
changes include identity documents, screening when traveling, health
care access, and more. These changes have happened at the local, state,
and federal levels. As a result, some TGNC people live in work in locations in which their basic human rights are protected. MHPs play a critical role in shaping policy. Chapter 12 explores the ways that MHPs can
engage in advocacy and being a strong ally to TGNC people.

Organization of This Book

We have organized this book to reflect the journey to becoming a trans-
affirming MHP, with the first chapters exploring gender diversity within
the TGNC community (Chapter 1) and TGNC people of color (Chapter 2)
to reflect the importance of intersectional identities in psychological
practice with TGNC people. The next chapter explores interdisciplinary
consultation and collaboration (Chapter 3), followed by the ethical and
legal concerns that commonly arise when working with TGNC people
(Chapter 4). Subsequent chapters explore TGNC-affirming psychological practice across the lifespan, with a focus on TGNC children and adolescents (Chapter 5), TGNC parents and family concerns (Chapter 6),
and TGNC aging and older adults (Chapter 7). Later chapters describe
the role of TGNC-affirming clinical supervision in health service psychology (Chapter 8), assessment and treatment of trauma from a feminist approach (Chapter 9), spirituality and religion (Chapter 10), and

TGNC-affirmative research (Chapter 11). The final chapter emphasizes the unique role of advocacy and social justice in TGNC-affirming psychological practice (Chapter 12), and this emphasis is also integrated across each chapter in the text.

Ultimately, we edited this book so that the specific importance of TGNC-affirming counseling and psychological practice was clearly described and defined. From affirming language to having knowledge of counseling to the major professional competencies, guidelines, and standards that exist and are constantly evolving, MHPs can draw from these sources of learning to develop a strong TGNC-affirming counseling approach. MHPs will also find counseling and psychological approaches with various groups within the TGNC umbrella that may be used to support TGNC-affirming practice, as well as address the protective and risk factors influencing TGNC mental health. Each chapter in this book provides a helpful overview and discussion of salient components of TGNC-affirming practice. Just as TGNC counseling has and will evolve and grow over time—often rapidly—we invite you to learn and grow with us as we seek to transform the ways that TGNC clients experience psychological practice.

References

American College of Obstetricians and Gynecologists. (2015). *Transgender health resource guide.* Retrieved from http://www.acog.org/About-ACOG/ACOG-Departments/Health-Care-for-Underserved-Women/Transgender-Health-Resource-Guide

American Counseling Association. (2010). American Counseling Association competencies for counseling with transgender clients. *Journal of LGBT Issues in Counseling, 4,* 135–159. http://dx.doi.org/10.1080/15538605.2010.524839

American Counseling Association. (2014). *ACA code of ethics.* Retrieved from https://www.counseling.org/resources/aca-code-of-ethics.pdf

American Psychiatric Association. (2013). *Diagnostic and statistical manual of mental disorders* (5th ed.). Washington, DC: Author.

American Psychological Association. (2010). *Ethical principles of psychologists and code of conduct (2002, amended June 1, 2010).* Retrieved from http://www.apa.org/ethics/code/index.aspx

American Psychological Association. (2014). *LGBT youth resources.* Retrieved from http://www.apa.org/pi/lgbt/programs/safe-supportive/lgbt/default.aspx

American Psychological Association. (2015). Guidelines for psychological practice with transgender and gender nonconforming people.

American Psychologist, 70, 832–864. http://dx.doi.org/10.1037/a0039906

Angello, M. (2013). *On the couch with Dr. Angello: A guide to raising & supporting transgender youth.* Philadelphia, PA: Author.

Bockting, W. O., Miner, M. H., Swinburne Romine, R. E., Hamilton, A., & Coleman, E. (2013). Stigma, mental health, and resilience in an online sample of the U.S. transgender population. *American Journal of Public Health, 103*, 943–951. http://dx.doi.org/10.2105/AJPH.2013.301241

Briere, J., & Scott, C. (2012). *Principles of trauma therapy: A guide to symptoms, evaluation, and treatment.* Thousand Oaks, CA: Sage.

Budge, S. L., Adelson, J. L., & Howard, K. A. (2013). Anxiety and depression in transgender individuals: The roles of transition status, loss, social support, and coping. *Journal of Consulting and Clinical Psychology, 81*, 545–557. http://dx.doi.org/10.1037/a0031774

Butler, J. (1990). *Gender trouble and the subversion of identity.* New York, NY: Routledge.

Byne, W., Bradley, S. J., Coleman, E., Eyler, A. E., Green, R., Menvielle, E. J., . . . Tompkins, D. A. (2012). Report of the American Psychiatric Association Task Force on Treatment of Gender Identity Disorder. *Archives of Sexual Behavior, 41*, 759–796. http://dx.doi.org/10.1007/s10508-012-9975-x

Clements-Nolle, K., Marx, R., & Katz, M. (2006). Attempted suicide among transgender persons: The influence of gender-based discrimination and victimization. *Journal of Homosexuality, 51*, 53–69. http://dx.doi.org/10.1300/J082v51n03_04

Coleman, E., Bockting, W., Botzer, M., Cohen-Kettenis, P., DeCuypere, G., Feldman, J., . . . Zucker, K. (2012). Standards of care for the health of transsexual, transgender, and gender-nonconforming people, 7th version. *International Journal of Transgenderism, 13*, 165–232. http://dx.doi.org/10.1080/15532739.2011.700873

dickey, l. m., Reisner, S. L., & Juntunen, C. L. (2015). Non-suicidal self-injury in a large online sample of transgender adults. *Professional Psychology: Research and Practice, 46*(1), 3–11. http://dx.doi.org/10.1037/a0038803

Ehrensaft, D. (2011). *Gender born, gender made: Raising healthy gender-nonconforming children.* New York, NY: The Experiment.

Fagan, P., King, G., Lawrence, D., Petrucci, S. A., Robinson, R. G., Banks, D., . . . Grana, R. (2004). Eliminating tobacco-related health disparities: Directions for future research. *American Journal of Public Health, 94*, 211–217. http://dx.doi.org/10.2105/AJPH.94.2.211

Grant, J. M., Mottet, L. A., Tanis, J., Harrison, J., Herman, J. L., & Keisling, M. (2011). *Injustice at every turn: A report of the national transgender discrimination survey.* Washington, DC: National Center for Transgender Equality & National Gay and Lesbian Task Force. Retrieved from http://endtransdiscrimination.org/PDFs/NTDS_Report.pdf

Harvey, M. R. (2007). Towards an ecological understanding of resilience in trauma survivors: Implications for theory, research, and practice. *Journal of Aggression, Maltreatment & Trauma, 14,* 9–32. http://dx.doi.org/10.1300/J146v14n01_02

Hembree, W. C., Cohen-Kettenis, P., Delemarre-van de Waal, H. A., Gooren, L. J., Meyer, W. J., III, Spack, N. P., . . . Montori, V. M., & the Endocrine Society. (2009). Endocrine treatment of transsexual persons: An Endocrine Society clinical practice guideline. *The Journal of Clinical Endocrinology and Metabolism, 94,* 3132–3154. http://dx.doi.org/10.1210/jc.2009-0345

Hendricks, M. L., & Testa, R. J. (2012). A conceptual framework for clinical work with transgender and gender nonconforming clients: An adaptation of the minority stress model. *Professional Psychology: Research and Practice, 43,* 460–467. http://dx.doi.org/10.1037/a0029597

Hock, R. R. (2012). *Human sexuality* (3rd ed.). Boston, MA: Pearson.

Jew, C. L., Green, K. E., & Kroger, J. (1999). Development and validation of a measure of resiliency. *Measurement and Evaluation in Counseling and Development, 32,* 75–89.

Lewis, J. A., Arnold, M. S., House, R., & Toporek, R. L. (2003). *Advocacy competencies.* Retrieved from http://www.counseling.org/docs/default-source/competencies/advocacy_competencies.pdf?sfvrsn=9

Masten, A. S. (2001). Ordinary magic. Resilience processes in development. *American Psychologist, 56,* 227–238.

Matarazzo, B. B., Barnes, S. M., Pease, J. L., Russell, L. M., Hanson, J. E., Soberay, K. A., & Gutierrez, P. M. (2014). Suicide risk among lesbian, gay, bisexual, and transgender military personnel and veterans: What does the literature tell us? *Suicide and Life-Threatening Behavior, 44,* 200–217. http://dx.doi.org/10.1111/sltb.12073

Mays, V. M., Cochran, S. D., & Barnes, N. W. (2007). Race, race-based discrimination, and health outcomes among African Americans. *Annual Review of Psychology, 58,* 201–225. http://dx.doi.org/10.1146/annurev.psych.57.102904.190212

Meyer, I. H. (1995). Minority stress and mental health in gay men. *Journal of Health and Social Behavior, 36,* 38–56. http://dx.doi.org/10.2307/2137286

Meyer, I. H. (2003). Prejudice, social stress, and mental health in lesbian, gay, and bisexual populations: Conceptual issues and research evidence. *Psychological Bulletin, 129,* 674–697.

Mollon, L. (2009). The forgotten minorities: Health disparities of the lesbian, gay, bisexual, and transgendered communities. *Journal of Health Care for the Poor and Underserved, 23,* 1–6. http://dx.doi.org/10.1353/hpu.2012.0009

Nadal, K. L. (2013). *That's so gay! Microaggressions and the lesbian, gay, bisexual, and transgender community.* Washington, DC: American Psychological Association. http://dx.doi.org/10.1037/14093-000

National Center for Transgender Equality. (2015). *Know your rights.* Retrieved from http://transequality.org/know-your-rights

Nuttbrock, L., Hwahng, S., Bockting, W., Rosenblum, A., Mason, M., Macri, M., & Becker, J. (2009). Lifetime risk factors for HIV/STI infections among male-to-female transgender persons. *Journal of Acquired Immune Deficiency Syndromes, 52,* 417–421. http://dx.doi.org/10.1097/QAI.0b013e3181ab6ed8

Pickering, D., & Leinbaugh, T. (2006). *Counselor self-efficacy with transgender clients* (Unpublished doctoral dissertation). Ohio University, Athens.

Ratts, M. (2011). Multiculturalism and social justice: Two sides of the same coin. *Journal of Multicultural Counseling and Development, 39,* 24–37. http://dx.doi.org/10.1002/j.2161-1912.2011.tb00137.x

Ratts, M. J., Singh, A. A., Nassar-McMillan, S., Butler, S. K., & McCullough, J. R. (2015). *Multicultural and social justice counseling competencies.* Retrieved from http://www.counseling.org/docs/default-source/competencies/multicultural-and-social-justice-counseling-competencies.pdf?sfvrsn=20

Reisner, S. L., White, J. M., Bradford, J. B., & Mimiaga, M. J. (2014). Transgender health disparities: Comparing full cohort and nested matched-pair study designs in a community health center. *LGBT health, 1,* 177–184. http://dx.doi.org/10.1089/lgbt.2014.0009

Richmond, K., Burnes, T. R., & Carroll, K. (2012). Lost in trans-lation: Interpreting systems of trauma for transgender clients. *Traumatology, 18*(1), 45–57. http://dx.doi.org/10.1177/1534765610396726

Serano, J. (2007). *Whipping girl: A transsexual woman on sexism and the scapegoating of femininity.* Emeryville, CA: Seal.

Singh, A. A. (2013). Transgender youth of color and resilience: Negotiating oppression and finding support. *Sex Roles, 68,* 690–702. http://dx.doi.org/10.1007/s11199-012-0149-z

Singh, A. A., & Burnes, T. R. (2010). Translating the *Competencies for Counseling with Transgender Clients* into counseling, practice, research, and advocacy. *Journal of LGBT Issues in Counseling, 4,* 126–134. http://dx.doi.org/10.1080/15538605.2010.524837

Singh, A. A., Hays, D. G., & Watson, L. (2011). Strategies in the face of adversity: Resilience strategies of transgender individuals. *Journal of Counseling & Development, 89,* 20–27. http://dx.doi.org/10.1002/j.1556-6678.2011.tb00057.x

Singh, A. A., & McKleroy, V. S. (2011). "Just getting out of bed is a revolutionary act": The resilience of transgender people of color who have survived traumatic life events. *Traumatology, 20*(10), 1–11.

Singh, A. A., Meng, S., & Hansen, A. (2013). "I am my own gender": Resilience strategies of trans youth. *Journal of Counseling & Development, 92,* 208–218. http://dx.doi.org/10.1002/j.1556-6676.2014.00150.x

Sue, D. W., Arredondo, P., & McDavis, R. J. (1992). Multicultural counseling competencies and standards: A call to the profession. *Journal of Multicultural Counseling and Development, 20,* 64–88. http://dx.doi.org/10.1002/j.2161-1912.1992.tb00563.x

Walinsky, D., & Whitcomb, D. (2010). Using the ACA Competencies for counseling with transgender clients to increase rural transgender well-being. *Journal of LGBT Issues in Counseling, 4,* 160–175. http://dx.doi.org/10.1080/15538605.2010.524840

World Health Organization. (2016). *ICD-10 Version: 2016: F64 Gender Identity Disorders.* Retrieved from: http://apps.who.int/classifications/icd10/browse/2016/en#/F64

Sand C. Chang, Anneliese A. Singh, and Kinton Rossman

Gender and Sexual Orientation Diversity Within the TGNC Community

1

Transgender and gender nonconforming (TGNC) people identify and express themselves in numerous ways with regard to gender identity and sexual and/or relational orientation. In this chapter, we provide an in-depth discussion of the gender diversity existing underneath the TGNC umbrella of identities and how this may inform sexual and/or relational orientation identities. Emphasis is placed on people with nonbinary gender identities and the many challenges that exist for these individuals, in addition to their needs in TGNC-affirming practice. In this chapter, we use the term *gender nonbinary* as an umbrella term to describe people for whom the labels *man* and *woman* are not accurate or not sufficient in describing their gender identities. Gender nonbinary people may or may not identify as TGNC men or women. Some gender nonbinary people define themselves in relation to the concepts of male/man and female/woman (e.g., fluidly moving between, neither, both, in the middle), whereas others do not (Wilchins, 2002). Within the broader realm of nonbinary

http://dx.doi.org/10.1037/14957-002
Affirmative Counseling and Psychological Practice With Transgender and Gender Nonconforming Clients, A. A. Singh and l. m. dickey (Editors)

gender identities, there are many other specific gender identities, labels, and descriptors (Wilchins, 2002). This chapter seeks to educate the reader about the variety of gender identities that exist underneath the TGNC umbrella and highlight the underrepresented needs of those who identify outside of the gender binary system. In doing so, sexual orientation and relational diversity of TGNC communities are reviewed, including misconceptions and microaggressions this community faces. The chapter concludes with a discussion of how mental health providers (MHPs) may work with this community and a case vignette.

Key Concepts

The *gender binary system*, which assumes that all people fall into categories of either male/man/masculine or female/woman/feminine (Burdge, 2007), is time specific and culturally informed; therefore, it varies over time and across cultures and countries around the globe (Stryker, 2008). Very present in Western societies, it is essential to note that the gender binary is not a universal cultural construct (binaohan, 2014). There is growing awareness about TGNC people who fit the narrative of being assigned one sex at birth and transitioning to the other binary gender (Brill & Pepper, 2008; Ehrensaft, 2011), and there are increasingly more health care systems available to these people (Williamson, 2010). Although this may be the authentic experience for a number of people under the TGNC umbrella, the dangers of applying this medicalized narrative as a one-size-fits-all approach in conceptualizing TGNC experience (Spade, 2006) include reinforcing a gender binary by assuming that all TGNC people seek medical transition (e.g., hormones, surgery), and continuing to pathologize TGNC identity as a mental illness. Such a model universalizes and necessitates distress (and a formal psychiatric diagnosis) to access medical transition. The act of pathologizing gender transition denies the existence of the many groups of TGNC people who do not fit into the gender binary system.

In opposition to the medicalized narrative of gender and gender identity is the idea of self-identification. Self-identification is related to self-determination and is the ability, right, and freedom of each individual to make decisions about their[1] gender identity and/or expression in a manner that is authentic. Clients' self-identification is respected

---

[1]The singular form of the pronouns *they/them/their* are used in place of the standard *he/him/his* and *she/her/hers* pronouns to demonstrate the use of gender neutral pronouns when the client-identified gender pronoun is unknown or unspecified. These pronouns are also self-designated as a third person pronoun by some people who identify as nonbinary or genderqueer.

regardless of the sex to which they were assigned at birth, how others may perceive them, their legally recognized name or gender marker, the extent to which one has socially transitioned from one gender role to another, or whether or not they have medically transitioned (de Vries, 2012). Exploring and respecting TGNC individuals' self-identification is not only key in building effective working relationships but also a way to undermine the systemic dismissal and pathologization of TGNC individuals from within the mental health industry. This also includes using correct self-designated pronouns, which may be the common pronouns of he/him/his and she/her/hers, alternative gender-neutral pronouns of they/them/theirs (Budge et al., 2013), and/or pronouns that change in relation to the presenting gender. TGNC people often use as much creativity in designating their appropriate pronouns as they do their authentic gender identities (Beemyn & Rankin, 2011). Although not encompassing all of the pronouns used by nonbinary individuals, a pocket-size card created by the LGBT Resource Center at the University of Wisconsin–Milwaukee provides guidance to usage when someone prefers an alternative to (a) he/she, (b) him/her, (c) his/her, (d) his/hers, or (e) himself/herself (see https://lgbt.wisc.edu/documents/LGBTCC-Gender_pronoun_guide.pdf).

Nonbinary (Gender) Identities

Though the term *TGNC* is intended to be inclusive of people whose gender identities do not fall within the gender binary system, some nonbinary people identify as TGNC, whereas others do not (Davidson, 2007; McLemore, 2015). It is important to recognize that the existence of nonbinary identities is not a new, modern, or solely Western phenomenon. Reducing gender into two binary categories is an act of colonization and is firmly rooted in a history of racial oppression and erasure of indigenous people and/or people of color (binaohan, 2014). Historical accounts show evidence of people who did not conform to traditional genders dating back centuries within Northern America (e.g., Native American two-spirit people) and beyond, including in Thailand, India, China, and Greece (Feinberg, 1996; Halberstam, 1998; Nanda, 2014; Scholz, 2001; Totman, 2011). One could consider nonbinary identities predating the more commonly known TGNC identities as they emerged in the 20th century (Feinberg, 1996; Halberstam, 1998).

The following is a brief review of some of the terms that are in popular usage today in the United States to describe gender identity outside of the binary. This is by no means an exhaustive list, and conventional usage of these terms is always evolving and varies depending on region and culture (Hill, 2007). It is important to respect the identity terms or labels that are self-designated or used by each particular person. The term *genderqueer* emerged as an individual identity label in the mid-1990s and has been associated with the writings of Wilchins (2002). Although accurate population estimates are not known, in a 2008 large national survey of TGNC people, 22% of 6,450 respondents reported using genderqueer as at least one term to describe their gender identity (Grant et al., 2011). In addition, over half of the 292 participants in a 2012 study of people who fall under the broader umbrella of TGNC identified as genderqueer (Kuper, Nussbaum, & Mustanski, 2012).

Some genderqueer people consider themselves as not conforming to the sex they were assigned at birth, whereas others consider themselves as not conforming to any notions of binary gender. Genderqueer people have a wide array of gender expressions, and two people who use the term to describe their gender identities may outwardly express this very differently, even if they use the same identity term. One person may identify as neither man nor woman, whereas someone else may identify as both or vacillating between the two. *Nonbinary* is an overarching term that includes any number of gender identities that do not fit with the dichotomous categories of male/man/masculine and female/woman/feminine and is sometimes used interchangeably with the term genderqueer (McLemore, 2015).

Gender nonconforming (GNC) describes people who feel their gender identity does not fully align with their sex assigned at birth. It is also frequently used to describe young children who exhibit an appearance or behaviors that seem to break, bend, or deviate from gender roles expected for boys or girls. Some, but not all, of these young people may eventually grow up to be TGNC (Ehrensaft, 2011). There are cisgender people who may consider themselves as GNC, including gay, lesbian, bisexual, and queer cisgender people, and may even have identity labels related to this variance in gender expression (e.g., butch, femme, stud; Kuper, Wright, & Mustanski, 2014). *Third gender* refers to people who see themselves and their gender identities as existing outside the realm of male and female (Namaste, 2000). People who identify as third gender do not usually view themselves as being on the same continuum or spectrum as men and women, but rather as a separate, distinct point. This notion is best captured by the quote "Gender is a universe and we are all stars," which has been associated with activist, educator, and artist Micah Bazant (2006, p. 7).

Gender neutral is a term used to refer to people who see themselves as having a neutral gender identity and/or expression (Ehrensaft, 2011). People who identify as *agender* see themselves as not having a gender. This term is sometimes used interchangeably with *genderless, neutrois, null-gender,* or *nongendered* (Barker & Richards, 2012; Zimmer, Solomon, & Carson, 2014). There are also people do not want any labels pertaining to gender (Bulldagger, 2006), while other communities have evolved language to be more reflective of their gender identity. *Masculine of center* (MOC; Cole & Han, 2011) is a term that has become more popular, especially in communities of color, to describe people assigned female at birth who identify as being on the more masculine side of a continuum between masculinity and femininity. Some people who identify as MOC also identify as transgender or under the TGNC umbrella, while others consider themselves simply as gender nonconforming (without a TGNC identity). *Androgyne*, which is sometimes used interchangeably with *intergender*, refers to someone who views their gender identity as existing somewhere between man and woman, or both (Zimmer et al., 2014). *Multigender, polygender, bigender,* and *genderfluid* are all terms that may describe someone whose experience of gender identity is more dynamic, sometimes moving between or simultaneously having more than one gender at one time (Kuper et al., 2012). This fluidity may be dependent on context, such as in different settings, at different times, or within different relationships.

Gender-Affirming Medical Interventions for Nonbinary Identified People

Although nonbinary identified people may not identify strictly as men or women, this does not mean that many are not interested in accessing medical transition services. Some people with nonbinary genders seek out medical services such as masculinizing/feminizing hormone therapy and/or surgeries to feel more affirmed in their bodies; however, their transitions may or may not resemble those of people who consider themselves as having binary genders. In addition, nonbinary individuals may not experience gender dysphoria or not experience it as has been conceptualized for binary identified TGNC individuals. Some people who transition or seek gender-affirming medical interventions still identify as nonbinary, so this label may be used regardless of one's social or medical transition status. When gender nonbinary people desire to medically alter their bodies they are often met with skepticism by the health care establishment (Ansara & Hegarty, 2012; Bradford, Reisner, Honnold, & Xavier, 2013), especially if they do not exhibit characteristics similar to people who identify as having a more binary gender identity. For example, if a client uses nonbinary pronouns (e.g., they, their) and/or desires surgeries but not hormones, these actions may be interpreted as not fitting the medical model of TGNC care. In these situations, it is possible that a provider will deny care

(Denny, 2004) either because of a lack of understanding and/or provider bias (Puckett, Cleary, Rossman, Newcomb, & Mustanski, 2015). These kinds of reactions from providers may leave nonbinary clients feeling that they are "not trans enough" to be approved for services. Even highly experienced MHPs and health care providers who consider themselves "gender specialists" are not always knowledgeable about or accepting of people who exist beyond the binary gender system, as the medical and psychiatric literature tends to represent only those who have binary identities or fit a traditional medicalized narrative (Denny, 2004). The World Professional Association for Transgender Health's "Standards of Care for the Health of Transsexual, Transgender, and Gender-Nonconforming People" (Coleman et al., 2012) is now more inclusive of people who are GNC and do not subscribe to binary identities; however, this does not mean that all providers have the training or competence to work with these individuals. Encountering assumptions from health care providers and MHPs about one's identity or how and if one desires to medically transition can create stress and unnecessary pressure on gender nonbinary people who already face similar pressures by others in their lives or even strangers (Ansara & Hegarty, 2012; Bradford et al., 2013). Fearing discrimination, nonbinary people may avoid seeking health care services (Harrison, Grant, & Herman, 2012).

Models of Gender Identity and Sexual Orientation Development

This section discusses models of gender identity and sexual orientation as they pertain to TGNC people. The most prominent model for gender identity development is Kohlberg's (1966) gender constancy model, which suggests that children establish *gender identity*, or awareness that they and others are male or female by the age of 3. They then achieve a sense of *gender stability*, recognition that gender is stable across time, by the age of 4 or 5. By the age of 6 or 7, children achieve *gender consistency*, a sense of knowing that their sex is fixed and unchangeable over time and across situations (Siegal & Robinson, 1987). TGNC children may similarly come into awareness about their gender identity at a young age. However, coming into gender stability and gender consistency and realizing that their bodies cannot change to match gender identity may be the catalyst for feelings of distress (Brill & Pepper, 2008). Kohlberg's model is controversial and has been criticized for underestimating the role of parental or societal reinforcement of gendered behaviors (Shaffer

& Kipp, 2013). Although Kohlberg's model may be applicable for many TGNC people, especially those who report having an early awareness of gender identity not aligning with societal expectations related to sex assigned at birth, it does not fully account for people whose gender identities are experienced as fluid or for people who are not aware of TGNC identity until adolescence, early adulthood, or even later in life.

Some attempts have been made to describe gender identity development in a way that is inclusive of TGNC people (Bilodeau & Renn, 2005; Bockting & Coleman, 2007; Burdge, 2007; Devor, 2004; Hill, 2007). These models propose that TGNC people undergo various stages, including awareness, expression, exploration, and identity integration (Bockting & Coleman, 2007; Devor, 2004). Although many TGNC and gender nonbinary people may be aware of gender identity when they are toddlers, many do not come into awareness of being TGNC until later in childhood or during adolescence or adulthood. Developmental pathways for gender identity and sexual orientation are distinct, with gender identity typically forming prior to sexual orientation (Devor, 2004). Many stage models for sexual orientation, based on Eurocentric models of "coming out" as a uniform process, do not take into account the fluidity and complexity that may be present for many nonheterosexual, non-White, non-Western, and noncisgender individuals (Bilodeau & Renn, 2005). D'Augelli's (1994) model of sexual orientation development accounts environmental and biological factors and may be more inclusive of a wider range of identities and experiences. Though it refers to sexual orientation identity development, D'Augelli's model has been used to discuss TGNC identity formation (Bilodeau & Renn, 2005).

At this time, there is not a model of sexual orientation identity development specific to TGNC people. However, dickey, Burnes, and Singh (2012) present a model that addresses the influences for the development of sexual orientation identity development in female-to-male individuals. This model includes examples of antecedents, interactions between gender identity and sexual orientation, and consequences, as well as experiences of marginalization and resilience factors. Lurie's (2015) traditional and authentic gender models may be used to demonstrate how TGNC people may vary from societal expectations on the basis of sex assigned at birth. In the traditional gender model, people assigned male at birth are expected to adopt masculine gender roles, identify as men, and be attracted to women. Meanwhile, people assigned female at birth are expected to adopt feminine gender roles, identify as women, and be attracted to men. In contrast, the authentic gender model allows for a range of sexes, gender roles, gender identities, sexual orientations, and relationships between these constructs. It is far more inclusive of people who are not cisgender and heterosexual. One of the limitations of this model is that these constructs still exist on a continuum. Words and constructs such as *continuum, range,* and *spectrum* do not accurately represent the diversity, and, in some cases, the fluidity, that exists within the TGNC population (Bulldagger, 2006; McLemore, 2015).

Challenges and Barriers Faced by Gender Nonbinary People

People who identify as gender nonbinary have varied experiences in terms of how they are treated by others in society. These variations may exist within one individual (depending on how the person is read or perceived by others); may differ between individuals (with different gender expressions); or may be highly influenced by other markers of cultural identity, privilege, or marginalization, particularly race and class (Saketopoulou, 2011). Gender nonbinary people often face the intersecting challenges of sexism and nonbinary oppression (Serano, 2007), and this may lead to significant risks to physical safety and well being (Walton, 2004). Gender nonbinary people are more likely to be people of color (30% compared with 23%) and more likely to be multiracial (18% compared with 11%; Harrison et al., 2012) than TGNC people who do not identify as nonbinary. Compared with TGNC people with binary gender identities, genderqueer and other nonbinary individuals also face unique patterns of gender identity–based discrimination and violence, including higher rates of physical assault and police harassment (Harrison et al., 2012; Hill & Willoughby, 2005). The suicide rate for TGNC people is significantly higher than that of the general population (Grant et al., 2011), and the rates of suicidality and attempts for genderqueer and gender nonbinary people are even higher (Budge et al., 2013; Clements-Nolle, Marx, & Katz, 2006). Gender nonbinary people may have lower incomes despite having higher educational attainment and are more likely to work in underground economies (Harrison et al., 2012).

Gender nonbinary people face other environmental and institutional barriers. Examples include completing paperwork that only includes two options for gender, not having their names and pronouns respected by others, and difficulty accessing spaces that are typically sex-segregated (Budge, Tebbe, & Howard, 2010; Herman, 2013; Smith, Shin, & Officer, 2012). Some gender nonbinary people can comfortably choose to exercise options that afford privilege, whereas others do not have viable choices (Herman, 2013). Some gender nonbinary people may choose to use gendered restrooms (i.e., restrooms clearly delineated for men or women) and feel relatively comfortable doing so. For others faced with these binary options for restrooms, neither choice may be safe or truly reflective of their identity.

Creating a sense of belonging and community can, at times, be challenging for gender nonbinary people who do not have access to or do not know others who identify in similar ways (e.g., genderqueer). They may experience "androphobia" from cisgender and TGNC people who endorse the gender binary (Kern, 2012, p. 242). The experience of misrepresentation and invisibility in historical accounts, as well as popular culture, may be heightened for gender nonbinary people (Bornstein, 1994). They may also lack role models in the professional world, as most professional clothing is highly gendered. Workplace dynamics, including expression of gender through clothing, pose significant challenges for many TGNC people (Budge et al., 2010; Tobia, 2014).

Common Misconceptions and Microaggressions Experienced by Gender Nonbinary People

TGNC people often face discrimination in multiple areas of their lives (Bradford et al., 2013; Grant et al., 2011). This includes blatant violence, such as police brutality (Edelman, 2011), and more subtle, yet pervasive, experiences of bias in the form of microaggressions (Nadal, Rivera, & Corpus, 2010). The following are common challenges that are more specific to having a nonbinary or (perceived) nonbinary gendered identity and/or expression.

MISCONCEPTION 1: "YOU DO NOT EXIST"

People with nonbinary gender identities are, perhaps, the most misunderstood of all. The medicalized, universalized, and often sensationalized narrative for TGNC experience (de Vries, 2012; Spade, 2006) perpetuates the idea that all TGNC people identify as the opposite of what they were assigned at birth. The assumption is, for example, that if someone is not or does not want to be a boy, that person is or wants to be a girl. This narrative, unfortunately, allows no space for people who do not identify with either. Because this narrative is so engrained in what it is to be transgender, people who identify as genderqueer or as having a nonbinary gender are often met with disbelief and skepticism. This disbelief and skepticism is a by-product and indication of how deeply woven the gender binary is into the fabric of society's narrow conceptions of sex and gender. As a result, people with nonbinary or genderqueer identities do not feel seen or validated by others for what is true and authentic for them. Out of their own discomfort or inability to tolerate ambiguity, people often challenge or pressure gender nonbinary people to make a choice to identify as either a man or a woman.

MISCONCEPTION 2: GENDER NONBINARY AS PRETRANSGENDER

Gender nonbinary people are often seen as not being able to commit to being TGNC or transitioning. Like bisexual people, gender nonbinary people are seen as not yet at their ultimate destination (Eisner, 2013). They are viewed as identifying as gender nonbinary only temporarily or until they can make the decision to engage in a social and/or medical transition. Although some people do identify as nonbinary prior to identifying as TGNC, FTM, or MTF, some people have a nonbinary identity that is stable and consistent over time. These clients may never transition to a different gender. Common microaggressions related to this stereotype include pressuring a gender nonbinary person to choose a binary identity and pressuring them to socially or medically transition (Bradford et al., 2013).

MISCONCEPTION 3: GENDER NONBINARY PEOPLE HAVE PERSONALITY DISORDERS

Gender nonbinary people are assumed to be unstable or lack a sense of self because they cannot choose or identify with a binary gender. As a result, they may be labeled as having borderline personality disorder (Meyer-Bahlburg, 2010). Some people have stable genderqueer or nonbinary gender identities. Even people who identify as genderfluid or moving between genders may consider their experience of fluidity as consistent, stable, or predictable. These clients may experience MHPs dismissing their gender concerns and instead focusing on treatment for personality disorders.

MISCONCEPTION 4: BEING GENDER NONBINARY IS A NEW PHENOMENON

Because many people are not as familiar with gender nonbinary identities or transition trajectories, the existence of gender nonbinary identities or experiences may be perceived as a recent emergence or a social trend. This assumption is erroneous, as well as Eurocentric, as gender nonbinary people have existed throughout history in many different cultures (binaohan, 2014; Stryker, 2008). An associated microaggression is not being taken seriously by others who perceive nonbinary identity as a fad.

MISCONCEPTION 5: GENDER NONBINARY PEOPLE WANT SPECIAL TREATMENT

For the most part, society does not recognize the existence of gender nonbinary people (Harrison et al., 2012; Herman, 2013). When gender nonbinary people express the need for all gender restrooms, gender neutral pronouns, or more than two gender boxes on a form or application, they are presumed to be asking for special privileges rather than a right to exist and be recognized along with cisgender people and TGNC people who do identify as male or female (Herman, 2013). Nonbinary people may have to deal with others' complaints about having to change ways of thinking or communicating (e.g., "These gender neutral pronouns are too hard for me. Why do I have to change just to make you feel comfortable?").

MISCONCEPTION 6: GENDER NONBINARY PEOPLE ARE TAKING THE EASY WAY OUT

Because not all gender nonbinary people seek medical services to feel affirmed in their gender, they may be viewed as having a more privileged form of gender identity and/or expression than TGNC people who seek these services and encounter barriers or systemic discrimination. It is useful to recognize that these are overgeneralizations negating experiences each unique individual has. For some, it is more difficult to have an ambiguous or nonbinary gender expression, as this makes one a more visible target for anti-TGNC bias (Grant et al., 2011; Harrison et al., 2012). Others, including TGNC people with binary identities, may treat nonbinary people as if they do not know what it is like to deal with anti-trans bias or discrimination.

Sexual Orientation Diversity Within the TGNC Community

Just as gender presentation has been used to limit access to medical care for TGNC individuals, so has sexuality (Denny, 2004). During the 1950s and 1960s heterosexuality following medical transition was a requirement to access to gender-affirming medical care (Lawrence, 2005). Accounts in the literature of sexual orientation diversity in the TGNC community began to emerge in the late 1960s and 1970s, and research on sexuality pre- and posttransition was conducted during the 1980s and 1990s (Lawrence, 2005). Currently there is a better understanding of the sexual diversity within the TGNC community. However, it is essential to note that much of the literature on TGNC sexuality is pathologizing toward TGNC women (Serano, 2010) and there is very little research on the sexual experiences of nonbinary individuals (Constantinides, 2011).

Most sexual orientation labels are based either on binary notions of assigned sex at birth or gender identity in relation to the assigned sex or gender identity of the person to whom one is attracted (Budge, Rossman, & Howard, 2014; Davidson, 2007; de Vries, 2012). TGNC and gender nonbinary people may identify as gay, lesbian, heterosexual, bisexual, pansexual, omnisexual, queer, or something else altogether (Davidson, 2007; Hill, 2007; Kennedy, 2013; Kuper et al., 2012; Nadal et al., 2010). Some TGNC people identify as asexual or as not having interest in sex (Bogaert, 2006). For some people, shifts in gender identity and/or expression may affect one's desire to explore sexuality with people of various gender identities and/or expressions (Hill, 2007). Other people may make assumptions about a TGNC or gender nonbinary person's sexual orientation on the basis of the perceived gender identity of that person and that person's partner. Because assumptions about gender identity are not accurately perceived, the sexual orientation identities of TGNC people may be invisible (Kennedy, 2013).

Consider the example of Jude, who was assigned male at birth, identifies as gender neutral, and varies in terms of how zie[2] is perceived by others. At times, zie is perceived as a gay or feminine man, at other times as a woman. Hir partner, Kyle, was assigned female at birth, identifies as genderqueer and a TGNC male, and generally passes as a man in society. When Jude and Kyle are walking down the street as a couple, they may be perceived as heterosexual or gay, depending on how others perceive Jude's gender identity in a given instance. Neither Jude nor Kyle identifies as straight or gay; they both consider themselves queer in terms of sexual orientation because it allows for a broader definition that is inclusive of the ways in which their relationship does not operate within the gender binary system. This example illustrates the limitations of sexual orientation labels and the concept of sexual orientation.

Relational Structure Orientations

There are a variety of ways that TGNC people engage in sexual and romantic interactions or relationships. Some TGNC people have relationships that resemble those of the dominant culture and may even be

---

[2]In this case example, the client's self-designated gender neutral pronouns are *zie/hir/hirs*.

considered heteronormative, whereas others may vary from the norm. Many TGNC people have relationships that are *monogamous* (i.e., one exclusive sexual and/or romantic relationship between two people). In this way, they may fit in with the dominant cultural norms. However, some TGNC and gender nonbinary people may identify as *polyamorous*, which is an umbrella term to describe relationship configurations that allow for and even celebrate consensual *nonmonogamy* (Taormino, 2013). Polyamory is different from infidelity in that all parties involved are aware of and agree to the relationship structure. People who practice polyamory or identify as polyamorous choose to engage in romantic and/or sexual relationships with more than one person. Some people identify as polyamorous in ways somewhat similar to a sexual orientation, so this label may be applied regardless of behavior (e.g., dating, being single or celibate). In some forms of polyamory or consensual nonmonogamy, sexual involvements with more than one person are permitted, whereas romantic or emotional relationships are not (Labriola, 1999; Taormino, 2013).

An *open relationship* is one in which two or more people are in a relationship and have the freedom to engage sexually and/or romantically with others outside of the relationship (Taormino, 2013). In some relationships, one person may choose to be monogamous, whereas the other is polyamorous. These relationships may be considered blended polyamorous/monogamous relationships (Labriola, 1999).

Another aspect of relational orientation that may vary is involvement with *kink/BDSM*. BDSM is an acronym that stands for bondage and discipline, domination and submission, and sadomasochism. Along with the term kink, the term BDSM is generally used as an overarching term to describe a number of erotic activities or interpersonal dynamics that typically involve a consensual play of power dynamics (Ortmann & Sprott, 2012). This may involve enacting dynamics of dominance and submission, whereas for others it is about seeking specific physical sensations. In some instances, kink/BDSM may involve acting out fantasy roles or aspects of identity that may be different from what that person may usually express in their everyday life.

Gender play occurs when a person takes on a gender expression and/or role that is different from how they usually present themselves. Involvement in kink/BDSM may range from being an integral part of one's identity, an occasional part of their sex lives, or something of little to no interest whatsoever. Although the *Diagnostic and Statistical Manual of Mental Disorders, Fifth Edition* (*DSM–5*; American Psychiatric Association, 2013) includes diagnoses that involve clinically indicated distress or impairment related to sexual fetishes or paraphilias, the manual clearly states that kink/BDSM in itself is not an indication of pathology. When practiced with intention and consent, it can be a healthy and fulfilling part of a person's sex life (Easton, 2007).

Case Vignette

Devon is a 19-year old, multiracial (Black and Native American) person assigned male at birth who identifies as two-spirit, gender fluid, and bisexual. Devon uses gender-neutral they/them/their pronouns. Devon reported going to an MHP at an LGBT center to talk about safety concerns after being harassed on the street for having a GNC appearance. As soon as the MHP, who was a White cisgender gay man, heard that Devon had a TGNC identity, he proceeded to use she/her/hers pronouns to refer to Devon. He also asked inappropriate questions about whether Devon wanted "the surgery" or "how bad Devon's gender dysphoria" was. Devon reported that they did not relate to the concept of gender dysphoria, did not desire medical transition, and had gone there to get emotional support for a frightening interaction they had had. Feeling pigeonholed and misunderstood, Devon did not return to this MHP after the first session.

Through an acquaintance, Devon was able to find the name of an MHP who was sensitive to their unique needs as a person who has a nonbinary identity. This MHP, who is genderqueer and mixed race (Pacific Islander and White), helped Devon to work through their traumatic experience, to identify strengths and sources of resilience (e.g., dance and connections to spirituality rooted in their ancestries), and to collaboratively develop a safety plan. Devon felt seen and validated and felt that the MHP was attentive to their concerns. This allowed Devon to further explore experiences with the mainstream LGBT community that were not always affirming, including experiences of racism, biphobia, and the pressure to identify with a binary TGNC narrative. Devon and their MHP were also able to explore their relationship to each other as TGNC people with very different gender identities and expressions. This helped Devon be more assertive about how they wanted to be addressed by others.

Counseling With Gender Nonbinary People: Recommendations for Mental Health Professionals

Information about gender nonbinary people, such as Devon in the previous case vignette, is largely absent in academic literature. Existing scholarship on TGNC people tends to focus solely on individuals existing within the gender binary (Bilodeau, 2005). As a result, MHPs, along with other health professionals, often do not have the necessary skills, knowledge, or awareness to provide culturally sensitive and affirming services (Burdge, 2007). However, research does suggest that social support and coping is influential in the moderating experiences of psychological distress for gender nonbinary people, with higher levels of social support and help seeking associated with fewer symptoms of anxiety and depression (Budge et al., 2014). In addition, it is important to emphasize that not all gender nonbinary clients experience their gender identities in the same way, nor is there a singular, appropriate way for MHPs to provide services to them. These recommendations can be used broadly as guides for culturally sensitive care and as prompts for deeper exploration with each individual.

KEEP AN OPEN MIND

As there are many ways that a person can identify under the umbrella of nonbinary gender, each client who enters the counseling relationship is the expert on their own gender identity. Regardless of how many other TGNC people the MHP has encountered, clinical encounters should be approached with cultural humility and a willingness to learn about each client's unique identity and needs (Burdge, 2007; Smith et al., 2012).

ENGAGE IN SELF-EXAMINATION

Nonbinary identities challenge basic societal assumptions about gender and MHPs should actively explore and increase awareness of their own relationships to gender identity. MHPs should explore how their gender identities, whether cisgender TGNC or nonbinary, may contribute to assumptions about TGNC people (Singh & Burnes, 2009, 2010).

DO NOT ASSUME A DESTINATION

Although some gender nonbinary people may be questioning their gender identity and/or expression, some are happy existing in a nonbinary space. MHPs should be aware of unconscious bias toward the gender binary and how this may inadvertently create pressure for a nonbinary person to transition or adhere to the gender binary (Singh & Burnes, 2009, 2010). MHPs should refrain from assuming that gender nonbinary people are merely passing through this identity to a binary TGNC identity or expression.

PRIORITIZE CLIENT SELF-DETERMINATION OVER MHP FRUSTRATION, CONFUSION, OR OPINION

MHPs are encouraged to refrain from commenting on or sharing their opinions about someone's name, gender identity, or choice of pronoun, including going into detail about why gender neutral pronouns are so difficult to use. The frustration or confusion an MHP feels related to gender nonbinary identities is not the client's responsibility to manage.

CHALLENGE IDEAS OF WHAT IS A MAN OR A WOMAN

Challenging the gender binary includes knowing the ways in which gender identity or gender role may differ from gender expression. For example, there are butch-identified TGNC women and femme-identified TGNC men. Working with gender nonbinary people requires expanding one's definition of what it means to be a man, a woman, both, or neither, developing the ability to accept what appears to be ambiguous or unfamiliar. An MHP gender-inclusive framework is helpful for MHPs and clients (Singh & Burnes, 2009, 2010).

DO NOT ASSUME PASSING IS THE ULTIMATE GOAL

Passing as a man or a woman may be the goal for some TGNC people, but this desire is not universal. MHPs should refrain from encouraging blending or passing if that is not what the client wants. This encouragement may seem well-meaning, but it does not respect a person's self-determination. MHPs are encouraged to interrogate their own countertransference or desire to "save" the person by protecting them from the hazards of being in the middle/neither spaces (Singh & Burnes, 2009, 2010). In addition, it is important to be aware of the concept of passing privilege (Sevelius, 2013), or lack thereof, and how this may affect a gender nonbinary person.

BE AWARE THAT SOCIAL PRESENTATION OR TRANSITION MAY BE NUANCED AND COMPLEX

A person's gender role may vary among different facets of their life. It is important to not assume a client's gender role is the same at work as it is at home, with family, in romantic relationships, or in their sex life. MHPs should be aware that one's gender presentation or choices about identity disclosure are often relational, dependent on context, and sometimes safety-based.

UNDERSTAND BARRIERS AND BE WILLING TO ADVOCATE FOR CLIENTS

As noted earlier, nonbinary folks face an array of challenges in their daily lives. As an MHP, is it essential not only to help nonbinary clients gain skills in navigating systems but also to advocate for clients. Examples of places where MHPs can advocate for nonbinary range from creating more inclusive paper work to working directly with medical providers to assure that their clients have access to transition related services. MHPs working with nonbinary individuals need to be knowledgeable about the barriers that exist in their area and able to assist clients in finding solutions and alternative resources. MHPs are encouraged to act on their clients' behalf. This may include correcting other people (i.e., colleagues, other health professionals) who use the incorrect names or pronouns when referring to the client and by refraining from making excuses for people in the world who expect gender nonbinary people to conform to binary gender expectations.

Chapter Summary

In this chapter, we reviewed basic concepts related to the wide spectrum of gender identity with a special focus on gender nonbinary people. Gender nonbinary people vary in terms of gender identity and/or expression, if and how they transition, and sexual and/or romantic attractions and relationship orientations. MHPs seeking to provide affirmative care with gender nonbinary people are encouraged to be aware of the common misconceptions and counseling recommendations provided in this chapter.

References

American Psychiatric Association. (2013). *Diagnostic and statistical manual of mental disorders* (5th ed.). Washington, DC: Author.

Ansara, Y. G., & Hegarty, P. (2012). Cisgenderism in psychology: Pathologising and misgendering children from 1999 to 2008. *Psychology and Sexuality, 3*, 137–160. http://dx.doi.org/10.1080/19419899.2011.576696

Barker, M. J., & Richards, C. (2012). Further genders. In E. Kuhlmann & E. Annandale (Eds.), *The Palgrave handbook of the psychology of sexuality and gender* (pp. 166–181). London, England: Palgrave Macmillan.

Bazant, M. (2006). *Trans respect/etiquette/support 101*. Retrieved from http://www.jmu.edu/safezone/wm_library/3.TransRespect101.pdf

Beemyn, B. G., & Rankin, S. (2011). *The lives of transgender people*. New York, NY: Columbia University.

Bilodeau, B. (2005). Beyond the gender binary: A case study of two transgender students at a Midwestern research university. *Journal of*

Gay & Lesbian Issues in Education, 3, 29–44. http://dx.doi.org/10.1300/J367v03n01_05

Bilodeau, B. L., & Renn, K. A. (2005). Analysis of LGBT identity development models and implications for practice. *New Directions for Student Services, 2005*(111), 25–39. http://dx.doi.org/10.1002/ss.171

binaohan, b. (2014). *Decolonizing trans/gender 101.* Retrieved from: https://publishbiyuti.org/decolonizingtransgender101/

Bockting, W. O., & Coleman, E. (2007). Developmental stages of the transgender coming-out process. In R. Ettner, S. Monstrey, & A. Eyler (Eds.), *Principles of transgender medicine and surgery* (pp. 185–208). New York, NY: Haworth.

Bogaert, A. F. (2006). Toward a conceptual understanding of asexuality. *Review of General Psychology, 10*, 241–250. http://dx.doi.org/10.1037/1089-2680.10.3.241

Bornstein, K. (1994). *Gender outlaw: On men, women, and the rest of us.* New York, NY: Routledge.

Bradford, J., Reisner, S. L., Honnold, J. A., & Xavier, J. (2013). Experiences of transgender-related discrimination and implications for health: Results from the Virginia Transgender Health Initiative Study. *American Journal of Public Health, 103*, 1820–1829. http://dx.doi.org/10.2105/AJPH.2012.300796

Brill, S., & Pepper, R. (2008). *The transgender child: A handbook for families and professionals.* San Francisco, CA: Cleis Press.

Budge, S. L., Katz-Wise, S. L., Tebbe, E. N., Howard, K. A., Schneider, C. L., & Rodriguez, A. (2013). Transgender emotional and coping processes facilitative and avoidant coping throughout gender transitioning. *The Counseling Psychologist, 41*, 601–647. http://dx.doi.org/10.1177/0011000011432753

Budge, S. L., Rossman, H. K., & Howard, K. A. (2014). Coping and psychological distress among genderqueer individuals: The moderating effect of social support. *Journal of LGBT Issues in Counseling, 8*, 95–117. http://dx.doi.org/10.1080/15538605.2014.853641

Budge, S. L., Tebbe, E. N., & Howard, K. A. (2010). The work experiences of transgender individuals: Negotiating the transition and career decision-making processes. *Journal of Counseling Psychology, 57*, 377–393. http://dx.doi.org/10.1037/a0020472

Bulldagger, R. (2006). The end of genderqueer. In M. B. Sycamore (Ed.), *Nobody passes: Rejecting the rules of gender and conformity* (pp. 137–148). Berkeley, CA: Seal Press.

Burdge, B. J. (2007). Bending gender, ending gender: Theoretical foundations for social work practice with the transgender community. *Social Work, 52*, 243–250. http://dx.doi.org/10.1093/sw/52.3.243

Clements-Nolle, K., Marx, R., & Katz, M. (2006). Attempted suicide among transgender persons: The influence of gender-based discrimination and victimization. *Journal of Homosexuality, 51,* 53–69. http://dx.doi.org/10.1300/J082v51n03_04

Cole, B., & Han, L. (2011). *Freeing ourselves: A guide to health and self love for brown bois.* Oakland, CA: Brown Boi Project.

Coleman, E., Bockting, W., Botzer, M., Cohen-Kettenis, P., DeCuypere, G., Feldman, J., . . . Zucker, K. (2012). Standards of care for the health of transsexual, transgender, and gender-nonconforming people, 7th version. *International Journal of Transgenderism, 13,* 165–232. http://dx.doi.org/10.1080/15532739.2011.700873

Constantinides, D. M. (2011). *Intersections of gender and intimacy in the lives of transgender people with non-binary gender identities.* (Doctoral dissertation). Retrieved from ProQuest. (3456031)

D'Augelli, A. R. (1994). Identity development and sexual orientation: Toward a model of lesbian, gay, and bisexual development. In E. J. Trickett, R. J. Watts, & D. Birman (Eds.), *Human diversity: Perspectives on people in context* (pp. 312–333). San Francisco, CA: Jossey-Bass.

Davidson, M. (2007). Seeking refuge under the umbrella: Inclusion, exclusion, and organizing within the category transgender. *Sexuality Research & Social Policy, 4,* 60–80. http://dx.doi.org/10.1525/srsp.2007.4.4.60

Denny, D. (2004). Changing models of transsexualism. *Journal of Gay & Lesbian Psychotherapy, 8,* 25–40.

Devor, A. H. (2004). Witnessing and mirroring: A fourteen-stage model of transsexual identity formation. *Journal of Gay & Lesbian Psychotherapy, 8,* 41–67.

de Vries, K. M. (2012). Intersectional identities and conceptions of the self: The experience of transgender people. *Symbolic Interaction, 35,* 49–67. http://dx.doi.org/10.1002/symb.2

dickey, l. m., Burnes, T. R., & Singh, A. A. (2012). Sexual identity development of female-to-male transgender individuals: A grounded theory inquiry. *Journal of LGBT Issues in Counseling, 6,* 118–138. http://dx.doi.org/10.1080/15538605.2012.678184

Easton, D. (2007). Shadowplay: S/M journeys to ourselves. In D. Langdridge & M. Barker (Eds.), *Safe, sane and consensual: Contemporary perspectives on sadomasochism* (pp. 217–228). New York, NY: Palgrave MacMillan.

Edelman, E. A. (2011). "This area has been declared a prostitution free zone": Discursive formations of space, the state, and trans "sex worker" bodies. *Journal of Homosexuality, 58,* 848–864. http://dx.doi.org/10.1080/00918369.2011.581928

Ehrensaft, D. (2011). *Gender born, gender made: Raising healthy gender-nonconforming children.* New York, NY: The Experiment.

Eisner, S. (2013). *Bi: Notes for a Bisexual Revolution.* San Francisco, CA: Seal Press.

Feinberg, L. (1996). *Transgender warriors: Making history from Joan of Arc to Dennis Rodman*. Boston, MA: Beacon.

Grant, J. M., Mottet, L. A., Tanis, J., Harrison, J., Herman, J. L., & Keisling, M. (2011). *Injustice at every turn: A report of the national transgender discrimination survey*. Washington, DC: National Center for Transgender Equality & National Gay and Lesbian Task Force. Retrieved from http://endtransdiscrimination.org/PDFs/NTDS_Report.pdf

Halberstam, J. (1998). *Female masculinity*. Durham, NC: Duke University.

Harrison, J., Grant, J., & Herman, J. L. (2012). A gender not listed here: Genderqueers, gender rebels and otherwise in the National Transgender Discrimination Study. *LGBT Policy Journal at the Harvard Kennedy School, 2*, 13–24. Retrieved from http://www.thetaskforce.org/static_html/downloads/reports/reports/gender_not_listed_here.pdf

Herman, J. L. (2013). Gendered restrooms and minority stress: The public regulation of gender and its impact on transgender people's lives. *Journal of Public Management and Social Policy, 19*, 65–80.

Hill, D. (2007). Trans/gender/sexuality. *Journal of Gay & Lesbian Social Services, 18*, 101–109. http://dx.doi.org/10.1300/J041v18n02_06

Hill, D. B., & Willoughby, B. L. (2005). The development and validation of the genderism and transphobia scale. *Sex Roles, 53*, 531–544. http://dx.doi.org/10.1007/s11199-005-7140-x

Kennedy, N. (2013). Cultural cisgenderism: Consequences of the imperceptible. *Psychology of Women Section Review, 15*, 3–11.

Kern, R. (2012). Andro-phobia?: When gender queer is too queer for *L Word* audiences. In K. Ross (Ed.), *The handbook of gender, sex, and media* (pp. 241–259). Malden, MA: John Wiley & Sons. http://dx.doi.org/10.1002/9781118114254.ch15

Kohlberg, L. (1966). A cognitive-developmental analysis of children's sex-role concepts and attitudes. In E. E. Maccoby (Ed.), *The development of sex differences* (pp. 82–173). Stanford, CA: Stanford University.

Kuper, L. E., Nussbaum, R., & Mustanski, B. (2012). Exploring the diversity of gender and sexual orientation identities in an online sample of transgender individuals. *Journal of Sex Research, 49*, 244–254. http://dx.doi.org/10.1080/00224499.2011.596954

Kuper, L. E., Wright, L., & Mustanski, B. (2014). Stud identity among female-born youth of color: Joint conceptualizations of gender variance and same-sex sexuality. *Journal of Homosexuality, 61*, 714–731. http://dx.doi.org/10.1080/00918369.2014.870443

Labriola, K. (1999). Models of open relationships. *Journal of Lesbian Studies, 3*, 217–225. http://dx.doi.org/10.1300/J155v03n01_25

Lawrence, A. A. (2005). Sexuality before and after male-to-female sex reassignment surgery. *Archives of Sexual Behavior, 34*, 147–166. http://dx.doi.org/10.1007/s10508-005-1793-y

Lurie, S. (2015). *Alternative gender model*. Unpublished manuscript.

McLemore, K. (2015). Experiences with misgendering: Identity and misclassification of transgender spectrum individuals. *Self and Identity, 14,* 51–74. http://dx.doi.org/10.1080/15298868.2014.950691

Meyer-Bahlburg, H. F. (2010). From mental disorder to iatrogenic hypogonadism: Dilemmas in conceptualizing gender identity variants as psychiatric conditions. *Archives of Sexual Behavior, 39,* 461–476. http://dx.doi.org/10.1007/s10508-009-9532-4

Nadal, K. L., Rivera, D. P., & Corpus, M. J. H. (2010). Sexual orientation and transgender microaggressions in everyday life: Experiences of lesbians, gays, bisexuals, and transgender individuals. In D. W. Sue (Ed.), *Microaggressions and marginality: Manifestation, dynamics, and impact* (pp. 217–240). New York, NY: Wiley.

Namaste, V. K. (2000). *Invisible lives: The erasure of trans-sexual and transgendered people.* Chicago, IL: University of Chicago.

Nanda, S. (2014). *Gender diversity: Crosscultural variations.* Long Grove, IL: Waveland Press.

Ortmann, D. M., & Sprott, R. A. (2012). *Sexual outsiders: Understanding BDSM sexualities and communities.* Lanham, MD: Rowman & Littlefield.

Puckett, J. A., Cleary, P., Rossman, K. H., Newcomb, M., & Mustanski, B. (2015). *Barriers to gender affirming care for transgender and gender nonconforming individuals.* Unpublished manuscript.

Saketopoulou, A. (2011). Minding the gap: Intersections between gender, race, and class in work with gender variant children. *Psychoanalytic Dialogues, 21,* 192–209. http://dx.doi.org/10.1080/10481885.2011.562845

Scholz, P. O. (2001). *Eunuchs and castrati: a cultural history.* Princeton, NJ: Markus Wiener.

Serano, J. (2007). *Whipping girl: A transsexual woman on sexism and the scapegoating of femininity.* Emeryville, CA: Seal Press.

Serano, J. M. (2010). The case against autogynephilia. *International Journal of Transgenderism, 12,* 176–187. http://dx.doi.org/10.1080/15532739.2010.514223

Sevelius, J. M. (2013). Gender affirmation: A framework for conceptualizing risk behavior among transgender women of color. *Sex Roles, 68,* 675–689. http://dx.doi.org/10.1007/s11199-012-0216-5

Shaffer, D., & Kipp, K. (2013). *Developmental psychology: Childhood and adolescence.* Independence, KY: Cengage Learning.

Siegal, M., & Robinson, J. (1987). Order effects in children's gender-constancy responses. *Developmental Psychology, 23,* 283–286. http://dx.doi.org/10.1037/0012-1649.23.2.283

Singh, A. A., & Burnes, T. R. (2009). Creating developmentally appropriate, safe counseling environments for transgender youth: The critical role of school counselors. *Journal of LGBT Issues in Counseling, 3,* 215–234. http://dx.doi.org/10.1080/15538600903379457

Singh, A. A., & Burnes, T. R. (2010). Introduction to the special issue: Translating the competencies for counseling with transgender clients into counseling practice, research, and advocacy. *Journal of LGBT Issues in Counseling, 4*, 126–134. http://dx.doi.org/10.1080/15538605. 2010.524837

Smith, L. C., Shin, R. Q., & Officer, L. M. (2012). Moving counseling forward on LGB and transgender issues speaking queerly on discourses and microaggressions. *The Counseling Psychologist, 40*, 385–408. http://dx.doi.org/10.1177/0011000011403165

Spade, D. (2006). Mutilating gender. In S. Stryker & S. Whittle (Eds.), *The transgender studies reader* (pp. 315–332). New York, NY: Taylor & Francis.

Stryker, S. (2008). *Transgender history.* Berkeley, CA: Seal Press.

Taormino, T. (2013). *Opening up: A guide to creating and sustaining open relationships.* San Francisco, CA: Cleis Press.

Tobia, J. (2014, June 10). Why I'm genderqueer, professional and unafraid. *Huffington Post.* Retrieved from http://www.huffingtonpost.com/jacob-tobia/genderqueer-professional-_b_5476239.html

Totman, R. (2011). *The third sex: Kathoey: Thailand's ladyboys.* London, England: Souvenir Press.

Walton, G. (2004). Bullying and homophobia in Canadian schools: The politics of policies, programs, and educational leadership. *Journal of Gay & Lesbian Issues in Education, 1*, 23–36. http://dx.doi.org/10.1300/J367v01n04_03

Wilchins, R. A. (2002). Queerer bodies. In J. Nestle, C. Howell, & R. Wilchins (Eds.), *Genderqueer: Voices from beyond the sexual binary* (pp. 33–47). Los Angeles, CA: Alyson.

Williamson, C. (2010). Providing care to transgender persons: A clinical approach to primary care, hormones, and HIV management. *The Journal of the Association of Nurses in AIDS Care, 21*, 221–229. http://dx.doi.org/10.1016/j.jana.2010.02.004

Zimmer, B., Solomon, J., & Carson, C. E. (2014). Among the new words. *American Speech, 89*, 470–496. http://dx.doi.org/10.1215/00031283-2908233

Anneliese A. Singh, Sel J. Hwahng, Sand C. Chang, and Bali White

Affirmative Counseling With Trans/Gender-Variant People of Color

2

This chapter focuses on specific points to consider in meeting the needs of trans/gender-variant (TGV) people of color (POC) as part of this volume on how to ensure professional and empowering interactions with TGV people in counseling and psychological settings. Based on the authors' collective professional expertise and life experiences as TGV POC, these are some key points we consider to be vital when initiating counseling and psychological work with TGV POC. After considerable deliberation, we agreed to use the term *gender-variant,* rather than *gender nonconforming,* as we believe it as most appropriate and inclusive for the population we are discussing in this chapter. We chose this term for several reasons, including the fact that in many sex/gender systems indigenous to Africa, Asia, the Pacific Islands, and the Americas (Besnier, 1996; Costa & Matzner, 2007; Gilley, 2006; Gosling & Osborne, 2006; Harvey, 1979; Henriquez, 2002; Hwahng, 2011; Hwahng & Lin, 2009; M. Johnson, 1997; Lang, 1998;

http://dx.doi.org/10.1037/14957-003
Affirmative Counseling and Psychological Practice With Transgender and Gender Nonconforming Clients, A. A. Singh and l. m. dickey (Editors)

Morris, 1994; Murray & Roscoe, 1998; Nanda, 1999; Oetomo, 2000; Reddy, 2005; Roscoe, 1998; Schifter, 1999; Sinnott, 2004), TGV identities have long been established and recognized as "traditional." Thus, the term *gender nonconforming* does not appear to incorporate these POC historical genealogies of gender-variance and seems to be most applicable to U.S. and Euro Western sex/gender systems that have historically (and often coercively) enforced highly restrictive cisgender binary identifications and presentations. By privileging the term *gender-variant*, we wish to reference POC historical genealogies and also destabilize and decenter the narrative of U.S. and European sex/gender systems as the "standard" of sex/gender systems for the rest of the world.

Because there has been limited attention given to TGV POC within mental health literature (Singh, 2013; White, 2013), it is often necessary for mental health providers (MHPs) to reference public health literature to add to the knowledge base of how to engage TGV POC in counseling. Therefore, the integration of public health with counseling and psychological perspectives may augment the mental health literature involving these populations to effectively address the counseling needs of TGV POC, and that is what we aim to do with this chapter.

Intersectionality as a Framework for TGV POC Experiences

A starting point of counseling competence with TGV POC populations is to capture how intersecting identities, stigmas, and oppressions are conceptualized and examined. Within the context of the United States, TGV POC are often familiar with forms of marginalization they share with family and other members of their community; belonging to a group "of color" is something they experience from birth, as is their social class. TGV identity, then, is an added layer of marginalized experience. Consequently, the theory of intersectionality can be an important conceptual tool when examining the complexity of the several minority identities held by TGV POC clients. The term *intersectionality* has come to subsume a critical awareness and understanding of a number of cultural identities, including but not limited to race/ethnicity, sex, gender identity, class, disability, religion, and sexual orientation. To understand the magnitude of oppression from any one of these, they must be addressed in combination (Bowleg, 2012; King, 1988). Scholars have noted that research with TGV people has neglected the concept of intersectionality (Hwahng & Nuttbrock, 2007; Singh, 2013).

Researchers have yet to consider how people's intersecting identities influence how they perceive the world around them and, more important, how they cope with the many layers of stigma and adversity associated with these intersecting identities. Because the lives of TGV POC are affected by structural inequities around race/ethnicity, gender, and sexual identity and expression (Hwahng & Nuttbrock, 2007), considering these multiple intersecting identities will significantly contribute to literature on the intersectionality of identity, as well as the literature on resiliency and coping (White, 2013). For instance, a study of trans feminine spectrum individuals in New York City suggested that TGV POC may be greatly isolated from each other on the basis of race, ethnicity, and their socioeconomic status, ensconced within their ethnocultural communities (Hwahng & Nuttbrock, 2007). Research that monolithically groups TGV people runs the risk of obscuring racialized and gendered experiences of TGV POC in terms of access to needed resources. A critical consideration of how the specific intersections of racism, sexism, and transphobia correlate to physical and mental health risks, as well as an unpacking of how these systematically impact the lives of TGV POC, may allow MHPs to better understand the specific needs of this often neglected and vastly misunderstood segment of the TGV population. In turn, MHPs may be better prepared to provide culturally informed and affirmative mental health care.

Contexts Influencing the Lives of TGV POC

Researchers across disciplines agree that there are particular health disparities for TGV POC (Herbst et al., 2008; Hwahng & Nuttbrock, 2014; Nuttbrock et al., 2009, 2010; Singh & McKleroy, 2011). However, the limited attention given to them within the mental health literature is often attributed to the "invisibility" of these populations, and some argue that transnegativity in communities of color can influence individuals to conceal their gender identity (Bailey, 2011; Green, 2004). Many TGV people, especially those from poor and working class backgrounds are unable to choose safe spaces within their neighborhoods to live and move; the result is that many are forced to navigate environments that are unsafe—where they are easily identifiable and often known from before transition—and are forced to "negotiate violence and oppression as a part of the quotidian conditions in which they are situated" (Bailey, 2011, p. 366). Feelings of acute vulnerability, and a desire for invisibility deemed a requirement for their survival, seem warranted given the wave of murders that have occurred recently, especially against TGV women of color (WOC; Chatelain & Asoka, 2015; Teal, 2015). Multiple oppressions that TGV people experience may result in higher rates of traumatic life events (Richmond, Burnes, & Carroll, 2012). Transphobia, misogyny, and racism each singularly can result in violence and death for their targets, but for TGV WOC these effects seem to be cumulative as TGV WOC are the most targeted victims of violence in the lesbian, gay, bisexual, and transgender (LGBT) community (National Coalition of Anti-Violence Programs [NCAVP], 2011). The NCAVP reported that TGV women make up 72% of anti-LGBT homicide victims, and 89% of these victims were POC (Ahmed & Jindasurat, 2014). Multiple oppressions that TGV people experience may situate them at higher rates of police violence as well (2.59 times higher than for White cisgender people; NCAVP, 2011).

THE EXPERIENCES OF TGV POC

Historically, TGV POC have been an integral part of many sex/gender systems across the world and have often been part of genealogies of distinct TGV practices that are virtually unknown and unrecognized in the United States and Europe. In addition, these TGV POC communities indigenous to Africa, East and Southeast Asia, South Asia, the Pacific Islands, and the Americas have endured despite overlapping waves of patriarchalizations and colonizations (with colonization entrenching particularly rigid forms of patriarchalization; see Gilley, 2006; M. Johnson, 1997; Lang, 1998; Reddy, 2005; Roscoe, 1998) that have often diminished and/or trivialized the roles and values of TGV POC in their respective indigenous contexts (Gilley, 2006; M. Johnson, 1997; Lang, 1998; Reddy, 2005; Roscoe, 1998).

For instance, many Native American tribes and communities venerated TVG people as community leaders, healers, and artists (Gilley, 2006; Lang, 1998; Roscoe, 1998). In Juchitán, Mexico, TGV women are respected members of society who are viewed as hard-working and integral to an indigenous social fabric in which women control the economy, Zapotec (vs. Spanish) is the official language, 600 major celebrations take place each year, and progressive politics are heartily promoted (Gosling & Osborne, 2006; Henriquez, 2002; Islas, 2005). In India, trans feminine people engage in spiritual traditions that include integrating Islamic and Hindu religious practices, *nirvan* body modifications, and the formation of TGV families consisting of TGV female *gurus* and daughters (Nanda, 1999; Reddy, 2005). In Thailand, transfeminine- and transmasculine-spectrum people are recognized as having genders separate from their birth sex and historically have not been subjected to compulsory heterosexuality (Costa & Matzner, 2007; Morris, 1994;

Sinnott, 2004). In Korea, there is a tradition of TGV identities and practices among shamans, who are mostly anatomically assigned female and are historically recognized as the main spiritual leaders of Korean society (Harvey, 1979).

Within diasporic communities in Euro Western contexts, TVG POC have also been visible leaders and participants within the larger LGBT rights movement and have also been instrumental in developing strong LGBT communities within their own racial/ethnic communities (Moradi, DeBlaere, & Huang, 2010). The House/Ballroom community is one example of their leadership, comprising almost exclusively POC. Though this milieu is one constructed on the idea of competition between "houses" in categories of dance, fashion, beauty, and sexual appeal, among others, TGV women and TGV men are frequently house "mothers" and "fathers." In these chosen family roles, they assist their "children" through pivotal life issues, such as homelessness and other realities that result from poverty and oppression (Kubicek et al., 2013). These communities may face challenges similar to those of other TGV POC communities, such as drug use or survival sex work; however, they also foster much-needed social support for TGV POC, which their biological families are unwilling or unable to provide (Bailey, 2011; Hwahng, Messina, & Rivera, 2013; Hwahng & Nuttbrock, 2007).

TGV POC IN PUBLIC HEALTH AND PSYCHOLOGICAL RESEARCH

Despite their presence in these areas, the continued limited representation within all research areas, including mental health, continues to perpetuate misinformation and paint inaccurate pictures about TGV POC communities. When the "T" has been a simple "add-on" to the already limited number of studies focused on LGBT POC and there has been very little explanation as to if and how TGV people were included in the study, these representations become even more skewed (White, 2013).

MHPs should be aware that, currently, the vast majority of public health research funding for TGV POC has been in the area of HIV. In one way this makes sense; the epidemic disproportionally affects TGV POC. However, this research focuses on individual HIV-related risk behaviors and vulnerabilities and often fails to consider how larger socioeconomic barriers, such as lack of housing and education, can lead low-income and poor POC to engage in HIV-risky behaviors to satisfy immediate needs for survival. Another noteworthy point is that almost all of this research is conducted by White cisgender researchers and fails to foster the involvement of TGV POC through approaches such as community-based participatory research (Singh, Richmond, & Burnes, 2013). This dearth of expertise limits the design, conduct, and analyses of these research studies.

Public health literature as a whole tends to lack an intersectional lens—aside from that found in HIV literature—and is not very diverse in representation. For example, for several years the Fenway Institute in Boston has provided a summer program to teach research methods to graduate students and junior investigators within their Center for Population Research in LGBT Health. Although this is valuable program, most of the datasets that are analyzed consist overwhelmingly of White and economically privileged samples, resulting in analyses of secondary data in which TGV POC are vastly underrepresented. Analysis of such datasets that lack POC and people from lower incomes understandably cannot detect existing disparities. Thus, researchers who work with such datasets must be cautious when generalizing findings to the TGV population at large.

In addition, data from the 2008 National Transgender Discrimination Survey, a large study conducted by the National Center for Transgender Equality and the National Gay and Lesbian Task Force, clearly demonstrated that "racial bias presents a significant, additional risk of discrimination for TGV POC in virtually every major area making their health care access and outcomes dramatically worse" (Grant et al., 2011, p. 72). In this study, researchers found that although TGV individuals, in general, face significant challenges to accessing health care—19% of their sample reported being refused care because of their TGV status—the numbers were significantly higher amongst TGV POC (e.g., 32% of Latino/Latinas reported being refused care by a doctor or hospital). However, potential substantive data analysis on POC from that dataset is not viable because the sample was overwhelmingly White (83%). In fact, one of the coauthors of this book chapter was contacted by the primary researcher of the National Transgender Discrimination Survey with regard to how to sample more POC. At that point in time the survey was only being administered online, and it was advised that in-person, on-the-ground recruitment and data collection were necessary to access more low-income POC communities, which constituted "hidden populations" at that time (S. J. Hwahng, personal communication, July 22, 2014). One of the study sponsors, the National Gay and Lesbian Task Force, implemented some in-person recruitment and data collection to access POC participants. However, perhaps because of funding restrictions, the scope of POC participant recruitment and data collection was not sufficient to conduct any meaningful analysis of POC. Thus, once again, this type of recruitment and data collection may appear to include racial, ethnic, and class diversity but in reality does not contribute information that is reliable, applicable, or beneficial to POC and their communities.

When the number of TGV POC are so small, there is not enough statistical power to make meaningful comparisons between racial groups,

thus rendering the examination of racial, ethnic, and class health disparities unfeasible. Researchers use datasets such as these to demonstrate
incidence of specific health outcomes, such as substance use, in the TGV
community, yet findings are generalizable solely to a White and often
economically privileged subset of the community (de Vries, 2015). The
reason for large enough samples of TGV POC is to have statistical power
to compare against White samples or any other comparison group, such
as cisgender POC. It is these numerical comparisons that provide the
evidence for justifications of funding for programs and services, and for
new policies or policy changes. So it is very important to have large
enough samples of TGV POC that are similar in sample size to the White
(or another) comparison group in order for statistical comparisons to
be made so that there is at least a chance to generate evidence (and
consequently justification for funding for new programs, services, and
policies) specific to TGV POC if statistically significant differences or
disparities are identified. Nonscientific researchers often do not realize
the extensive impact of statistically significant research findings, and
any conclusions that are based on research in which the sample sizes
of POC are much smaller compared with the White sample (e.g., Grant
et al., 2010) will result in findings that are either merely descriptive or
do not capture all the possible statistically significant differences compared with when there are large samples of similar size for each group
being measured.

Although it is important to capture any information on TGV POC,
collecting information from much smaller samples of TGV POC probably
does very little to actually portray the lives and issues that TGV POC face.
In fact, this type of information can be detrimental to TGV POC because
uninformed health care and social service providers may assume data or
recommendations from data findings from a primarily White TGV study
are also applicable to TGV POC. This may result in the implementation
of services, programs, and policies that may be harmful or, at the very
least, ineffective and thus waste valuable resources that could have been
used to more constructively address the needs of TGV POC.

HISTORICAL CONTEXT OF COUNSELING
APPROACHES WITH TGV POC

When it comes to understanding the relationship between a TGV POC
and an MHP (of any racial/ethnic background or gender identity), it is
essential to understand the history of how mental health fields, particularly psychiatry and psychology, have played a role in undermining the
self-determination of TGV people and racial/ethnic minorities. Though
many MHPs today are affirming of TGV people's identities, this is not
and has not always been the case. The gatekeeping model of TGV health

care (Bouman et al., 2014; Singh & Burnes, 2010) is one in which TGV people are seen as lacking the ability to determine what is in their own best interest and "gatekeepers" (usually physicians and MHPs) assess and make these decisions for the patients. Denny (2002) wrote about the early gender clinics in university health centers (e.g., Johns Hopkins University) where strict requirements were made to regulate if and how TGV people were allowed to access medical care. For example, in some of these clinics, access to medical care was granted only under the condition that patients consented to being research subjects or participated in years of psychotherapy (Denny, 2002). Racial bias was also present in the assessment of which patients were deemed "appropriate candidates" for medical transition. For instance, Puerto Rican male-to-female TGV patients were often denied gender-affirming medical services on the basis of the homophobic and racist sentiment that labeled them as gay men, while their TGV identities were minimized or disregarded (Ophelian, 2009). These are just two examples of how bias on the part of medical and MHPs has been harmful or exclusionary to TGV POC.

Moreover, related to the latter example, public health research has shown that TGV WOC are statistically significantly more likely to be attracted to cisgender men, often considering themselves on an androphilic (i.e., attracted only to cisgender men) spectrum that they share with gay-identified cisgender men of color (Hwahng & Nuttbrock, 2007, 2014; Nuttbrock et al., 2011). In comparison, the majority of White TGV women are attracted to cisgender women and in many studies, the majority of these White TGV women are also middle-age and middle-class (Grant et al., 2011; Hwahng & Nuttbrock, 2007; Nuttbrock et al., 2011). Thus, if the norm for TGV women is modeled after a White, middle-age, middle-class woman who is attracted to women, or is bisexual or pansexual (Hwahng & Nuttbrock, 2007), then an uninformed health care provider could misidentify young, low-income, TGV WOC who are overwhelmingly attracted to cisgender men as they do not fit the norm for TGV women.

Due to these factors, TGV POC have historically been distrustful of the medical establishment (Polly & Nicole, 2011). Therefore, TGV POC may be less likely to consent to participate in TGV research, especially over lengthy periods of time (Singh et al., 2013). In addition, the counseling and psychological literature has long noted that POC are less likely to participate in counseling and psychotherapy (Alvidrez, 1999; Cheng, Kwan, & Sevig, 2013; Obasi & Leong, 2009) so TGV POC may experience overt or covert racism when working with counseling and psychological providers. Throughout this history of TGV counseling, the stories of TGV POC have been omitted, and there is little information on how much TGV POC accessed formal networks of mental health. The World Professional Association for

Transgender Health (WPATH) has published "Standards of Care for the Health of Transsexual, Transgender, and Gender Nonconforming People," which many health care providers consider best practices for treatment of TGV patients. Now in its seventh edition, the WPATH standards (Coleman et al., 2012) are arguably more inclusive of gender diversity, posing fewer barriers to care than previous versions, yet remain embedded within a Western cultural context that may not fit for all TGV people.

These treatment standards have several limitations when it comes to application with TGV POC. Though the WPATH standards no longer require TGV people to be in psychotherapy for a predetermined length of time to access services such as hormone therapy or gender-confirming surgeries, a mental health assessment in still required. In addition, these standards of care were based on norms for White people and may not be applicable for TGV POC (see Chapter 3, this volume). For TGV POC, many of whom do not have health insurance or the economic resources to see an MHP for an assessment, this poses an unreasonable and sometimes impossible barrier to self-actualization. Some TGV POC may prefer working with an MHP who is also a POC, and in some areas it may be difficult to locate a TGV-affirming provider of color. Though WPATH is an international organization, its membership is predominantly White and from Western countries. In addition, criteria for the gender dysphoria diagnosis (American Psychiatric Association, 2013), like those for most mental health diagnoses, are primarily based on research that was conducted with samples lacking racial/ethnic diversity (i.e., predominantly White).

Cultural bias exists not only in dominant treatment models but in the scholarly literature as well. Beemyn (2013) referred to this conspicuous absence of TGV POC in the scholarly literature as a "whitewashing" of the TGV experience. The result is a stereotype or universalizing of TGV identity as White (de Vries, 2012; Namaste, 2000). The lack of reliable information about the lives and experiences of POC affects training and cultural competency. Given the history of the mental health field's interactions with TGV people seeking medically necessary health care, as well as the implicit cultural biases in treatment standards, it is reasonable for TGV people of all backgrounds to feel cautious about entering a counseling relationship and to be very aware of the power that the MHP holds. To get their needs met, clients who seek counseling with the request of getting a letter for hormones or surgery may not feel that is possible to be completely honest or forthcoming with the MHP. A TGV POC may feel the minority stress of not only being TGV (Hendricks & Testa, 2012) and a POC (Harrell, 2000), but the minority stress specific to the intersection of these identities (de Vries, 2015; Singh & McKleroy, 2011; see also Bowleg, Huang, Brooks, Black,

& Burkholder, 2003; King, 1988, for origins of the multiple minority stress model). They may feel the need to overemphasize the ways in which the medicalized narrative (Spade, 2006) fits for them (e.g., ways in which they are "normal" TGV people, often coded as White and economically privileged) and to downplay other important aspects of their experience that are not addressed in the context of that narrative. The risk here is that integral parts of a person's life and culture may be denied, disregarded, or remain unaddressed, thereby reinforcing the power of a narrative that fits for some, but not all, TGV people.

TGV people facing racial discrimination and/or poverty may not feel that there is permission in the counseling room or within the counseling relationship to address these experiences, especially if the focus of counseling is evaluation for the purposes of providing a recommendation letter to a surgeon or prescribing physician. In such a situation, the opportunity for providing necessary support may be lost as the client toes the line between "too sick" and "too healthy." The client may have valid fears or concerns about being pathologized, judged, or denied services. For TGV POC who may have a history of being pathologized or discriminated against on the basis of racism and antitrans bias (and quite possibly classism and homophobia as well), there may be even more hesitancy to trust an MHP. Rather than label or diagnose this as paranoia, it is important that MHPs are aware of the contextual validity of these client concerns. To avoid inaccurately overestimating pathology and thereby causing harm, it is crucial that MHPs consider the environmental factors that clients face, which are often direct effects or by-products of systemic oppressions such as racism, classism, and ableism. In addressing clients' responses to these challenges, MHPs may be able to highlight clients' strengths and sources of resilience as exemplified in the following case vignette.

Case Vignette

This case vignette illustrates examples of some common concerns faced by TGV POC when seeking counseling, some of the specific ways that they may experience the intersections of race and gender, and the relational power dynamics that may arise when working with an MHP. Tianna is a 34-year-old, African American, transgender woman who works at a retail store. She reported that for as long as she could remember, she never felt identified with the sex that she was assigned at birth (male). Her family made allowances for her feminine gender expression growing up, and her father often introduced her as his daughter when she was a child. Tianna's father worked for a gas company, and her mother worked in the home. Tianna had two brothers and three sisters who used to "beat her up sometimes" when she would assert that she was a girl. The school system that Tianna attended from kindergarten through high school was tagged as a "low performing" school. Tianna was quite intelligent, but she got into "lots of fights" in school because of the relentless teasing from her peers. The schools and neighborhood where Tianna grew up were predominantly African American and low income. Tianna described her family instilling a sense of pride about her African American identity and was "grateful" for her father's affirmation of her gender identity. Tianna's mother and siblings instituted a "don't ask, don't tell" policy when it came to her gender identity. For instance, they were still in communication with Tianna and expressed their love and support for her, but they stopped inviting her to family gatherings. Tianna described getting "kicked out" of school in 11th grade after numerous fights at school. She wanted to get her GRE but felt it was time for her to move out of her family's home and try to "make it" on her own. Tianna described a history of engaging in underground economies of sex work and hormone use because she had trouble as a 17-year-old finding employment, stable housing, and accessing affordable and affirming health care. She had been on and off hormones procured from the underground economy for the past 10 years and was seeking counseling now to get a letter for hormones. She "never thought in a million years" she would be sitting in an MHP's office. As Tianna began counseling, she was unsure as to whether the MHP would be supportive of her gender identity, as her father was, or more similar to others who have rejected her. She felt like she had to play the part of being "put together" so that the MHP would write her a recommendation letter, and this pressure caused her to tell herself that she couldn't open up about the "tough times" she had experienced in her life. She hoped that the MHP, who had the power to recommend or deny her access to hormones, would not judge her for having taken hormones procured from the underground economy, as this was the most comfortable, readily available, and therefore the most viable option available to her at the time. Tianna was also worried that the MHP would only see her as a TGV woman, not as a low-income African American as well, and would not fully understand the complexity of her identity.

As Tianna's story illustrates, TGV POC experience many societal challenges in the world today in terms of oppression, discrimination, and other prejudice within and outside of their families and communities, as well as of resilience despite these negative experiences. MHPs must be aware of and explore the multiple barriers TGV POC clients have experienced and intentionally integrate a focus on removing these barriers. MHPs should focus not only on gender identity, but also on needs and overall well-being related to the intersections of race/ethnicity, social class, and other salient identities. MHPs can also play vital roles in supporting the development of TGV POC client and community resilience, while simultaneously being strong advocates for the removal of societal and psychological barriers.

Common Concerns TGV POC Have When Accessing Counseling

In addition to the intersectional focus on multicultural identities and social justice issues demonstrated in the previous case vignette, it may be useful for MHPs to acknowledge the history of the gatekeeping model in TGV counseling and to approach the counseling relationship with transparency about power dynamics with TGV POC. Some clients may be very candid about past negative or traumatic experiences of being labeled as "sick" or "crazy" by family members, peers, and health care providers. When this is the case, it is important for MHPs to validate the feelings that clients express about these experiences and to refrain from using approaches that may be further pathologizing. For example, some MHPs, out of their own discomfort in speaking about antiTGV bias or trauma, may attempt to rectify their clients' feelings by treating them as "irrational beliefs" or "cognitive distortions" that need to be challenged. Other MHPs with unexamined rescue needs/fantasies, out of a desire to be seen as "good" or as allies, may try to dismiss or write off negative experiences as coming from individuals rather than entire systems. We discuss other common concerns TGV POC may have when accessing counseling and mental health systems in the following sections.

MENTAL HEALTH PROFESSIONAL–CLIENT POWER DIFFERENTIALS

It is important to maintain awareness of differences between MHPs and clients regarding education and socioeconomic class background and how these differences may affect the counseling relationship (Chang & Singh, 2016). Though not all MHPs come from backgrounds of having class privilege, the very fact that they have obtained education and the status of being an MHP may create a barrier in the counseling relationship. This dynamic may make it difficult for some clients, particularly those who have not been afforded class privilege, to trust that the MHP can truly understand them. Furthermore, those who do in fact hold gatekeeping power are more likely to have some uninterrogated privileged identities (de Vries, 2015) and are sometimes less aware of issues related to race, class, or other systems of oppression. In other words, there may a exist a system of "gatekeeping for gatekeepers" that poses a challenge for TGV clients who are seeking to connect to an MHP who is similar to them with regard to racial/ethnic identity or class background.

EXPERIENCES OF TRAUMA

Due to the high rates of traumatic life events and the multiple oppression experiences that influence well-being, counseling with TGV POC often entails a thorough trauma assessment. It is important to note that trauma assessment must not only focus on the gender-related experiences of trauma but should also explore intergenerational trauma related to racism, colonization, and genocide (Balsam, Rothblum, & Beauchaine, 2005; Hwahng & Nuttbrock, 2014; Simoni, Walters, Balsam, & Meyers, 2006) and how these traumas intersect with other oppressions (e.g., classism, sexism, ableism). Trauma assessments should also include an exploration of the experiences of interpersonal (e.g., child physical, sexual, and/or psychological abuse; adult physical, sexual, and/or psychological assault; hate crimes) and intrapersonal (e.g., self-injury, suicide attempts) violence (e.g., Balsam et al., 2005; dickey, Reisner, & Juntunen, 2015; Hwahng & Nuttbrock, 2014; Nuttbrock et al., 2010, 2014; Simoni et al., 2006).

Because TGV POC may encounter and internalize multiple oppressions, trauma assessments should also include questions about social identity development and related internalized oppression experiences (e.g., internalized racism, internalized heterosexism). It can be common to develop safety plans with TGV POC who are vulnerable to violence intrapersonally (e.g., self-injury, suicide attempts) or interpersonally (e.g., intimate partner violence, sexual assault). These safety plans must entail holistic attention to multiple identities as well. For instance, a TGV Chicana who is experiencing intimate partner violence related to her gender identity may also be experiencing workplace violence in the form of harassment. Both experiences of violence multiply one another in terms of the stressors, coping, and needs this client may have in terms of developing a safety plan that is comprehensive and provides her with the resources she needs. In addition, because the incidence of trauma experiences for TGV POC is elevated, it is important that trauma assessment be continual and integrated into the overarching counseling process rather than occur as a one-time event. Chapter 9 of this volume has an extensive discussion of the assessment and treatment of trauma with TGNC people.

RESILIENCE AND COPING

Although TGV POC experience multiple forms of oppression, recent research has noted the important role of resilience and posttraumatic growth (Hendricks & Testa, 2012; Singh, Hays, & Watson, 2011). *Resilience* has been defined as the ability individuals and communities have to move through adverse experiences (Masten & Obradovic, 2006). TGV POC, therefore, may have developed resilience in response to multiple oppression experiences. Research suggested that TGV POC who have survived traumatic life events may have developed resilience in the following areas (Singh & McKleroy, 2011): (a) developing pride in one's gender and racial/ethnic identity, (b) recognizing and negotiating gender and racial/ethnic oppression, (c) accessing financial and health care resources, (d) connecting with a community of color, and (e) cultivating spirituality and hope for the future. Because TGV POC may have multiple experiences of trauma, integrating the minority stress model (Hendricks & Testa, 2012; Meyer, 2003) into counseling may be helpful in identifying a client's resilience and coping. For instance, components of the minority stress model include distal (e.g., societal threats to TGV safety) and proximal (e.g., a TGV POC's expectations of violence and discrimination and internalization of transphobia) sources of stress (Institute of Medicine, 2011). Resilience to distal and proximal sources of stress can be explored in counseling to identify how best to navigate and challenge oppression experiences.

Research has also suggested that TGV POC place great value on community building (Hwahng et al., 2012; Hwahng & Nuttbrock, 2007; Nuttbrock et al., 2015), which can include social capital comprised of *thick trust* formed through friendship and social network interactions and *thin trust* formed through interactions across disparate groups, including racial and class groups (Putnam, 2000). Community building can be a common source of resilience and coping in the absence of health care and other necessary resources, especially when TGV communities of color incorporate thick trust and thin trust and, thus, provide information, insights, and other resources for TGV POC clients to effectively navigate legal, health care, employment, housing, and other systems (Hwahng & Nuttbrock, 2007; Nuttbrock et al., 2015; Singh & McKleroy, 2011; White, 2013). For example, studies on urban Latina and African American TGV women (Hwahng et al., 2012, 2014; Hwahng, Allen, et al., 2013; Hwahng & Nuttbrock, 2007) revealed that these women found support and information to access hormones and medical feminizing procedures they identified as critical to reinforcing their gender identities through their TGV POC networks' connections. Services such as these are typically expensive and difficult to access. These networks were also opportunities for the women to share common concerns about threats to their lives and survival and could lead to participation in social and civic activities and even political action (Lombardi, 1999; Pinto, Melendez, & Spector, 2008).

TGV WOC often experience optimal health care from an integration of thick trust in the form of emotional support and sharing and thin trust in the form of information distribution across disparate groups (Hwahng et al., 2014; Rostila, 2011). TGV WOC access the greatest forms and amounts of thick trust within neighborhoods and communities of color (Hwahng et al., 2014; Hwahng, Allen, et al., 2013; Hwahng & Nuttbrock, 2007). In one study (Hwahng et al., 2012, 2014), thick trust was observed among TGV WOC in behaviors such as close physical proximity and body contact with each other, finishing each other's sentences, affectionate teasing, offering unrequested advice to one another, referring to each other as "baby" and other pet names, and appropriating formerly derogatory terms in an affectionate or playful manner. In this same study, one African American TGV woman referred to her social network of other African American TGV women in Brooklyn, New York, as a "sister circle" and stated that their daily interactions of sharing stories and experiences with each other kept all of them psychologically "grounded" (Hwahng et al., 2012, 2014). In another social network consisting of immigrant trans Latinas in Jackson Heights, New York, over 100 of them gathered in an informal peer-delivered hormone injection and syringe exchange for several years before this group was able to meet formally and access services from a local harm-reduction center. During these informal gatherings, one TGV woman would host all the other women in her home, another provided the syringes, and another would inject all the TGV women present. Immense amounts of thick trust had been built among these immigrant TGV women through frequent communication and sharing of survival resources, which had resulted in the development of great trust. They were thus able to rapidly convene in large groups and provide frequent assistance to each other (Hwahng et al., 2012; Hwahng, Allen, et al., 2013). As indicated by these examples, health care provision, including counseling provision, that only focuses on distributing information and thin trust will not effectively reach TGV WOC. MHPs can instead build on TGV POC social support networks that are often based on thick trust and enhance the informal and peer networks that often already incorporate thick trust and thin trust in many TGV POC communities and social networks. MHPs can work in tandem with thick trust networks by building relationships with network members and engaging in services, programs, and advocacy-related activities together, instead of working separately and outside of thick trust networks.

In addition, TGV POC may also experience resilience when engaging in system-change efforts, such as advocacy and street-level activism. For instance, in December 2014, queer and TGV POC and allies across North America raised funds to donate to organizations supporting the Black Lives Matter movement (Polak, 2014). Organizers designated one day during which health care providers and healers of different disciplines donated some or all of their wages to the Black Lives Matter movement after the events in Ferguson, MO, in which a White police officer shot and killed Michael Brown, an African American male who was unarmed. Protests mounted after he was killed, and queer and TGV people of color joined in the protests that took place around the United States. In addition, queer and TGV POC mobilized to create group healing spaces across North America and India on that same day. As a result, over 157 healing professionals or organizations participated in fundraising for this cause over one day (Polak, 2014). This is an example of the activism and movement building that occur within queer and TGV POC communities to strive for racial justice and empowerment. This event enlisted allies, donated money to social justice funds, and also created healing spaces for queer and TGV POC.

DISCRIMINATION AND EXCLUSION IN EDUCATION, EMPLOYMENT, AND SOCIAL SERVICES

Access to health care is not the sole concern of TGV POC who face economic hardship. Conditions of multigenerational poverty and employment discrimination often create situations in which the only viable option is participation in street economies or survival crime. In addition, attention has been increasingly brought to the school-to-prison pipeline that most adversely affects youth who are LGBT, POC, or both (GSA Network, 2011). The *school-to-prison pipeline* is a term used to refer to the funneling of mostly students of color into the juvenile justice system, as opposed to ensuring these students have the resources and supports they need in their schools and communities. Even when they are the victims of bullying and hate violence, TGV youth are more likely to be seen as the perpetrators and often sent to jail if they are prosecuted (A. G. Johnson, 2006). Because of these interruptions and barriers to education, when these youths become adults they may have difficulties with employment based on lack of skills or having a criminal record. In addition, there are high rates of incarceration among homeless TGV youth, the majority of which are TGV POC (Quintana, Rosenthal, & Krehely, 2010), and among undocumented immigrants (Hwahng et al.,

2012; Hwahng, Allen, et al., 2013). All of these barriers to education and stable employment thus reinforce stereotypes of TGV people as socially deviant or as "criminals" (Mogul, Ritchie, & Whitlock, 2011; Skolnik, 2014). Another example of exclusion is in admission to women's shelters, where a requirement of being postoperative (i.e., having had genital reconstructive surgery) often exists for admission. This requirement is most harmful to TGV WOC and those who are low income, as it assumes this costly medical care is preferred and available (Hwahng & Nuttbrock, 2007; Namaste, 2000; Spicer, Schwartz, & Barber, 2010). It also assumes that all TGV women must desire and achieve surgery to be seen as women.

IMMIGRATION HISTORY

Immigration, or one's family's immigration history, could have a significant effect on a TGV POC's experience (Bazargan & Galvan, 2012; Cerezo, Morales, Quintero, & Rothman, 2014; Hwahng et al., 2012; Hwahng, Allen, et al., 2013; Hwahng & Nuttbrock, 2007; Pinto et al., 2008; Rhodes et al., 2013). TGV POC who have immigrant status must negotiate gender norms in their country of origin, in the country they now reside in, and in the intersections that exist within a bicultural immigrant experience. There may not be a direct translation for words used to describe one's gender experience, and this may lead to misunderstanding within the counseling relationship. It is recommended that MHPs listen closely to the reasons for immigrating, the conditions the person faced, and how these factors may be related to gender identity or expectations. It is also important to be attuned to the unique needs of TGV POC who are the first generation to grow up in the United States and may experience a cultural barrier with their parents or family. For some of these individuals, the divide already posed by having a different cultural experience or socialization from their parents may render gender nonconforming expression or behavior less visible. They may differ from their parents and their country of origin's expectations in multiple ways, of which gender expression is only one. For this reason, MHPs should refrain from over-relying on traditional medicalized narratives for the identification or validation of TGV identity or experience with TGV clients of color.

In one study that included immigrant TGV Latinas (Hwahng et al., 2012; Hwahng, Allen, et al., 2013) a staff person at a harm-reduction program noted that the majority of immigrant TGV Latinas accessing her organization's services had originally emigrated from poor rural areas. She stated that many of the immigrant TGV Latinas did not understand when caseworkers would give them a referral to call a provider and, as a result, experienced alienation. She explained that immigrant

TGV Latinas were not comfortable going to appointments with health care providers by themselves because they often came from cultures where relatives and friends would support and accompany each other to doctor's visits or even to visit a drugstore to buy aspirin. Immigrant trans Latinas also expressed their need for Spanish-speaking companions from their communities for their visits with providers to feel comfortable in unfamiliar settings outside of their immigrant Latina communities. It is thus important to situate immigrants within their particular ethnocultures (Hwahng & Nuttbrock, 2007). A task such as purchasing aspirin from a drugstore, which would be considered incidental and often undertaken individually in U.S. mainstream society, was often an opportunity to reinforce relationships, and maintaining interpersonal connection with others was an integral part of the experience of accessing health services. Understanding what may facilitate or occlude access to health services, including MHP services, can lead to more effective service provision. In addition, immigrants who are undocumented face additional layers of barriers to service provision, education, and employment, which can result in a large mental health burden.

TGV POC–AFFIRMATIVE GENDER TRANSITION ACCESS

Besides the various mental and physical health issues discussed in the previous sections, guidelines for medical transition often cater to people with economic resources. TGV POC, many of whom experience poverty and disproportionate workplace discrimination, may have greater difficulty accessing the financial resources that make this care possible. For example, they may not have health insurance that provides gender-affirming medical services as a covered benefit, and they may not be able to pay out-of-pocket for this care. They may not be able to take time off work for extensive interviews or evaluations regarding their appropriateness for care. When discussions of fertility preservation are relevant to an assessment for surgical intervention, it is important to understand the harm that may be caused when offering suggestions or choices that are extremely costly and not financially feasible, such as egg or sperm banking. In other words, it is crucial to explore the contextual factors (e.g., financial resources, employment discrimination) that influence what these options are in actuality.

To get their medical needs met, some TGV POC may opt for buying hormones from underground market economies because they do not have the economic resources to access health care professionals who will provide a gender dysphoria diagnosis (Hwahng & Nuttbrock, 2007; Namaste, 2000). Even when TGV POC have access to obtaining hormones through the legal medical system, some prefer obtaining hormones through an underground economy because these are often based on thick trust within communities of color (Bourgois, 2002; Hwahng, Allen, et al., 2013; Pinto et al., 2008). Thus, TGV POC often make choices on the basis of building and preserving resilience and a need for self-determination. Unfortunately, TGV POC are often pathologized for using these options, which are often more accessible than networks available in most mainstream health care systems.

AGE, COHORT, AND GENERATIONAL DIFFERENCES

Age and cohort differences may have a significant influence on the ways TGV POC experience the world around them. To begin with, a person is affected by the prevalent gender norms of a given generation. Moreover, these norms are shaped by one's racial or ethnic background. Therefore, specific expectations often exist for specific intersections of age and race/ethnicity. For example, what was considered normative or acceptable for Black men growing up in the 1950s is substantially different from what was considered so for White men of the same generation or for Black men growing up in a different generation (e.g., the 1990s). In addition to their own culture and generation's gender norms, POC in the United States are typically bombarded with whitewashed gender ideals (Beauchamp & D'Harlingue, 2012).

A person's generation may have an effect on how a person goes about expressing gender. Much of the literature discussing characteristics of people being categorized under various generations (e.g., baby boomers, Generation X, Generation Y/Millennials) addresses different orientations to authority figures and the degree to which it is acceptable to assert oneself in the face of authority (Gursoy, Maier, & Chi, 2008). This may affect a person's relationship to health care providers and MHPs who hold power in relation to a person's treatment options or outcome. This further adds complexity to the racialized power dynamics that a TGV person may already face in medical settings. For instance, people who are considered Generation X or Millennials may be socialized to challenge authority, and this may have positive benefits when it comes to advocating for themselves in medical settings. However, the option to challenge authority may not feel tenable for a TGV POC who interfaces with predominantly White providers and/or has been taught a cultural value of always deferring to the opinions of authority (e.g., adults, teachers, doctors; Chang & Singh, 2016).

Another important factor is the time at which a person is first exposed to TGV identity/experience as an option and how viable it is to pursue this option. For example, in the 1950s, people across the world became aware of the medical transition undergone by Christine Jorgensen, a White TGV woman. For some people, this gave them hope of something that could be done to help them attain gender congruence. For TGV WOC, this image (and most of the images of White TGV women) may not have been attainable or relatable. Access to such medical treatments was, and still is, costly and unobtainable by most TGV people (APA, 2015; Herbst et al., 2008) including TGV POC, and some research suggests many TGV WOC prefer not to pursue gender confirmation surgery (Hwahng & Nuttbrock, 2007; Nemoto, Operario, Keatley, Han, & Soma, 2004).

Older TGV POC who have medically transitioned may be more likely to be stealth or to be isolated from other members of the TGV community. They may not feel that they can easily access spaces in which it is safe to discuss the salient aspects of their identity. This may mean that the counseling relationship, if it is one in which the person feels comfortable disclosing TGV status/experience and/or discussing race, may take on great importance in meeting the need for identity integration. However, the very small but growing body of scholarly literature on TGV older adults fails to address racial identity. This is partially because of the difficulty in even identifying TGV older adults, let alone TGV older adults of color in the research literature because of methodological limitations in studies. In a recent survey of TGV older adults (Witten, 2014), 15% of respondents identified themselves as POC (Biracial/Multiracial, Other, Hispanic, Asian/Pacific Islander, all other racial identifications); however, African American/non-Hispanic identities were not captured. Therefore, even when MHPs are educated about some of the issues of aging and TGV concerns, they may remain uninformed about and unprepared to address the specific needs and experiences of TGV older adults of color.

Chapter Summary

TGV POC experience many societal challenges in the world today in terms of oppression, discrimination, and other prejudice within and outside of their families and communities, in addition to experiencing resilience despite these negative experiences. MHPs must be aware of and explore the multiple barriers TGV POC clients have experienced, while intentionally integrating a focus on addressing how these barriers influence overall well-being and mental health. MHPs should focus not only on gender identity but also on the specific needs TGV POC have related to their intersections of race/ethnicity, social class, and other salient identities. MHPs can also play vital roles in supporting the development of TGV POC client and community resilience, while simultaneously being strong advocates for the removal of societal and psychological barriers.

References

Ahmed, O., & Jindasurat, C. (2014). *Lesbian, gay, bisexual, transgender, Queer and HIV-affected hate violence 2013.* Retrieved from http://avp.org/storage/documents/2013_ncavp_hvreport_final.pdf

Alvidrez, J. (1999). Ethnic variations in mental health attitudes and service use among low-income African American, Latina, and European American young women. *Community Mental Health Journal, 35,* 515–530. http://dx.doi.org/10.1023/A:1018759201290

American Psychiatric Association. (2013). *Diagnostic and statistical manual of mental disorders* (5th ed.). Washington, DC: Author.

American Psychological Association. (2015). Psychological practice guidelines with transgender and gender nonconforming clients. *American Psychologist, 70,* 832–864. http://dx.doi.org/10.1037/a0039906

Bailey, M. M. (2011). Gender/racial realness: Theorizing the gender system in ballroom culture. *Feminist Studies, 2,* 365–386.

Balsam, K. F., Rothblum, E. D., & Beauchaine, T. P. (2005). Victimization over the life span: A comparison of lesbian, gay, bisexual, and heterosexual siblings. *Journal of Consulting and Clinical Psychology, 73,* 477–487. http://dx.doi.org/10.1037/0022-006X.73.3.477

Bazargan, M., & Galvan, F. (2012). Perceived discrimination and depression among low-income Latina male-to-female transgender women. *BioMed Central Public Health, 12,* 663. http://dx.doi.org/10.1186/1471-2458-12-663

Beauchamp, T., & D'Harlingue, B. (2012). Beyond additions and exceptions: The category of transgender and new pedagogical approaches for women's studies. *Feminist Formations, 24*(2), 25–51. http://dx.doi.org/10.1353/ff.2012.0020

Beemyn, G. (2013). A presence in the past: A transgender historiography. *Journal of Women's History, 25,* 113–121. http://dx.doi.org/10.1353/jowh.2013.0062

Besnier, N. (1996). Polynesian gender liminality through time and space. In G. Herdt (Ed.), *Third sex, third gender: Beyond sexual dimorphism in culture and history* (pp. 285–328). New York, NY: Zone Books.

Bouman, W. P., Richards, C., Addinall, R. M., Arango de Montis, I., Arcelus, J., Duisin, D., . . . Wilson, D. (2014). Yes and yes again: Are standards of care which require two referrals for genital reconstructive surgery ethical? *Sexual and Relationship Therapy, 29,* 377–389. http://dx.doi.org/10.1080/14681994.2014.954993

Bourgois, P. (2002). *In search of respect: Selling crack in El Barrio* (2nd ed.). New York, NY: Cambridge University Press.

Bowleg, L. (2012). The problem with the phrase *women and minorities*: Intersectionality—An important theoretical framework for public health. *American Journal of Public Health, 102,* 1267–1273. http://dx.doi.org/10.2105/AJPH.2012.300750

Bowleg, L., Huang, J., Brooks, K., Black, A., & Burkholder, G. (2003). Triple jeopardy and beyond: Multiple minority stress and resilience among Black lesbians. *Journal of Lesbian Studies, 7,* 87–108.

Cerezo, A., Morales, A., Quintero, D., & Rothman, S. (2014). Trans migrations: Exploring life at the intersection of transgender identity and immigration. *Psychology of Sexual Orientation and Gender Diversity, 1,* 170–180. http://dx.doi.org/10.1037/sgd0000031

Chang, S., & Singh, A. A. (2016). Affirming psychological practice with transgender and gender nonconforming people of color. *Psychology of Sexual Orientation and Gender Diversity, 3,* 140–147. http://dx.doi.org/10.1037/sgd0000153

Chatelain, M., & Asoka, K. (2015). Women and Black Lives Matter. *Dissent, 62,* 54–61. http://dx.doi.org/10.1353/dss.2015.0059

Cheng, H. L., Kwan, K. L. K., & Sevig, T. (2013). Racial and ethnic minority college students' stigma associated with seeking psychological help: Examining psychocultural correlates. *Journal of Counseling Psychology, 60,* 98–111. http://dx.doi.org/10.1037/a0031169

Coleman, E., Bockting, W., Botzer, M., Cohen-Kettenis, P., DeCuypere, G., Feldman, J., . . . Zucker, K. (2012). Standards of care for the health of transsexual, transgender, and gender-nonconforming people, 7th version. *International Journal of Transgenderism, 13,* 165–232. http://dx.doi.org/10.1080/15532739.2011.700873

Costa, L., & Matzner, A. J. (2007). *Male bodies, women's souls: Personal narratives of Thailand's transgendered youth.* New York, NY: Haworth Press.

de Vries, K. M. (2012). Intersectional identities and conceptions of the self: The experience of transgender people. *Symbolic Interaction, 35*(1), 49–67. http://dx.doi.org/10.1002/symb.2

de Vries, K. M. (2015). Transgender people of color at the center: Conceptualizing a new intersectional model. *Ethnicities, 15,* 3–27. http://dx.doi.org/10.1177/1468796814547058

Denny, D. (2002). The politics of diagnosis and a diagnosis of politics: How the university-affiliated gender clinics failed to meet the needs of transsexual people. *Transgender Tapestry, 98,* 17–27.

dickey, l. m., Reisner, S. L., & Juntunen, C. L. (2015). Non-suicidal self-injury in a large online sample of transgender adults. *Professional Psychology: Research and Practice, 46.* Advance online publication. Retrieved from http://psycnet.apa.org/journals/pro/46/1/3.pdf

Gilley, B. J. (2006). *Becoming two-spirit: Gay identity and social acceptance in Indian country.* Lincoln: University of Nebraska Press.

Gosling, M., & Osborne, E. (Directors). (2006). *Blossoms of fire* [Motion picture]. United States: New Yorker Films.

Grant, J. M., Mottet, L. A., Tanis, J., Harrison, J., Herman, J. L., & Keisling, M. (2011). *Injustice at every turn: A report of the national trans-*

gender discrimination survey. Washington, DC: National Center for Transgender Equality & National Gay and Lesbian Task Force. Retrieved from http://endtransdiscrimination.org/PDFs/NTDS_Report.pdf

Grant, J. M., Mottet, L. A., Tanis, J., Herman, J. L., Harrison, J., & Keisling, M. (2010). National transgender discrimination survey report on health and health care. *National Center for Transgender, 5,* 23. Retrieved from http://www.thetaskforce.org/static_html/downloads/resources_and_tools/ntds_report_on_health.pdf

Green, J. (2004). *Becoming a visible man.* Nashville, TN: Vanderbilt University Press.

GSA Network. (2011). *The school to prison pipeline and the pathways for LGBT youth.* Retrieved from http://www.gsanetwork.org/files/resources/STPPdiagram.pdf

Gursoy, D., Maier, T. A., & Chi, C. G. (2008). Generational differences: An examination of work values and generational gaps in the hospitality workforce. *International Journal of Hospitality Management, 27,* 448–458. http://dx.doi.org/10.1016/j.ijhm.2007.11.002

Harrell, S. P. (2000). A multidimensional conceptualization of racism-related stress: Implications for the well-being of people of color. *American Journal of Orthopsychiatry, 70,* 42–57. http://dx.doi.org/10.1037/h0087722

Harvey, Y. K. (1979). *Six Korean women: The socialization of shamans.* St. Paul, MN: West.

Hendricks, M. L., & Testa, R. J. (2012). A conceptual framework for clinical work with transgender and gender nonconforming clients: An adaptation of the minority stress model. *Professional Psychology: Research and Practice, 43,* 460–467. http://dx.doi.org/10.1037/a0029597

Henriquez, P. (Director). (2002). *Juchitán Queer Paradise* [Motion picture]. Canada and Chile: Filmakers Library.

Herbst, J. H., Jacobs, E. D., Finlayson, T. J., McKleroy, V. S., Neumann, M. S., & Crepaz, N., & the HIV/AIDS Prevention Research Synthesis Team. (2008). Estimating HIV prevalence and risk behaviors of transgender persons in the United States: A systematic review. *AIDS and Behavior, 12,* 1–17. http://dx.doi.org/10.1007/s10461-007-9299-3

Hwahng, S. J. (2011). The Western "lesbian" agenda and the appropriation of non-Western transmasculine people. In J. Fisher (Ed.), *Gender and the science of difference: Cultural politics of contemporary science and medicine* (pp. 164–186). New Brunswick, NJ: Rutgers University Press.

Hwahng, S. J., Allen, B., Zadoretzky, C., Barber, H., McKnight, C., & Jarlais, D. D. (2012). *Resiliencies, vulnerabilities, and health disparities among low-income transgender people of color at New York City Harm Reduction Programs.* New York, NY: Baron Edmond de Rothschild Chemical Dependency Institute, Mount Sinai Beth Israel.

Hwahng, S. J., Allen, B., Zadoretzky, C., Barber, H., McKnight, C., & Jarlais, D. D. (2013, May). *Immigrant trans Latinas in New York City: Resiliencies, vulnerabilities, and health disparities.* Paper presented at the National Transgender Health Summit, Oakland, CA.

Hwahng, S. J., Allen, B., Zadoretzky, C., Barber, H., McKnight, C., & Jarlais, D. D. (2014, November). *Thick trust, thin trust, HIV, and health outcomes among transwomen of color in New York City.* Paper presented at the American Public Health Association, New Orleans, LA.

Hwahng, S. J., & Lin, A. (2009). The health of lesbian, gay, bisexual, transgender, queer, and questioning people. In C. Trinh-Shevrin, N. Islam, & M. Rey (Eds.), *Asian American communities and health: Context, research, policy, and action* (pp. 226–282). San Francisco, CA: Jossey-Bass.

Hwahng, S. J., Messina, M., & Rivera, A. (2013, March). *Hangin' in Harlem: low-income transfeminine and transmasculine people of color in New York City.* Paper presented at the Fifth Annual Health Disparities Conference, Columbia University, Teacher's College, New York City.

Hwahng, S. J., & Nuttbrock, L. (2007). Sex workers, fem queens, and cross-dressers: Differential marginalizations and HIV vulnerabilities among three ethnocultural male-to-female transgender communities in New York City. *Sexuality Research & Social Policy, 4,* 36–59. http://dx.doi.org/10.1525/srsp.2007.4.4.36

Hwahng, S. J., & Nuttbrock, L. (2014). Adolescent gender-related abuse, androphilia, and HIV risk among transfeminine people of color in New York City. *Journal of Homosexuality, 61,* 691–713. http://dx.doi.org/10.1080/00918369.2014.870439

Institute of Medicine. (2011). *The health of lesbian, gay, bisexual, and transgender people: Building a foundation for better understanding.* Washington, DC: National Academy of Sciences.

Islas, A. (Director). (2005). *Muxes: Authentic, intrepid seekers of danger* [Motion picture]. Mexico: Ethnoscope Film and Video.

Johnson, A. G. (2006). *Privilege, power, and difference* (2nd ed.). Boston, MA: McGraw Hill.

Johnson, M. (1997). *Beauty and power: Transgendering and cultural transformation in the southern Philippines.* New York, NY: Berg.

King, D. (1988). Multiple jeopardy, multiple consciousness: The context of a black feminist ideology. *Signs: Journal of Women in Culture and Society, 14*(1), 42–72. http://dx.doi.org/10.1086/494491

Kubicek, K., Beyer, W. H., McNeeley, M., Weiss, G., Ultra Omni, L. F., & Kipke, M. D. (2013). Community-engaged research to identify house parent perspectives on support and risk within the House and Ball scene. *Journal of Sex Research, 50,* 178–189. http://dx.doi.org/10.1080/00224499.2011.637248

Lang, S. (1998). *Men as women, women as men: Changing gender in Native American cultures.* Austin: University of Texas Press.

Lombardi, E. L. (1999). Integration within a transgender social network and its effect upon members' social and political activity. *Journal of Homosexuality, 37*(1), 109–126. http://dx.doi.org/10.1300/J082v37n01_08

Masten, A. S., & Obradovic, J. (2006). Competence and resilience in development. *Annals of the New York Academy of Sciences, 1094,* 13–27. http://dx.doi.org/10.1196/annals.1376.003

Meyer, I. H. (2003). Prejudice, social stress, and mental health in lesbian, gay and bisexual populations: Conceptual issues and research evidence. *Psychological Bulletin, 129,* 674–697. http://dx.doi.org/10.1037/0033-2909.129.5.674

Mogul, J. L., Ritchie, A. J., & Whitlock, K. (2011). *Queer injustice: The criminalization of LGBT people in the United States.* Boston, MA: Beacon Press.

Moradi, B., DeBlaere, C., & Huang, Y. P. (2010). Centralizing the experiences of LGB people of color in counseling psychology. *The Counseling Psychologist, 38,* 322–330. http://dx.doi.org/10.1177/0011000008330832

Morris, R. C. (1994). Three sexes and four sexualities: Redressing the discourses on gender and sexuality in contemporary Thailand. *Positions, 2*(1), 15–43. http://dx.doi.org/10.1215/10679847-2-1-15

Murray, S. O., & Roscoe, W. (1998). *Boy-wives and female husbands: Studies in African homosexualities.* New York, NY: Palgrave.

Namaste, V. K. (2000). *Invisible lives: The erasure of transsexual and transgendered people.* Chicago, IL: University of Chicago Press.

Nanda, S. (1999). *Neither man nor woman: The hijras of India.* Belmont, CA: Wadsworth.

National Coalition of Anti-Violence Programs. (2011). *Hate violence against lesbian, gay, bisexual, transgender, queer, and HIV-affected communities in the United States in 2011: A report from the National Coalition of Anti-Violence Programs.* New York, NY: Author. Retrieved from http://avp.org/storage/documents/Reports/2012_NCAVP_2011_HV_Report.pdf

Nemoto, T., Operario, D., Keatley, J., Han, L., & Soma, T. (2004). HIV risk behaviors among male-to-female transgender persons of color in San Francisco. *American Journal of Public Health, 94,* 1193–1199. http://dx.doi.org/10.2105/AJPH.94.7.1193

Nuttbrock, L., Bockting, W., Mason, M., Hwahng, S., Rosenblum, A., Macri, M., & Becker, J. (2011). A further assessment of Blanchard's typology of homosexual versus non-homosexual or autogynephilic gender dysphoria. *Archives of Sexual Behavior, 40,* 247–257. http://dx.doi.org/10.1007/s10508-009-9579-2

Nuttbrock, L., Bockting, W., Rosenblum, A., Hwahng, S., Mason, M., Macri, M., & Becker, J. (2014). Gender abuse and major depression among transgender women: A prospective study of resilience and vulnerability. *American Journal of Public Health, 104*, 2191–2198. http://dx.doi.org/10.2105/AJPH.2013.301545

Nuttbrock, L., Bockting, W., Rosenblum, A., Hwahng, S., Mason, M., Macri, M., & Becker, J. (2015). Gender abuse and incident HIV/STI among transgender women in New York City: Buffering effect of involvement in a transgender community. *AIDS and Behavior, 19*, 1446–1453. http://dx.doi.org/10.1007/s10461-014-0977-7

Nuttbrock, L., Hwahng, S., Bockting, W., Rosenblum, A., Mason, M., Macri, M., & Becker, J. (2009). Lifetime risk factors for HIV/sexually transmitted infections among male-to-female transgender persons. *Journal of Acquired Immune Deficiency Syndromes, 52*, 417–421. http://dx.doi.org/10.1097/QAI.0b013e3181ab6ed8

Nuttbrock, L., Hwahng, S., Bockting, W., Rosenblum, A., Mason, M., Macri, M., & Becker, J. (2010). Psychiatric impact of gender-related abuse across the life course of male-to-female transgender persons. *Journal of Sex Research, 47*(1), 12–23. http://dx.doi.org/10.1080/00224490903062258

Obasi, E. M., & Leong, F. T. L. (2009). Psychological distress, acculturation, and mental health-seeking attitudes among people of African descent in the United States: A preliminary investigation. *Journal of Counseling Psychology, 56*, 227–238. http://dx.doi.org/10.1037/a0014865

Oetomo, D. (2000). Masculinity in Indonesia: Genders, sexualities, and identities in a changing society. In R. Parker, R. M. Barbosa, & P. Aggleton (Eds.), *Framing the sexual subject: The politics of gender, sexuality, and power* (pp. 46–59). Los Angeles: University of California Press.

Ophelian, A. (2009). *Diagnosing difference* [Motion picture]. United States: Floating Ophelia Productions.

Pinto, R. M., Melendez, R. M., & Spector, A. Y. (2008). Male-to-female transgender individuals building social support and capital from within a gender-focused network. *Journal of Gay & Lesbian Social Services, 20*, 203–220. http://dx.doi.org/10.1080/10538720802235179

Polak, J. (2014, December 25). "We're here! We're queer! Black lives matter!" *Breitbart*. Retrieved from http://www.breitbart.com/big-government/2014/12/25/were-here-were-queer-black-lives-matter/

Polly, R., & Nicole, J. (2011). Understanding the transsexual patient: Culturally sensitive care in emergency nursing practice. *Advanced Emergency Nursing Journal, 33*, 55–64. http://dx.doi.org/10.1097/TME.0b013e3182080ef4

Putnam, R. D. (2000). *Bowling alone: The collapse and revival of American community*. New York, NY: Simon & Schuster. http://dx.doi.org/10.1145/358916.361990

Quintana, N. S., Rosenthal, J., & Krehely, J. (2010). *On the streets: The federal response to gay and transgender homeless youth*. Washington, DC: Center for American Progress.

Reddy, G. (2005). *With respect to sex: negotiating hijra identity in South India.* Chicago, IL: University of Chicago Press. http://dx.doi.org/10.7208/chicago/9780226707549.001.0001

Rhodes, S. D., Martinez, O., Song, E. Y., Daniel, J., Alonzo, J., Eng, E., . . . Reboussin, B. (2013). Depressive symptoms among immigrant Latino sexual minorities. *American Journal of Health Behavior, 37,* 404–413. http://dx.doi.org/10.5993/AJHB.37.3.13

Richmond, K., Burnes, T. R., & Carroll, K. (2012). Lost in trans-lation: Interpreting systems of trauma for transgender clients. *The Journal of Trauma, 18,* 45–57. http://dx.doi.org/10.1177/1534765610396726

Roscoe, W. (1998). *Changing ones: Third and fourth genders in native North America.* New York, NY: St. Martin's Press.

Rostila, M. (2011). A resource-based theory of social capital for health research: Can it help us bridge the individual and collective facets of the concept? *Social Theory & Health, 9,* 109–129. http://dx.doi.org/10.1057/sth.2011.4

Schifter, J. (1999). *From toads to queens: Transvestism in a Latin American setting.* New York, NY: Harrington Park Press.

Simoni, J. M., Walters, K. L., Balsam, K. F., & Meyers, S. B. (2006). Victimization, substance use, and HIV risk behaviors among gay/bisexual/two-spirit and heterosexual American Indian men in New York City. *American Journal of Public Health, 96,* 2240–2245. http://dx.doi.org/10.2105/AJPH.2004.054056

Singh, A. A. (2013). Transgender youth of color and resilience: Negotiating oppression, finding support. *Sex Roles, 68,* 690–702. http://dx.doi.org/10.1007/s11199-012-0149-z

Singh, A. A., & Burnes, T. R. (2010). Shifting the counselor role from gatekeeping to advocacy: Ten strategies for using the ACA Competencies for Counseling Transgender Clients for individual and social change. *Journal for Lesbian, Gay, Bisexual, and Transgender Issues in Counseling, 4,* 241–255.

Singh, A. A., Hays, D. G., & Watson, L. (2011). Strategies in the face of adversity: Resilience strategies of transgender individuals. *Journal of Counseling and Development, 89,* 20–27. http://dx.doi.org/10.1002/j.1556-6678.2011.tb00057.x

Singh, A. A., & McKleroy, V. S. (2011). "Just getting out of bed is a revolutionary act": The resilience of transgender people of color who have survived traumatic life events. *Traumatology, 20,* 1–11.

Singh, A. A., Richmond, K., & Burnes, T. (2013). Feminist participatory action research with transgender communities: Fostering the practice of ethical and empowering research designs. *International Journal of Transgenderism, 14,* 93–104. http://dx.doi.org/10.1080/15532739.2013.818516

Sinnott, M. J. (2004). *Toms and Dees: Transgender identity and female same-sex relationships in Thailand.* Honolulu: University of Hawaii Press.

Skolnik, A. A. (2014). *The burden of suspicion: A grounded theory study on the psychological and interpersonal consequences of criminalizing stereotypes* (Unpublished doctoral dissertation). Teacher's College, Columbia University, New York, NY.

Spade, D. (2006). Compliance is gendered: Struggling for gender self-determination in a hostile economy. In P. Currah, R. M. Juang, & S. P. Minter (Eds.), *Transgender rights* (pp. 217–241). Minneapolis: University of Minnesota Press.

Spicer, S. S., Schwartz, A., & Barber, M. E. (2010). Special issue on homelessness and the transgender homeless population. *Journal of Gay & Lesbian Mental Health, 14,* 267–270. http://dx.doi.org/10.1080/19359705.2010.509004

Teal, J. L. (2015). *"Black trans bodies are under attack": Gender nonconforming homicide victims in the US 1995–2014.* St. Arcata, CA: Humboldt State University. Retrieved from http://hdl.handle.net/10211.3/143682

White, M. G. (2013). *Resiliency factors among transgender people of color* (Doctoral dissertation). Retrieved from http://dc.uwm.edu/etd/182

Witten, T. M. (2014). It's not all darkness: Robustness, resilience, and successful aging in the trans-community. *LGBT Health, 1,* 24–33. http://dx.doi.org/10.1089/lgbt.2013.0017

Kelly Ducheny, Michael L. Hendricks, and Colton L. Keo-Meier

TGNC-Affirmative Interdisciplinary Collaborative Care

3

I n this chapter, we discuss how mental health providers (MHPs) contribute to transgender and gender nonconforming (TGNC)–affirmative interdisciplinary collaborative care (ICC) and how they add value to the holistic care of TGNC clients. We explore different models of ICC and the crucial role MHPs play in securing needed interdisciplinary care for TGNC clients. Various disciplines and systems with which MHPs might interact are addressed, including school and child care, religious and spiritual, legal and correctional, work and travel, and medical, with a focus on hormone therapy (HT), puberty suppression, surgery, and primary care. MHPs working with TGNC communities are regularly called on to help their clients navigate oppressive, demeaning, and damaging systems (American Counseling Association [ACA], 2010). Through this work, MHPs become progressively more aware of TGNC prejudice and systems that block or ignore gender diversity. To effectively serve the TGNC community, MHPs must become proficient at helping clients navigate and access necessary

http://dx.doi.org/10.1037/14957-004
Affirmative Counseling and Psychological Practice With Transgender and Gender Nonconforming Clients, A. A. Singh and l. m. dickey (Editors)

services typically outside of their areas of expertise (e.g., medical treatments, legal concerns, identity documentation). Through advocacy and collaborative care, MHPs become a strong voice for TGNC-affirmative care and help lay a foundation for the safest passage through the range of obstacles and barriers clients regularly encounter.

Intensive work with the TGNC community is necessarily complex and interdisciplinary (American Psychological Association [APA], 2015; Bockting, Knudson, & Goldberg, 2007) and requires that MHPs engage in ICC. ICC is care that actively blends input from a combination of professionals from different disciplines to provide best care for a common client (Brucker & Shields, 2003). Expertise in ICC allows MHPs to offer accurate, effective assessment and treatment to TGNC clients, collaborate with other professionals to offer the best possible care, and incrementally improve the ability of systems, organizations and individuals to provide TGNC-affirmative treatment.

Interdisciplinary Collaborative Care

MHPs are well positioned to serve an important role in ICC and to facilitate respectful communication across disciplines that result in improved treatment for TGNC people (Bockting et al., 2007). MHPs have a fluid understanding of the interplay of biological, psychological, and social factors that affect clients' lives and others' understanding of gender identity and gender expression (Hendricks & Testa, 2012). In addition to sharp assessment and diagnostic skills, MHPs possess several abilities which aid in the development and cohesion of interdisciplinary teams and make them extremely effective collaborators. These abilities include identifying contextual factors and barriers that may be impacting treatment effectiveness; understanding the language, values, and perspectives of different disciplines; understanding and integrating the intersectionality of each client's cultural identities into treatment planning; and educating others to improve multicultural competence.

Interdisciplinary communication to coordinate care can be oral or written, bidirectional (exchange), multidirectional (collaboration of multiple disciplines) or unidirectional (release of information from one provider to another). Best practice offers clients full informed consent about the information to be shared and actively engages clients as members of the interdisciplinary care team. Perhaps the simplest and most common form of ICC occurs when an MHP and a medical provider or psychiatrist discuss issues related to a client's medication regimen, or when an MHP conducting individual therapy with a client collaborates with an MHP conducting partners or family therapy with the same client. Typically, many MHPs have engaged in some kind of ICC even if it is not focused on TGNC-affirmative care (Torrence et al., 2014).

When working with the TGNC community, ICC is a more involved and more consistent part of working with clients (Bockting et al., 2007). Because many TGNC clients require services from a broad range of professionals including endocrinologists, primary care providers, surgeons, school personnel, employers, religious leaders, and attorneys, it is important that MHPs are in communication with others involved in their clients' care. Additionally, the MHP will likely interact with systems through which clients obtain necessary documentation to maneuver through daily activities (APA, 2015). These may include local, state and federal offices that issue identification documents (i.e., driver's license, ID, birth certificate, passport, U.S. permanent resident card, social security card), school record offices, and the Transportation Security Administration (World Professional Association for Transgender Health [WPATH], 2015).

There are two main structures within which TGNC-affirmative ICC occurs. One main structure includes clinics, hospitals, or health care centers that employ an interdisciplinary group of health care professionals to work as a treatment team providing care to TGNC clients (Edwards-Leeper & Spack, 2012; Reisner et al., 2015). Examples of such health care centers or hospitals include the LA LGBT Center in Los Angeles, California; Howard Brown Health in Chicago, Illinois; the T-Clinic at Randall Children's Hospital in Portland, Oregon; and Legacy Community Health in Houston, Texas. Many TGNC clients receive their care from these types of organizations, with some lesbian, gay, bisexual, transgender, and queer/questioning health care centers providing medical and behavioral health care for thousands of TGNC clients per year. Although many services can be coordinated under one roof at such health care centers, these organizations still coordinate care with outside providers when clients require care or resources that are not provided by the health care center (i.e., surgery, oncology, electrolysis, legal assistance).

A second main structure includes providers who are in separate locations (e.g., private practice or hospital-based) that establish working relationships and collaborative networks to facilitate efficient cross-referral and communication to ensure the best coordinated care for TGNC clients. In some major cities, providers across a range of disciplines have formed formal or informal networks. Networks expand as new TGNC-affirmative providers are identified and shrink as other providers leave the area or change their practice availability. Such networks facilitate cross-referral and prompt care as clients navigate the complex and often daunting health care system to obtain needed services (Stroumsa, 2014). Within the range of structures, ICC may take many forms for

MHPs. Among the various health care professionals working with TGNC clients, MHPs often have the most contact with clients and are in the best position to understand how care across multiple domains should be linked. MHPs may also have more contact with family members, be more aware of the lived experiences of clients and have a deeper awareness of important cultural issues that must be incorporated into care.

WHY INTERDISCIPLINARY COLLABORATIVE CARE IS CRITICAL FOR TGNC-AFFIRMATIVE CARE

ICC improves client health outcomes and the quality of care that clients receive. A range of professional organizations have strongly endorsed the need for interdisciplinary care and comprehensive, integrated services for TGNC clients (ACA, 2010; APA, 2015; Byne et al., 2012; Coleman et al., 2012). In addition, multiple studies have demonstrated that ICC enhances the effectiveness of treatment for TGNC clients (Hembree et al., 2009; Spack et al., 2012). Client health outcomes and service quality are enhanced by improved continuity of care and better communication between shared providers facilitated by ICC. Without ICC, clients are sometimes expected to carry messages and questions between providers, often leading to confusion and frustration on the part of the client and providers. When health care providers work collaboratively, colleagues can communicate to develop a comprehensive treatment plan that coordinates the client's biopsychosocial care and more efficiently addresses client needs (Mizock & Fleming, 2011). When health care providers collaborate, client engagement and retention are also improved. Many, if not most, TGNC clients have at some point had to obtain services from providers who were ill-informed about gender identity and their needs as TGNC people (Grant et al., 2011). As a result, TGNC people have often felt dissatisfied with or hurt by the health care they received (Bradford, Xavier, Hendricks, Rives, & Honnold, 2007). When clients feel that their providers are attentive, competent, and respectful, clients may more actively engage in their treatment and remain in care. Interdisciplinary teams can reduce client frustration and fear, while amplifying clients' voices and needs.

When care involves contact with TGNC clients' families, significant others, or chosen intimate circles, ICC can facilitate the management of complex systems issues. Close collaboration is also especially important in complex cases that require careful consideration and consistent communication to provide clients with affirmative, empowering care that effectively addresses the causes of any distress or dysfunction clients may be experiencing. In such cases, a TGNC client's history or diagnosis may be complicated and problems that clients face might not be resolved without the close collaboration that comes with ICC.

As in all instances of ICC, it is important to clarify and secure any release of information needed for collaborative communication between providers, the family, and other systems. Within integrated care systems, a separate release of information may not be required for communication between providers. In addition, different disciplines work under different requirements for release of information outside of their respective care system. For example, it is standard practice for medical providers to exchange information with an external referral source without a signed release. MHPs involved in an ICC team should ensure that they have met their legal requirements for release from clients and/or their guardians as necessary.

Although ICC may require more administrative time from providers on the front end of treatment, it can provide care that is ultimately more efficient, effectively utilizing funding and other scarce resources. As insurance carriers increasingly cover TGNC-affirmative care (Stroumsa, 2014), the costs of the various treatments and procedures will come under closer scrutiny. Because much TGNC health care involves providers across a range of health care disciplines, ICC will be a necessary component in ensuring coverage for this medically necessary care and providing such care in the most cost-efficient way possible.

ICC enhances professional and organizational growth and development in ways that ultimately benefit TGNC clients as well as the providers and organizations that serve them. ICC allows professional colleagues to teach and learn from each other, rather than relying on clients to teach their providers how to offer TGNC-affirmative care (Hopwood & dickey, 2014). Providers grow professionally from participation in other disciplines' cultures and systems. Through this interdisciplinary exposure, providers become progressively more informed and better prepared to facilitate communication and transitions between disciplines. The knowledge and skills gained as a result of ICC offers providers the ability to better prepare their clients for interaction with different disciplines and to identify circumstances that may warrant a specific interdisciplinary referral or course of action. Through ICC, MHPs are also in a position to reinforce care instructions offered by other providers. For example, an MHP who regularly collaborates with surgeons might speak with a client who has chosen to disregard the vaginal dilation directions received from their surgeon following a vaginoplasty. As a result of ICC, the MHP understands the significant impact of such a decision (permanent closure of the newly formed vagina) and can facilitate communication between the client and their surgeon to clarify and discuss the long term physical, psychological, and sexual impact of this decision.

By working in close collaboration with an interdisciplinary team, providers constantly hone and update their knowledge and clinical skills. This is especially critical in the area of TGNC health in which the knowledge and evidence base is growing rapidly (Mayer et al., 2008). This continually improves providers' ability to guide and inform clients. In this way, ICC minimizes barriers to care for current and future TGNC clients and makes care more TGNC-affirmative. Because the learning that is gained from working with the ICC team impacts all team members, the systems in which they work are also impacted. This facilitates the process by which systems and organizations move away from positions and practices that are driven by TGNC-prejudice and toward TGNC-affirmative care. The learning that is gained through ICC can also positively impact colleagues in other organizations and other providers, inform current practice models and the field as a whole, and inform policy and advocacy efforts.

Finally, it is important to note that, despite an increasing amount of information available about TGNC people and the care that they require, only a small percentage of health care providers across disciplines have developed the expertise needed to provide TGNC-affirmative care (Dewey, 2013). At this point in time, clinicians with solid expertise in working with TGNC clients are uncommon and are unique in their respective fields. At the same time, the lack of training opportunities for health care professionals in TGNC health has resulted in some providers across disciplines offering services to TGNC clients without adequate training or exposure. With the ICC model, it becomes possible to include practitioners who are at different levels of development and knowledge, allowing them to learn from providers who are more experienced in offering TGNC-affirmative care. This provides a training and supervision mechanism leading to more health care providers adequately trained to work with TGNC clients.

COMMON ROLES OF MENTAL HEALTH PROVIDERS IN INTERDISCIPLINARY COLLABORATIVE CARE

ICC teams may be made up of a variety of professionals, within and outside of the health care professions. Depending on the setting and the situation, ICC teams may include MHPs (e.g., psychologists, psychiatrists, mental health counselors, social workers, family therapists, case managers, school counselors, university counseling staff), medical professionals (e.g., endocrinologists, surgeons, primary care providers, nurses, dieticians), and allied professionals (e.g., electrologists, laser hair removal technicians, voice coaches, school personnel, religious or spiritual leaders, lawyers, massage therapists; APA, 2015). The role of the MHP is influenced by the client's willingness to consent to release information outside of the provider's health care system and the client's comfort working with an ICC team. Many TGNC clients enthusiastically support ICC models if they believe their providers are honest, transparent, and genuinely invested in supporting their access to necessary care. In this way, TGNC clients often view MHPs, in particular, as advocates for their overall health care. It is important for the client and MHP to specifically discuss and agree to any limitations on the information that will be shared with the ICC team, as well as possible outcomes.

Schools and Child Care Settings

Special expertise in child and adolescent mental health, in addition to expertise in providing TGNC-affirmative care, is required when working with TGNC and gender-questioning youth (Coleman et al., 2012). TGNC and gender-questioning youth can present with a complicated clinical picture and with complex system issues (Ehrensaft, 2011). MHPs may be called on to assist young clients and their families to coordinate a care and education plan with a youth's school system or, for younger children, a youth's child care setting. The collaboration may include participation in a meeting with the youth, the youth's parents or guardians, school administrators, and school counselors to create a plan for respectful, supportive treatment of the youth in the educational or child care setting (APA, 2015; APA & National Association of School Psychologists, 2014). The development and implementation of a plan can help the school better understand the youth's situation, educate school staff about gender identity and gender expression, and solicit support for the youth. The plan might define the youth's experience of gender, specify names and pronouns to be used when addressing the youth, clarify bathroom and locker room use, and describe conditions that would facilitate a more affirmative learning environment for the youth in the school. MHPs may also be asked to provide education about gender identity to staff, teachers, parents, and/or students (Case & Meier, 2014; Singh & Burnes, 2009).

Religious and Spiritual Systems

Many TGNC people were raised in a faith tradition that they may wish to maintain throughout their lives. Although quite a few faith traditions openly discourage, ignore, or pathologize TGNC lives, MHPs may be able to assist their clients in the process of reconciling their faith with their gender identity or finding new outlets for spiritual growth. MHPs can create a network of gender-affirming religious and spiritual guides, including pastoral counselors, chaplains, priests, rabbis, nuns, pastors, and shamans. MHPs can gather information about how sacred texts discuss gender identity and TGNC people and different faiths' comfort in welcoming TGNC people into their community, discuss issues of gender identity with religious/spiritual leaders, or facilitate a meeting with the client and their religious/spiritual leader to improve communication and understanding. Common intrapersonal challenges include internalized transphobia related to a belief that being TGNC is inherently sinful or disordered, trauma resulting from excommunication or religious ritual, exorcism or prayer to change one's TGNC identity, and families feeling that they have to choose between supporting their TGNC family member or maintaining their faith and adherence to anti-TGNC doctrine.

Legal and Correctional Systems

MHPs may be called on to interact with various personnel in correctional or legal systems to ensure the well-being of their clients. A client who has been incarcerated or jailed may request that an MHP provide a letter to the jail or correctional setting staff. The letter can describe the client's gender identity, specify names and pronouns to be used when addressing the client, clarify bathroom and shower use, offer housing recommendations (e.g., general population housing, women's section, men's section) and describe conditions that would facilitate a safe and respectful environment for the client. In particular, it can be important to specifically address the possibility that the correctional system will chose to place a TGNC client in isolation, instead of general population housing, as a protective measure. If the client will be incarcerated for a lengthy period of time, it may also be necessary to inform medical personnel at the facility of the client's need for continuation of HT and facilitate proof of prescription through the client's medical provider to support the client's access to necessary medication. In some cases, clients who are facing sentencing on criminal charges may require a letter to the judge that describes the client's gender identity and treatment needs.

When a TGNC or gender-questioning youth or TGNC parent or caregiver is the subject of a child custody evaluation, an MHP may be asked to offer documentation to inform the evaluation. Typically, the child custody evaluator will not be trained in TGNC-affirmative care and may not understand whether gender identity and gender expression are significant issues that should influence the evaluation. Whenever a TGNC or gender-questioning youth is the subject of such an evaluation, the role of the MHP can involve educating the evaluator about gender identity issues, describing the youth's gender identity and expression, identifying the level of support received from different caregivers, and describing the work that has been done with the youth and/or caregivers. A similar communication will typically occur with the guardian ad litem (GAL) who has been assigned to represent the child or adolescent's best interests. In this case, it is important that the GAL understand the youth's best interests from the perspective of the youth. A letter can also be provided to the evaluator when a TGNC parent or caregiver is involved in a child custody evaluation. A helpful addition to the letter can include a notation that research shows that children of TGNC parents do not appear to suffer long-term negative impact as a result of their parent's gender identity (Minter & Wald, 2012; White & Ettner, 2004) and that loss of a parent's presence in a child's life creates more distress than the gender transition (White & Ettner, 2007).

In other cases, an MHP may be called on to write a letter or complete a form to assist a client to change their gender marker on vital documents, such as a driver's license, social security card, passport, or birth certificate. Information regarding the specific requirements for various identity documents in different states can be found on websites, such as the National Center for Transgender Equality (http://www.transequality.org/). It is important to determine whether there is a prescribed format that must be followed and whether information must be submitted on a specific form. There may also be verbatim language that must be included in a letter for it to be considered valid; this may differ by federal, state, county, and city regulations. For example, some department of motor vehicle offices require that a letter include designation of the client's current gender, that this gender is stable, and that it is not likely to change in the foreseeable future before revising identification documents. As another example, the U.S. State Department will only accept a verbatim letter from a physician to change the gender marker on a U.S. passport.

Work and Travel Settings

At times, clients may struggle with how to express their gender identity at work. In these situations, communication between an MHP and human resources personnel or the client's supervisor may be instructive and helpful in gaining understanding and support in the work environment. For clients who decide to transition while remaining at their current place of employment, this can help prepare the employer for upcoming changes (APA, 2015). Communication with an employer might explain gender identity, describe the client's experience of gender, specify correct client names and pronouns, clarify bathroom and locker room use, and describe conditions facilitating an affirmative work environment. In certain high-security jobs (e.g., law enforcement, security, airline pilots), additional information may be required to ensure that the client is allowed to continue working in their position during and after transition.

MHPs may also write a letter to assist clients with "safe passage" when traveling, particularly when using commercial airlines or crossing international borders. Because current screening procedures can reveal anatomical features that may not conform to the client's gender presentation, a safe passage letter can help to explain the discrepancy that may be observed to security staff. Clients can carry such a letter and produce it if necessary. The same letter can be used if a client is detained by police or pulled over for a traffic violation, or if a client is approached in a gender-specific public space or bathroom and asked about the appropriateness of their presence.

Medical Systems and Access to Medical Procedures

Collaboration with medical professionals is perhaps the most common instance of ICC. The MHP's role is often to ensure readiness and understanding of the medical procedures or treatments; evaluate a client's ability to grant informed consent, advocate for informed and TGNC-affirmative medical care; assist the client to integrate the medical procedures and body changes into their identity; help prepare the client for mental; physical and social changes that may occur; maximize the success of medical interventions and the client's satisfaction with those interventions; assist the client to access necessary care; and help the ICC team interpret and apply the client's unique needs and desires (APA, 2015). Appendix 3.1 lists common gender-affirming medical procedures with which an MHP should be familiar.

Historically, MHPs have been placed in the role of gatekeepers rather than ICC team members. The role of gatekeeper occurred because many medical providers would not prescribe HT or perform surgery without approval letters from MHPs that indicated that clients were ready for these procedures and had demonstrated their readiness by meeting certain prescribed criteria, including lived experience as the "opposite" gender (Hastings & Markland, 1978). Thus, clients often reported a rigid, stereotypical gender binary narrative allowing them to access the letter they needed, disregarding their own gender identity and expression (Lev, 2006). More recently, models of TGNC-affirmative care have improved and clinical practice has evolved to include a nonbinary understanding of gender focused on informed consent (see Chapter 1). Revised systems of care actively include clients as ICC team members, avoid strict gatekeeping roles for any ICC team member, apply a broader understanding of gender identity and expression, recognize that there is no correct process of transition, and position clients to play a much larger role in deciding the procedures they will undergo. The development of the ICC model has the potential of reducing the MHP gatekeeping role through addressing substantial barriers in the ability of clients to obtain needed services. Collaborative team members should seek to trust each other enough to identify challenges and barriers, working together to improve and innovate the way they offer TGNC-affirmative care (Deutsch, 2012; Mizock & Fleming, 2011). Some providers and systems, however, still utilize a gatekeeper process (Ehrbar & Gorton, 2011) and reify the gender binary.

Within medical systems, the most common collaboration involves working with primary care providers, endocrinologists and surgeons to facilitate clients' access to HT and surgical procedures. The focus of the ICC interaction is the same whether providers work as a preexisting interdisciplinary team or constitute a network of independent professionals, although formality of the documentation may differ (i.e., a short, internal health record note vs. a letter to include in the health record). The content of HT and surgery letters is impacted by the medical provider's requirements, with some medical providers having strict qualification requirements for MHPs providing letters (i.e., only a doctoral level MHP or only a psychiatrist). It is prudent for a client to confirm which, if any, credentials are required before seeking a letter from an MHP.

Letters provided to clients for HT or surgery follow a fairly standard format, with surgical letters offering greater detail and depth (Coleman et al., 2012). Letters should clearly identify the author and briefly describe the training and experience that the MHP has working with TGNC individuals. Letters should indicate the amount of time that the provider has known and/or worked with the client, the frequency with which or the number of times the client has been seen, and the nature of the relationship with the client. A description of the client's gender identity and gender expression, some gender history, and a comment about how the requested treatment will help the client to achieve congruence and authenticity are commonly included. The MHP should describe any psychological or psychiatric conditions with which the client has been diagnosed, intensity of ongoing symptoms and whether these present a complication or contraindication for HT or surgery.

Hormone Therapy for Adults

There are two basic models of HT: a more traditional standard of care (SOC) model and an informed consent model (Deutsch, 2012; Ehrbar & Gorton, 2011). The two models are not in conflict but are instead at different places on a continuum of assessment for HT. A *traditional SOC model* requires the MHP to conduct a psychosocial assessment that evaluates whether a client meets specific criteria that would warrant a referral for HT, one element of which is the client's ability to grant informed consent (Coleman et al., 2012). An *informed consent model* reduces the requirements for an adult client to access HT and does not require a justification for HT on the basis of gender history. A growing number of health care centers and interdisciplinary teams are utilizing an informed consent model for HT prescription for adults 18 and over (Coleman et al., 2012). An informed consent model requires that clients requesting HT receive comprehensive, accessible information about the effects and risks of HT, and are screened to ensure their ability to understand the information and to apply it in their decision making process. Providers or MHPs screen for conditions that may interrupt informed consent and actively work with clients to expeditiously establish informed consent when possible. An MHP's role in an informed consent process may include screening to ensure clients can grant informed consent, offering information about HT effects and risks, and identifying any suggestions to maximize a positive HT experience.

Many providers prescribing HT are not located in an informed consent clinic and may require a letter from an MHP. Most endocrinologists or primary care providers request letters from MHPs because they lack adequate training in mental health to determine whether there are any psychological or psychiatric concerns that might be exacerbated by HT and whether HT is psychologically appropriate for the client. In such cases, interdisciplinary colleagues are working to ensure that the care they are rendering will have the intended beneficial effect. The length and level of detail will depend on the requirements of each HT provider. MHPs may need to offer information about a client's unique experience and transition plan, helping providers to understand clients' need and readiness for HT when they do not offer stereotypical narratives or goals, MHPs, however, should include only the amount of psychosocial assessment information required by the health care provider and not disclose unnecessary client medical history. MHPs can also support HT providers in understanding clients' unique transition plans that may include a request for low levels of HT to achieve a more androgynous appearance or certain psychological benefits, or a plan to discontinue HT after specific permanent physical changes have occurred.

When working with clients who are seeking HT, MHPs can be especially helpful in preparing clients for its effects. This may include helping clients to understand the effects of HT (including what it will not do); which effects are permanent and which are temporary; and the influence of HT on mood, identity, and expression. MHPs can collaborate with medical professionals who are prescribing HT by educating and ensuring clients are able to make fully informed decisions prior to starting HT (Coleman et al., 2012; Deutsch, 2012). MHPs can help clients understand HT can cause infertility and facilitate a discussion about whether clients want to cryogenically store eggs or sperm. Once clients have begun HT, MHPs can assist them in understanding the effects, and the changes, they can expect across time, including HT's impact on emotional functioning (Keo-Meier et al., 2015). MHPs can also help clients understand when it may be appropriate to contact their medical provider if they experience an unusual response pattern or prepare for the loss of the temporary changes induced by HT if HT is discontinued.

Puberty Suppression and Hormone Therapy for Youth

In the past, HT and puberty suppression have followed a very formal SOC process in clinical settings that serve TGNC and gender-questioning youth. However, as some of these clinical settings mature, providers have adapted the decision-making process to the needs and situation of each youth or family (Edwards-Leeper & Spack, 2012), and there is a greater infusion of informed consent elements in the care of youth ages 17 and under. The interplay of psychological, physical, and social development has made it critical to have interdisciplinary care teams involved when working with TGNC or gender-questioning youth (Olson, Forbes, & Belzer, 2011). MHPs working with youth play an important role on the interdisciplinary team due to considerations of cognitive and social development, as well as family dynamics, including the degree of support within the family for the youth's gender identity and expression. This role is especially crucial when conducting a mental health evaluation to determine the appropriateness and timeliness of a medical intervention (APA, 2015). MHPs can also be very helpful when adolescents present with a late-onset (i.e., postpubertal) gender nonconforming identification with no history of gender role nonconformity or gender questioning in childhood (Edwards-Leeper & Spack, 2012). In these cases, parents, school staff, and medical providers are often caught off guard and a thorough and accurate assessment can establish the appropriateness of HT or puberty suppression. MHPs can assist the ICC team when complex family dynamics exist, especially if parents and youth disagree about the speed or type of medical care the youth has requested. MHPs can also assist the ICC team in acknowledging the fear and burden of responsibility that parents and caregivers may feel as they make decisions about the health of their child or adolescent (Grossman, D'Augelli, Howell, & Hubbard, 2005).

Surgeries

Surgeons typically require at least one letter from an MHP prior to initiating gender-affirming surgery. For some surgeries or as a preference by some surgeons, two letters from independent MHPs may be required. Surgeons request letters from MHPs because they lack adequate training in mental health to determine whether there are any psychological or psychiatric concerns that might be exacerbated by the surgical procedure and to discern whether these procedures are psychologically appropriate for the client. Many surgeons require a very detailed letter that follows SOC protocol and may only accept letters from specific types of MHPs. This type of letter may be difficult to write for a gender-queer client who does not endorse a binary gender identity because some surgeons may require assurance that the client has an established identity that stereotypically aligns with the surgery being considered (i.e., a client requesting vaginoplasty is a TGNC woman, has consistently identified as a woman, and dresses as a woman). Nonetheless, if the client wishes to utilize this surgeon, the letter must conform to the surgeon's expectations. MHPs can offer surgeons information about a client's unique experience and transition plan, helping surgeons to understand clients' readiness for and the appropriateness of gender-affirming surgery when clients do not offer stereotypical narratives or goals. Surgery letters for genderqueer clients should carefully balance a client's unique identity and needs with the information surgeons need to feel confident that surgery is psychologically appropriate and that the client will not retroactively regret their decision to undergo the procedure. Involving the client as an active ICC team member (Maguen, Shipherd, & Harris, 2005) and discussing letter requirements can empower clients to participate in the creation of the letter and the personal gender narrative it presents.

When working with clients planning surgical procedures, MHPs help clients develop a realistic expectation of the costs, logistics, risks, and potential results of surgery (e.g., appearance, use, sensate response). Discussion may also include what to expect in the recovery period after surgery, including the length of time that recovery is expected to take. Clients should be aware that there are different surgical techniques in common practice, only some of which retain nerve connection following surgery (i.e., nipples, clitoris).

Primary Care and Other Specialty Care

When communicating with a medical provider offering HT, puberty suppression, or gender-affirming surgery, an MHP frequently speaks to an informed colleague. MHPs who work within an ICC model interact regularly with clients' primary care providers, gynecologists, endocrinologists, and other medical or allied professionals, such as fertility specialists, nurses, speech therapists, occupational therapists, and health educators. Collaboration in an ICC model can be bidirectional, and just as medical providers may rely on MHPs to provide documentation that TGNC clients will use to initiate a medical transition and to address the psychological and social aspects of transition with the client before, during, and after HT or surgery, MHPs often refer clients to medical providers for assessment and treatment of medical issues (Coleman et al., 2012; Hembree et al., 2009; Lev, 2009).

Given the lack of informed, TGNC-affirmative medical and allied health providers, clients will frequently receive care from providers who have never previously worked with TGNC people. Communicating and collaborating with colleagues who are unfamiliar with, and possibly intimidated by, TGNC health care requires a supplemental set of skills.

MHPs may need to offer support, information, and education to interdisciplinary colleagues who are unfamiliar with issues of gender identity and gender expression to assist their clients in obtaining TGNC-affirmative care (Holman & Goldberg, 2007; Lev, 2009). For example, an MHP who is assisting a TGNC person to obtain a vaginoplasty could contact the client's new gynecologist in preparation for the client's first office visit. This contact could include providing the gynecologist with general information about the client's gender history, coaching on respectful ways to communicate with and about the client, and discussing how both providers could most affirmatively raise the continued need for appropriate health checks to ensure the client's best physical health (APA, 2015; Unger, 2014; van Trotsenburg, 2009).

It can be important to help interdisciplinary colleagues who are less familiar with TGNC-affirmative care understand TGNC clients' presentations and reframe their behavior, if necessary, to assist the colleague in providing the best care possible. In particular, many TGNC clients have fought extremely hard to access care with uninformed providers in a system that fails to appreciate the medical necessity of their requests (Bradford et al., 2007). As a result, TGNC clients may seem aggressive, insistent, angry, and unwilling to compromise. In these instances, it can be helpful to reframe their presentation as stemming from fear, a fight for body integrity, and self-advocacy in a predominantly oppressive, discriminatory health care system.

When communicating with providers who may not regularly engage in ICC, MHPs should be intentional about the mode of the communication they choose and the method in which information is given, received, and shared. It may help to clarify how the information exchange could improve the care provided to the client by all treating professionals, clearly define roles and discuss the various levels of expertise in TGNC care that each provider brings to the exchange. It can also be of assistance to offer the interdisciplinary colleague the opportunity to communicate with an ICC team member in the same profession, if available, especially if the colleague is in need of specific treatment guidance that an MHP may not have or if the colleague fails to value the expertise and support an MHP can offer. MHPs should remember that learning and expanding one's understanding of the gender spectrum can be uncomfortable and anxiety provoking, and that some providers may find it difficult to manage issues of gender identity while also recognizing and respecting other cultural identities of the client. Providing TGNC-affirmative care may require difficult or uncomfortable personal and professional change by the colleague. In providing care to TGNC clients, colleagues will need to confront previously unexamined stereotypes, fears, and anti-TGNC prejudice (Vanderburgh, 2007), and it may take years for a colleague to become competent in TGNC-affirmative care.

For MHPs, it may be particularly difficult to work with colleagues who say or do things that are not TGNC-affirmative, that diminish TGNC clients' lives and choices, or who disregard how difficult it can be for TGNC clients to remain in care. MHPs are encouraged to lead by example, remaining alert for any receptive teaching moments with their colleagues, using affirmative language and gently suggesting ways for colleagues to improve care of TGNC clients. Using a colleague's professional language and couching elements of TGNC-affirmative care in language that aligns with their values (i.e., health outcomes, client's ability to consent to pelvic exam, improve patient retention in care, treatment adherence, reduced no-show rate) can also slowly improve the care they offer to TGNC clients. When things get difficult, it can often be helpful to seek consultation from a trusted colleague who can offer support and a reminder of why the effort will ultimately improve the care clients receive.

SPECIAL CONSIDERATIONS IN INTERDISCIPLINARY COLLABORATIVE CARE

Although still uncommon, an increasing number of health insurance plans now explicitly cover gender-affirmative treatment and various procedures (Stroumsa, 2014). However, because insurance plans are unfamiliar with TGNC-affirmative care and are slow to revise previous exclusions and restrictions, clients may encounter difficulty obtaining reimbursement for health care costs, including prescribed medications, procedures, and surgery. In these cases, a letter to an insurance company representative from an ICC team member can sometimes facilitate the reimbursement process. Before communicating with an insurance company, it is important to know exactly what the client's insurance policy says about coverage for gender-related procedures and to then pair that language with treatment protocols received by the client.

The experience of practicing as an ICC team within the same organization and across a range of organizations or practices can differ. Preexisting relationships can enhance the MHP's ability to discuss TGNC-affirmative care issues, but they can also create pressure and discomfort when those discussions affect all of the professional activities that the colleagues share. MHPs may have less ability to influence a system from the outside, but they can partner with key colleagues with whom they work well and who enhance their ability to provide quality care to their clients.

When MHPs are not part of an existing interdisciplinary setting or team, and especially when they practice in isolated or rural communities, it is still possible to identify interdisciplinary colleagues with whom they may collaborate and/or refer, if only by phone or video conference (Walinsky & Whitcomb, 2010). For example, a rural MHP could identify a TGNC-affirmative pediatrician in a surrounding area and collaborate with the pediatrician to work with parents raising concerns about their gender-questioning or TGNC youth. It can be especially helpful to create a network of resources that can be used for referral to assist clients (i.e., support groups, community centers, hair stylists, makeup artists, tailors, electrologists, lawyers, intimate apparel fitters, massage therapists). MHPs may also be able to collaborate with social service colleagues to provide their clients with TGNC-affirmative referrals for housing, financial support, vocational/educational counseling and training, TGNC-affirming religious or spiritual communities, peer support, and other community resources (Gehi & Arkles, 2007).

ICC with and for TGNC clients is challenging on many levels, but it can also be profoundly rewarding. Whenever needed, it is important to seek consultation and support from other TGNC-affirmative MHPs or providers. Those clinicians who are fortunate enough to work on a preexisting ICC team are encouraged to make great use of the available resources. Those who do not have the benefit of an in-house ICC team will need support and consultation as they do this work. It will be essential to intentionally create a network of interdisciplinary colleagues who can be consulted to discuss issues of treatment and to exchange resources. Not only will this support improve the care MHPs can offer, it can reduce and soothe the secondary traumatization and occasional discouragement MHPs encounter as they champion TGNC-affirmative care. Training opportunities and guidance from professional organizations (APA, 2015) is increasingly available. Recently, WPATH initiated a certification process to credential providers in transgender health, although no providers have yet been certified.

CASE VIGNETTES

ICC can be complex and multidimensional, requiring strong foundational knowledge about TGNC-affirmative care mixed with the ability to cultivate unique approaches to address the needs and context of each client. It can have dramatic, transformative impact and can support clients, their families, and the TGNC community. ICC can catalyze comprehensive, culturally competent care and assist systems to affirmatively meet the needs of TGNC people. For example, consider the fictional case of Michael, a 17-year-old TGNC young man who began counseling with an MHP at his parents' insistence. Michael's parents emigrated from Pakistan, and Michael was born and educated in the United States. Michael began assertively requesting HT after being attacked and severely hurt at a school social event. Michael's parents told the MHP that they were hesitant to proceed with medical transition, believing that "their daughter" had not carefully explored gender identity issues, and they did not want Michael to discuss gender identity issues with anyone outside the immediate family. The high school administration contacted Michael's parents to identify concerns about Michael's bathroom choice; his request that others call him "Michael" instead of his legal name, Maria; his increasing anger and frustration in the classroom, and the bullying and fights that are occurring as other youth become aware of Michael's requests. In the first contact, the MPH learned that the primary care provider was concerned with the discord in the family, would not prescribe HT without parental consent and was growing progressively more worried about Michael's use of nonprescribed medications and supplements to effect physical changes he desperately wants.

ICC places the MHP in an ideal position to concurrently communicate with multiple systems and develop a shared treatment plan. The MHP began by coordinating a series of meetings with Michael and his parents, sometimes in family sessions, to discuss their concerns and negotiate an initial treatment plan Michael and his parents found agreeable. Issues addressed included acculturation, the families' beliefs about the cause and impact of a TGNC identity, basic education about TGNC identities, the parents' fears of loss of their child and their community, and their spiritual beliefs. The MHP spoke with the medical provider to identify the health behaviors of greatest concern and worked with Michael in therapy to reduce the use of nonprescribed substances. The MHP spoke with school administrators to offer basic education about TGNC identities and gender-questioning youth and, with Michael and his parents, created a plan to increase Michael's safety and comfort at school while reducing his disruptive behaviors in the classroom. After almost a year in therapy, Michael's parents used his self-identified name and developed a greater understanding of Michael's identity. With this, Michael's acting out behaviors in school decreased. The medical provider's concerns abated when Michael ended his use of nonprescribed medications and began therapy, and the provider agreed to prescribe starting doses of HT when Michael turned 18, although Michael's parents did not support this decision.

Another example of effective ICC is the case vignette of Vanessa, a 29-year-old African American transwoman who was incarcerated at a local jail for sexwork. On her third day, after being cleared for housing in general population and placed on a male unit, she sought an emergency mental health appointment. Vanessa reported that she had been taking black market hormones for 15 years. For the last 5 years, she had engaged in sex work to support herself and in that time more than a dozen of her friends (also transwomen of color) had been brutally assaulted, two had been stabbed, and one had been murdered. Vanessa had not taken HT in several days and was reporting symptoms consistent with early menopause. More urgently, she had received three serious threats from male inmates on her new housing unit, causing her to reexperience trauma-related symptoms and to fear for her safety. When she reported her concerns to the correctional officers on her unit, she was told that she belonged on a male unit and that she would have to solve her own problems with the placement.

The MHP had to carefully navigate a rigid jail system to advocate for the client's previously undocumented medical and mental health needs and address the immediate safety issues in her assigned jail unit. The MHP worked with jail officials across multiple contacts to advocate for the client's placement on a female unit to improve the client's safety. This involved providing education to correctional staff on the client's new housing unit. In addition, the MHP collaborated with the jail's medical director to offer HT and ensure Vanessa's receipt of HT as well as to improve her access to other medically necessary care.

Chapter Summary

As the case vignettes demonstrate, ICC is an integral aspect of care when working with TGNC clients and communities. It significantly improves health outcome and TGNC people's quality of life. The specifics of surgery and hormone therapy change quickly and will require MHPs to frequently refresh their knowledge. Although those specifics may shift, the need for this work is deep and abiding, and will only grow in the next decade as more TGNC people seek care and as more systems learn to offer this care in a TGNC-affirmative way.

Appendix 3.1. Common Gender-Affirming Medical Procedures

In the course of aligning the body to be more congruent with gender identity, transgender and gender nonconforming (TGNC) people may use a number of gender-affirming procedures. Described very briefly here are the most common procedures. Mental health providers (MHPs) are encouraged to seek out the most current literature about medical procedures, as new developments occur at a rapid pace.

Hormone Therapy and Puberty Suppression: Hormone therapy (HT) can either feminize or masculinize the body, sometimes in combination with a testosterone blocker. HT is typically used after the individual has reached the age of 16 or 18 years old (depending on the facility, provider, and Tanner stage of physical development). Masculinizing HT involves administration of testosterone through intramuscular (IM) or subcutaneous injection (typically self-injected), pills, creams, or transdermal patches. Feminizing HT can involve an antiandrogen agent or testosterone-blocker (e.g., spironolactone) that suppresses the effect of the testosterone that the body produces and/or the administration of feminizing hormones (e.g., estradiol) with IM injections or oral medication. The combination allows feminizing hormones introduced to the body to have an effect because existing testosterone can generally overpower them. Masculinizing and feminizing agents are titrated until the desired clinical effects are achieved.

Another hormone-related treatment involves administration of gonadotropin-releasing hormone (GnRH) analogues to adolescents, beginning shortly after the onset of puberty (typically when the adolescent is at Tanner Stage 2 or 3), to block sexual maturation and the effects of sex hormones. The use of this approach is increasing because it has been shown to result in positive treatment outcomes and can serve a diagnostic purpose, allowing an ICC team to work with adolescent clients to assess whether gender dysphoria and/or co-occurring psychological issues improve or resolve when puberty is halted and the adolescent feels supported in their gender exploration (de Vries, Steensma, Doreleijers, & Cohen-Kettenis, 2011). The cost of GnRH analogues is much higher than HT and may not be affordable for many clients.

In addition to the physical effects of HT and GnRH analogues, clients also experience psychological effects, particularly emotional effects (Keo-Meier et al., 2015). For example, people taking testosterone may experience fewer symptoms of depression and anxiety, along with an increased sex drive. They may experience a quicker temper and become angry more easily, although this is likely to decrease over time as they become accustomed to higher levels of testosterone. People taking feminizing hormones may experience a wider range of emotions and become more sensitized to emotional stimuli. In both cases, the typical pattern is similar to that experienced during puberty; framing clients' experiences this way can facilitate their adjustment to new emotional experiences.

Gender-Affirming Surgery: There are several surgical procedures that can be undertaken. These include chest masculinization or breast augmentation, frequently referred to as *top surgery*, to either reduce or enhance breast size; vaginoplasty and labiaplasty to feminize the genitalia; and a tracheal shave to reduce the visible presence of an Adam's apple. Techniques to masculinize the genitalia, including metoidioplasty and phalloplasty, are used less frequently, mostly because many individuals are not satisfied with the typical functioning and sensitivity of the resulting tissue. Genital surgery is frequently referred to as *bottom surgery.* In addition, there are a number of facial surgical techniques that can be used to either feminize or masculinize facial appearance.

Other Physical Procedures: For individuals seeking to feminize their appearance, electrolysis and laser hair removal are often used to remove hair on the face, chest, or back. For those individuals who wish to have feminizing genital surgery, removal of the hair and hair follicles on the scrotum is necessary because this tissue is used in the surgical procedure to create the vaginal walls. Additionally, voice training is sometimes undertaken to elevate the pitch of the voice for those who are seeking feminization procedures.

References

American Counseling Association. (2010). American Counseling Association competencies for counseling with transgender clients. *Journal of LGBT Issues in Counseling, 4*, 135–159. http://dx.doi.org/10.1080/15538605.2010.524839

American Psychological Association. (2015). Guidelines for psychological practice with transgender and gender nonconforming people. *American Psychologist, 70*, 832–864. http://dx.doi.org/10.1037/a0039906

American Psychological Association & National Association of School Psychologists. (2014). *Resolution on gender and sexual orientation diversity in children and adolescents in schools.* Retrieved from http://www.apa.org/about/policy/orientation-diversity.aspx

Bockting, W. O., Knudson, G., & Goldberg, J. M. (2007). Counseling and mental health care for transgender adults and loved ones. *International Journal of Transgenderism, 9*, 35–82. http://dx.doi.org/10.1300/J485v09n03_03

Bradford, J., Xavier, J., Hendricks, M., Rives, M. E., & Honnold, J. A. (2007). The health, health-related needs, and lifecourse experiences of transgender Virginians. *Virginia Transgender Health Initiative Study Statewide Survey Report.* Retrieved from http://www.vdh.state.va.us/epidemiology/DiseasePrevention/documents/pdf/THISFINALREPORTVol1.pdf

Brucker, P., & Shields, C. (2003). Collaboration between mental and medical healthcare providers in an integrated primary care medical setting. *Families, Systems, & Health, 21*, 181–191. http://dx.doi.org/10.1037/1091-7527.21.2.181

Byne, W., Bradley, S. J., Coleman, E., Eyler, A. E., Green, R., Menvielle, E. J., . . . Tompkins, D. A., & the American Psychiatric Association Task Force on Treatment of Gender Identity Disorder. (2012). Report of the American Psychiatric Association Task Force on Treatment of

Gender Identity Disorder. *Archives of Sexual Behavior, 41,* 759–796. http://dx.doi.org/10.1007/s10508-012-9975-x

Case, K., & Meier, C. (2014). Developing allies to transgender and gender non-conforming youth: Training for counselors and educators. *Journal of LGBT Youth, 11,* 62–82. http://dx.doi.org/10.1080/19361653.2014.840764

Coleman, E., Bockting, W., Botzer, M., Cohen-Kettenis, P., DeCuypere, G., Feldman, J., . . . Zucker, K. (2012). Standards of care for the health of transsexual, transgender, and gender-nonconforming people, 7th version. *International Journal of Transgenderism, 13,* 165–232. http://dx.doi.org/10.1080/15532739.2011.700873

Deutsch, M. B. (2012). Use of the informed consent model in provision of cross-sex hormone therapy: A survey of the practices of selected clinics. *International Journal of Transgenderism, 13,* 140–146. http://dx.doi.org/10.1080/15532739.2011.675233

de Vries, A. L., Steensma, T. D., Doreleijers, T. A., & Cohen-Kettenis, P. T. (2011). Puberty suppression in adolescents with gender identity disorder: A prospective follow-up study. *Journal of Sexual Medicine, 8,* 2276–2283. http://dx.doi.org/10.1111/j.1743-6109.2010.01943.x

Dewey, J. M. (2013). Challenges of implementing collaborative models of decision making with trans-identified patients. *Health Expectations: An International Journal of Public Participation in Health Care & Health Policy.* Advance online publication. Retrieved from http://onlinelibrary.wiley.com/doi/10.1111/hex.12133/pdf

Edwards-Leeper, L., & Spack, N. P. (2012). Psychological evaluation and medical treatment of transgender youth in an interdisciplinary "Gender Management Service" (GeMS) in a major pediatric center. *Journal of Homosexuality, 59,* 321–336. http://dx.doi.org/10.1080/00918369.2012.653302

Ehrbar, R. D., & Gorton, R. N. (2011). Exploring provider treatment models in interpreting the standards of care. *International Journal of Transgenderism, 12,* 198–210. http://dx.doi.org/10.1080/15532739.2010.544235

Ehrensaft, D. (2011). *Gender born, gender made: Raising healthy gender nonconforming children.* New York, NY: The Experiment.

Gehi, P. S., & Arkles, G. (2007). Unraveling injustice: Race and class impact of Medicaid exclusions of transition-related health care for transgender people. *Sexuality Research & Social Policy, 4,* 7–35. http://dx.doi.org/10.1525/srsp.2007.4.4.7

Grant, J. M., Mottet, L. A., Tanis, J., Harrison, J., Herman, J. L., & Keisling, M. (2011). *Injustice at every turn: A report of the national transgender discrimination survey.* Washington, DC: National Center for Transgender Equality and National Gay and Lesbian Task Force.

Grossman, A. H., D'Augelli, A. R., Howell, T. H., & Hubbard, A. (2005). Parent reactions to transgender youth gender nonconforming expression and identity. *Journal of Gay & Lesbian Social Services, 18*, 3–16. http://dx.doi.org/10.1300/J041v18n01_02

Hastings, D., & Markland, C. (1978). Post-surgical adjustment of twenty-five transsexuals (male-to-female) in the University of Minnesota study. *Archives of Sexual Behavior, 7*, 327–336. http://dx.doi.org/10.1007/BF01542041

Hembree, W. C., Cohen-Kettenis, P., Delemarre-van de Waal, H. A., Gooren, L. J., Meyer, W. J., III, Spack, N. P., . . . & Montori, V. M. (2009). Endocrine treatment of transsexual persons: An Endocrine Society clinical practice guideline. *The Journal of Clinical Endocrinology and Metabolism, 94*, 3132–3154. http://dx.doi.org/10.1210/jc.2009-0345

Hendricks, M. L., & Testa, R. J. (2012). A conceptual framework for clinical work with transgender and gender nonconforming clients: An adaptation of the minority stress model. *Professional Psychology: Research and Practice, 43*, 460–467. http://dx.doi.org/10.1037/a0029597

Holman, C., & Goldberg, J. M. (2007). Social and medical transgender case advocacy. *International Journal of Transgenderism, 9*, 197–217. http://dx.doi.org/10.1300/J485v09n03_09

Hopwood, R. A., & dickey, l. m. (2014). Mental health services. In L. Erickson-Schroth (Ed.), *Trans bodies, trans selves: A resource for the transgender community* (pp. 291–305). New York, NY: Oxford University Press.

Keo-Meier, C. L., Herman, L. I., Reisner, S. L., Pardo, S. T., Sharp, C., & Babcock, J. C. (2015). Testosterone treatment and MMPI-2 improvement in transgender men: A prospective controlled study. *Journal of Consulting and Clinical Psychology, 83*, 143–156. http://dx.doi.org/10.1037/a0037599

Lev, A. I. (2006). Disordering gender identity: Gender identity disorder in the DSM-IV-TR. *Journal of Psychology & Human Sexuality, 17*, 35–69. http://dx.doi.org/10.1300/J056v17n03_03

Lev, A. I. (2009). The ten tasks of the mental health provider: Recommendations for revision of the World Professional Association for Transgender Health's standards of care. *International Journal of Transgenderism, 11*, 74–99. http://dx.doi.org/10.1080/15532730903008032

Maguen, S., Shipherd, J. C., & Harris, H. N. (2005). Providing culturally sensitive care for transgender patients. *Cognitive and Behavioral Practice, 12*, 479–490. http://dx.doi.org/10.1016/S1077-7229(05)80075-6

Mayer, K. H., Bradford, J. B., Makadon, H. J., Stall, R., Goldhammer, H., & Landers, S. (2008). Sexual and gender minority health: What we know and what needs to be done. *American Journal of Public Health, 98*, 989–995. http://dx.doi.org/10.2105/AJPH.2007.127811

Minter, S. M., & Wald, D. H. (2012). Protecting parental rights. In J. L. Levi & E. E. Monnin-Browder (Eds.), *Transgender family law: A guide to effective advocacy* (pp. 63–85). Bloomington, IN: AuthorHouse.

Mizock, L., & Fleming, M. Z. (2011). Transgender and gender variant populations with mental illness: Implications for clinical care. *Professional Psychology: Research and Practice, 42,* 208–213. http://dx.doi.org/10.1037/a0022522

Olson, J., Forbes, C., & Belzer, M. (2011). Management of the transgender adolescent. *Archives of Pediatrics & Adolescent Medicine, 165,* 171–176. http://dx.doi.org/10.1001/archpediatrics.2010.275

Reisner, S. L., Bradford, J. B., Hopwood, R., Gonzalez, A., Makadon, H., & Todisco, D. (2015). Comprehensive transgender healthcare: The gender affirming clinical and public health model of Fenway Health. *Journal of Urban Health. Bulletin of the New York Academy of Medicine.* Advance online publication. Retrieved from http://www.ncbi.nlm.nih.gov/pmc/articles/PMC4456472/

Singh, A. A., & Burnes, T. R. (2009). Creating developmentally appropriate, safe counseling environments for transgender youth: The critical role of school counselors. *Journal of LGBT Issues in Counseling, 3,* 215–234. http://dx.doi.org/10.1080/15538600903379457

Spack, N. P., Edwards-Leeper, L., Feldman, H. A., Leibowitz, S., Mandel, F., Diamond, D. A., & Vance, S. R. (2012). Children and adolescents with gender identity disorder referred to a pediatric medical center. *Pediatrics, 129,* 418–425. http://dx.doi.org/10.1542/peds.2011-0907

Stroumsa, D. (2014). The state of transgender health care: Policy, law, and medical frameworks. *American Journal of Public Health, 104,* e31–e38. http://dx.doi.org/10.2105/AJPH.2013.301789

Torrence, N. D., Mueller, A. E., Ilem, A. A., Renn, B. N., DeSantis, B., & Segal, D. L. (2014). Medical provider attitudes about behavioral health consultants in integrated primary care: A preliminary study. *Families, Systems, & Health, 32,* 426–432. http://dx.doi.org/10.1037/fsh0000078

Unger, C. A. (2014). Care of the transgender patient: The role of the gynecologist. *American Journal of Obstetrics and Gynecology, 210,* 16–26. http://dx.doi.org/10.1016/j.ajog.2013.05.035

van Trotsenburg, M. A. A. (2009). Gynecological aspects of transgender healthcare. *International Journal of Transgenderism, 11,* 238–246. http://dx.doi.org/10.1080/15532730903439484

Vanderburgh, R. (2007). *Transition and beyond: Observations on gender identity.* Portland, OR: Q-Press.

Walinsky, D., & Whitcomb, D. (2010). Using the ACA Competencies for counseling with transgender clients to increase rural transgender well-being. *Journal of LGBT Issues in Counseling, 4,* 160–175. http://dx.doi.org/10.1080/15538605.2010.524840

White, T., & Ettner, R. (2004). Disclosure, risks and protective factors for children whose parents are undergoing a gender transition. *Journal of Gay & Lesbian Psychotherapy, 8,* 129–147.

White, T., & Ettner, R. (2007). Adaptation and adjustment in children of transsexual parents. *European Child & Adolescent Psychiatry, 16,* 215–221. http://dx.doi.org/10.1007/s00787-006-0591-y

World Professional Association for Transgender Health. (2015). *WPATH statement on legal recognition of gender identity.* Retrieved from http://www.wpath.org/uploaded_files/140/files/WPATH%20Statement%20on%20Legal%20Recognition%20of%20Gender%20Identity%201-19-15.pdf

Linda F. Campbell and Gabriel Arkles

Ethical and Legal Concerns for Mental Health Professionals

4

I n 2009, the American Psychological Association (APA) Task Force on Gender Identity and Gender Variance found that fewer than 30% of psychologists surveyed viewed themselves as familiar with concerns of transgender and gender nonconforming (TGNC) individuals, far from the question of competence to treat or conceptual understanding. Although recognition of access to services has gained visibility, many psychologists continue to conflate TGNC clinical concerns with those of sexual orientation. Practitioners unknowingly generalized their competence to work with other diverse groups, particularly lesbian, gay, and bisexual (LGB) individuals with the TGNC population. The importance of knowledge, skill, and competence acquisition for practitioners has become only too evident. For several reasons, including (a) recognition of special needs for treatment, (b) lack of

The authors wish to thank Molli Freeman-Lynde, Elana Redfield, Anya Mukarji-Connolly, and Harper Jean Tobin for their input and assistance with this chapter.

http://dx.doi.org/10.1037/14957-005
Affirmative Counseling and Psychological Practice With Transgender and Gender Nonconforming Clients, A. A. Singh and l. m. dickey (Editors)

subject matter expertise and TGNC-affirmative care, (c) level of stigma and discrimination experienced by TGNC individuals, and (d) resulting mental health consequences, the call for professional practice guidelines was realized. The guidelines were in process for 4 years and were adopted during the APA Council of Representatives meeting in August 2015.

The APA guidelines are highlighted in this chapter as a standard of care as defined by ethical practice and the legal context[1] in which clinical practice with TGNC individuals takes place. Provision of psychological services to TGNC populations requires an understanding of the intersection of standards of care, ethics, and law that are not applicable in the same way to other populations. For example, clinical understanding of decisions regarding identity transition, social transition, medical transition, and the distinctions of each; complexities of gender identity on legal documents; and standards of care regarding intersection of gender identity with other cultural identities cannot be compartmentalized in therapeutic work but rather must be understood as aspects of the integrated work to be conducted.

In this chapter, ethical standards that are particularly significant in working with TGNC individuals are linked to supporting guidelines and the compatibility of ethical standards and the TGNC guidelines are highlighted, and a brief case scenario illustrates a common decision factor. Practical legal aspects of working with TGNC clients are described and linked to the clinical competency needs for practitioners. This chapter strives to make evident the distinctiveness of psychological services with the TGNC population yet also conveys that the application of ethical standards and guidelines of respect for people's rights and dignity, doing no harm, and ensuring clinical competence are familiar standards of care in working with all populations. In doing so, this chapter draws from the APA Code of Ethics to provide examples of how MHPs across helping professions can apply ethical standards to TGNC-affirming guidelines for practice.

Ethical Dimensions: Case Example

Professional practice with TGNC people entails complexities and perspectives that are critical to competent practice. Ethical judgments take many forms in application to practice with TGNC individuals. The following scenario offers but one example. This hypothetical case illustrates some of the important factors typically embedded in working with TGNC clients.

---

[1]Practitioners should keep in mind that this book cannot serve as legal advice and, if needed, professionals should seek legal advice from a licensed attorney.

Dr. B. is an independent practitioner who works with adults and families on relational, workplace, and behavioral health concerns. He had been seeing his client David for several months for workplace stressors, moderate depression, and increasing anxiety. David, who is a 23-year-old Latino man, had made reference to a major factor that was impacting his well-being that he was not yet ready to discuss. Dr. B. has often dealt with the phenomena of clients needing time to develop trust, pacing the disclosure of a past experience such as childhood abuse and trauma, or achieving a level of readiness in disclosing for the first time.

During one session, David disclosed to Dr. B. that he "is a person of transgender identity" and needed help with deciding how he wanted to incorporate his authentic self into his life, how he may most fruitfully reflect on this transition, and how to discuss his identity with his family. Dr. B. had frequently worked with gay and lesbian clients, particularly adolescents and young adults who were coming to terms with their sexual orientation. Therapeutic goals with these LGB clients address the changes necessary to achieve congruence in their lives. What Dr. B. was hearing from David, however, brought him to the realization that he did not have the knowledge, skill set, or clinical experience to work effectively with David. He and David had developed a solid working alliance and had processed very significant experiences; however, Dr. B. had mistakenly assumed that the therapeutic relationship signaled a competency level which he then knew he did not have. Ethical responsibility to competence requires awareness of the need for continued professional development particularly in areas of diversity. Diversity is not a specialty, such as eating disorders or neuropsychology, but rather is an aspect of culture, identity and individuality that is incumbent on all mental health providers (MHPs) to acquire.

As exemplified in this vignette MHPs are becoming increasingly aware of the ethical and professional obligations to achieve competence in working with clients of diverse backgrounds (Hendricks & Testa, 2012). MHPs are committed to the welfare of their clients, but may find themselves at a crossroads in the absence of training for practice with a particular diverse population. Clinical competence in working with LGB individuals regarding sexual orientation has become more common in general practice than has work with TGNC clients and gender identity. Practitioners cannot ethically declare a scope of practice that precludes services to a specific population for discriminatory reasons (APA, 2010). Such a stance defies the meaning of competence and professional integrity, and presents great risk of harm to vulnerable populations.

The desire to be competent and the motivation to work with TGNC people can be overshadowed by risk management fears. Anticipation of working with new populations can generate great trepidation for MHPs (Raj, 2002). The initiative to increase awareness, understanding, and sensitivity to sexual orientation has had an earlier educational start than the same initiative for TGNC clients. The priority of overcoming prejudice and discrimination against sexual orientation status has gained momentum. MHPs in recent years understand that knowledge acquisition, clinical competencies, and sensitivity to TGNC populations are distinct and differentiated from competencies in working with matters of sexual orientation (APA, 2012). Further, TGNC concerns may not be the primary reason an individual seeks psychological services, nor does the MHP necessarily know, when a client is engaging in therapy for work or family-of-origins reasons, that gender identity will later emerge as a factor in the therapeutic work (Budge, Adelson, & Howard, 2013). Consequently, MHPs cannot decide up front, by virtue of their scope of competence, that they will compartmentalize their scope of practice (APA, 2010, Standard 3.01). An MHP may be treating a TGNC client before the client brings the issue into the treatment. None of the diversity factors (e.g., ethnicity, age, gender, gender identity, race/ethnicity, disability, religion, culture, national origin, sexual orientation, language, socioeconomic status) should be presumed to be the reason individuals seek mental health services. Clients understandably may need to develop trust and a working alliance before engaging in personal disclosures. Importantly, however, clients may also be unaware of the role their diverse identity will play in their clinical work (Bess & Stabb, 2009). A challenge for MHPs is not to be presumptive and to be competently prepared.

Because gender identity is increasingly recognized as a type of diversity rather than a pathological state (Institute of Medicine, 2011; World Professional Association for Transgender Health, 2010) due to the increase in social acceptance, more TGNC persons are choosing to enter counseling (Borden, 2015). A paradigm shift is occurring in which MHPs view counseling with TGNC persons as dealing with environmental, relational, or stress related problems rather than counseling for gender identity reasons per se (Buehler, 2014). However, TGNC persons may also seek counseling in support of their decision making about how they want to pursue congruence and achieve a way of life that respects and incorporates their gender identity.

APA Guidelines for Psychological Practice With TGNC People

The APA guidelines were developed to assist MHPs in providing culturally competent services for TGNC clients. Several guidelines are particularly pertinent to elements of the APA (2010) *Ethical Principles of Psychologists and Code of Conduct* (Ethics Code) and are essential in working with TGNC persons. Three important aspects of practice with TGNC clients are competence, avoiding harm, and informed consent. The legal aspects are access to identification, asylum, and access to gender affirming care.

COMPETENCE

Practicing within one's scope of practice and simultaneously developing broad ranges of competence to serve the multiple diverse identities of clients is a challenge, a caution, and a professional imperative. Practitioners may declare a treatment scope of practice (e.g., individuals with eating disorders) and in certain circumstances a population scope of practice (e.g., children). MHPs ensure their competence to work with diverse populations when an understanding of diversity is essential for a service (APA, 2010, Standard 2.01b). A critical yet often overlooked section of the Ethics Code gives practitioners multiple paths to competence through supervision, consultation, continuing education, and other means (APA, 2010, Standard 2.01c).

MHPs are encouraged to understand that gender is not a binary construct but rather allows for a wide spectrum of gender identities (APA, 2015, Guideline 1). Making this fundamental, conceptual shift is most important in order for practitioners to provide affirmative care. An MHP may know the client is coming to counseling, in part with regard to TGNC status, and assume a goal of medical transition, which may or may not be what the client wants. Equally important is the awareness that gender identity intersects with other cultural identities and often is not the primary current concern in counseling (APA, 2015, Guideline 3). A client may be conflicted regarding the incongruence of religious beliefs and gender identity with greater need to reconcile with incompatible religious teachings than with gender identity (see Chapter 10, this volume). The competent MHP supportively follows the lead of the client in determining the focus of the problem. Incorporation of these constructs informs the practitioner's frame of reference and therapeutic stance, promotes a healthy working alliance, and initially may be more important than knowledge and information. The therapeutic relationship makes way for additional formal education and informal education on learning through one's clients. MHPs are aware, however, that education is their independent responsibility and not that of the clients.

For MHPs, competence in working with TGNC clients most essentially includes (a) shedding the gender binary construct and understanding the unique gender expression of their clients which may reside at any point on the gender identity spectrum and (b) realizing that the intersection of multiple identities is complex and gender identity should not be assumed to be the primary concern. Medical and social transition can bring significant changes in privilege and social treatment on the basis of intersections of stigmatized identities (Singh, 2013).

AVOIDING HARM

MHPs' responsibility to avoid harm or to minimize harm when it is foreseeable (APA, 2010, Standard 3.04) is uniquely challenged in working with TGNC clients because of the potential for unintentional harm on the basis of empathic efforts that further stereotype or stigmatize the client. TGNC individuals have suffered harm from unknowing MHPs who targeted the TGNC status as the focus of therapy instead of accurately identifying workplace difficulties or relational problems, for example. MHPs may confuse gender identity and sexual orientation, which are distinctly different constructs (APA, 2015, Guideline 2). Clients may also have difficulty distinguishing between aspects of sexual orientation and gender identity in relation to their own identity on the gender spectrum (Singh & Burnes, 2009). Affirming practitioners may unintentionally do great harm to clients through microaggressions based on a failure to understand their own gendered assumptions related to privilege, power, or marginalization (APA, 2010, Standard 3.01; APA, 2015, Guideline 4) or, for example, by making assumptions about the degree or type of transition the client may choose (Nadal, 2013). TGNC clients may be confused about their incongruence between sex assigned at birth, societal expectations, and gender identity, for example. The MHP may inadvertently direct the exploration to sexual orientation or to the need to develop a goal of clarifying identity before the client is ready. Practitioners who take the stance of affirming exploration of gender identity and sexual orientation as related but different constructs enable clients to adopt a broader perspective and develop an authentic and congruent identity within themselves and between both constructs.

Two ethical principles are particularly aligned with Guideline 4 which focuses on provider attitudes and the resulting effect on quality of care provided to TGNC clients and their families. These principles specifically underscore the foundational value of doing no harm through Principle A (Beneficence and Nonmaleficence) in which MHPs pledge to benefit those with whom they work and to safeguard their rights. Principle E (Respect for People's Rights and Dignity) further commits MHPs to protect the rights and the dignity of all people with particular care to marginalized or vulnerable people. These principles must be firmly planted in the ethical obligation of competence so that MHPs, however well intended, do not harm their clients.

ADVOCACY

An important competency emerging in many mental health models is advocacy. Advocacy is a key characteristic of professional identity, particularly for those training programs and MHPs who are committed to social justice, the underserved, and being a voice against marginalization, prejudice, and discrimination. MHPs can instruct clients in the skills to challenge stereotypes. Further, they can teach clients how to model advocacy to their allies, family, and support groups through education and proactive participation in awareness and safety programs (APA, 2015, Guideline 7). Although not an Ethics Code standard, advocacy is woven through the Ethics Code in Principles B (Fidelity and Responsibility), C (Integrity), and D (Justice). Advocacy for TGNC clients may take different paths than advocacy for other stigmatized groups and may well call on MHPs to act in specific supportive ways. MHPs, for example, may assist TGNC clients in (a) providing documentation that affirms gender identity in accessing public accommodations (Lev, 2009); (b) being sensitive to special cautions necessary in working with military clients (APA, 2015, Guideline 4); (c) being sensitive to the impact on the therapeutic relationship when asked to provide an endorsement letter attesting to the stability of the client in acquiring a referral to an endocrinologist, surgeon, or legal institution (APA, 2015, Guideline 7; Lev, 2009); and (d) offering information and assistance in the process of legal name change, gender marker change, or accessing other gender-affirming documents (APA, 2015, Guideline 6).

MHPs need to be aware and prepared for the inevitable multiple role occurrences in advocacy. Regardless of community population, advocacy in a committed role for any marginalized group is an identifiable group of individuals. MHPs may easily find themselves involved in advocacy initiatives with clients, friends of clients, and clients who are friends of the MHP's friends or colleagues. MHPs may navigate these circumstances by being continually alert for the potential for exploitation or loss of objectivity. These dynamics are most frequently at the root of unethical multiple roles. Peer consultation is an effective way to self-monitor and draw on colleagues' professional judgment.

As the legal section of the chapter and the advocacy chapter in this book (Chapter 12) make clear, advocacy on the basis of good intentions alone may represent an unacceptable risk of harm. Advocacy on the basis of competence is essential for MHP working with TGNC clients. MHPs have a responsibility to be knowledgeable of federal, state, and local laws and regulations that may affect their work with clients. Some areas of practice are likely to intersect with legal or regulatory implications such that to be unfamiliar could be viewed as absence of due diligence and failure to maintain competence. These areas of practice include custody evaluations, competency to stand trial, fitness for duty evaluations, evaluations of parental fitness, immigration, divorce counseling, and mediation. These and other areas often require interaction with the court that requires understanding of not only law and regulations but also judicial proceedings and navigation of the court setting.

INFORMED CONSENT

Informed consent speaks to the value of respect for others in ensuring that recipients of our services understand fully the purpose and course of treatment, involvement of third parties, limits of confidentiality, potential outcomes, and expectations the client may reasonably have of the MHP (APA, 2010, Standard 3.10, Standard 10.1a). In working with TGNC clients, MHPs are aware of being the stewards of clients' personal disclosures, fears and anxieties, and trust that may not have been granted to another person regarding the clients' TGNC experience. The informed consent process may take on special ethical and clinical importance in the treatments of TGNC clients. MHPs will not only want to be specific about limits of confidentiality, and other legal or ethical demands (e.g., court orders, requests for creation of documents) that could be seen by the client as harmful or violating trust, but would also include the actions, positions, and advocacy that the MHP is willing to commit that might not otherwise be included in an informed consent, such as working with children or parents of the client during transition or collaborating with medical or school professionals on the client's behalf. Knowledge of one's jurisdictional laws and regulations regarding confidentiality and the rights of parents is most important not only for risk management but for informed assent of the minor client. Even though the minor client cannot legally give consent, MHPs want their minor clients to be fully informed of the role of the MHPs, the role of parents, and the range of decision making possible for the youth. Support for minor clients without understanding the legal, medical, and ethical parameters can lead to harmful consequences for the client.

MHPs maintain a delicate balance in content and detail of informed consent. Full explanation of the factors noted in the informed consent to therapy promotes a trusting working alliance and demonstrates commitment to the welfare of the client (Campbell, Vasquez, Behnke, & Kinscherff, 2010). Confidentiality in the course of treatment, however, is critical to the well-being of TGNC clients who (for employment, family, or personal reasons) are putting themselves at risk to seek therapy. Informed consent is typically in written form, although the APA Ethics Code does not require that it be so (Koocher & Campbell, 2016). Oral discussion of the trajectory of treatment and the reasonable expectations the client may have of therapy can be preferable (Campbell et al., 2010). For example, planning for transition or discussing the impact of disclosure of gender identity to one's family are personal experiences that should be treated with sensitivity in clinical notes and in informed consent (APA, 2010, Standard 4.02a).

RECORDKEEPING

MHPs are alert to the importance of thoughtful selection for content in recordkeeping, and retain records that clearly explain the treatment plan and would allow a transfer practitioner to read and understand the case. In working with TGNC clients, recordkeeping decisions are critical (APA, 2010, Standard 6.02a). For example, issues of employment discrimination are threats to TGNC people in the military and to TGNC veterans. Insurance plans may exclude coverage for trans-affirmative primary healthcare, which may result in a lack of preventative health maintenance. MHPs working with TGNC clients must be aware of the likely implications in the event that outside entities (e.g., family, employer, insurance company) have access to client records.

Provision of health services to the TGNC community carries a responsibility and a commitment to education, skill acquisition, and ongoing self-reflection (APA, 2015). Although the ethical standards of competence, informed consent, avoiding harm, and recordkeeping have been highlighted here, psychologists must understand and practice broadly applied ethics principles, standards, and the APA guidelines in working with TGNC individuals.

Legal Concerns
and TGNC People

MHPs working with TGNC people often want to know how to support their clients as they navigate legal systems and how to protect themselves from liability. This section first addresses a number of common legal issues for TGNC people, with a focus on the role of MHPs. Then the emphasis shifts to address key areas of law regulating MHPs working with TGNC people, with a focus on general recommendations for preventing legal risk.

The legal issues that TGNC people face encompass the full range of issues that anyone may face, but may involve additional dimensions and unique obstacles. MHPs play an important role as advocates, counselors, experts, and mediators with regard to many of these legal issues. This section focuses on legal aspects of access to gender-appropriate identification, asylum, and access to gender-affirming health care. Laws change frequently and vary from place to place. MHPs will want to access updated information specific to their jurisdiction whenever assisting a client navigating these systems. These issues are only a fraction of the ways in which the law may affect TGNC clients relevant to mental health treatment. This discussion should therefore be understood as illustrative, rather than as comprehensive.

ACCESS TO IDENTIFICATION DOCUMENTS

Many TGNC people seek to change their gender designation on their identity documents and records. These changes matter a great deal, not only to affirm gender identity but also to permit navigation of day-to-day life with less exposure to harassment, discrimination, and violence. Particularly in the current era of ever-increasing scrutiny on immigrants, poor people, and other politically unpopular groups, people face pervasive demands for identity documents (Gehi, 2009). The consequences of having the wrong gender on one's identity documents can range from humiliating interactions, such as getting turned away from a bar, to life-threatening ones, such as getting denied public assistance. Even for people with nonbinary gender identities, changing a gender designation from assigned male to female or assigned female to male can make the difference between employment and joblessness, a trip to see family or isolation, or a violent encounter with police or an uneventful one. Unfortunately, MHPs and medical professionals remain forced into an uncomfortable gatekeeper role. That is, TGNC people must acquire support from professionals before obtaining legal affirmation of their gender identity, which can introduce a dynamic into the professional–client interaction that neither the professional nor the client had any role in choosing. With a solid understanding of the rules and appropriate respect and support for clients' decisions, professionals can help their clients navigate these systems successfully.

Many people assume that everyone has one clear, consistent legal gender, but the reality is more complex (Spade, 2008). Government agencies have different rules about when and if they will change gender in someone's records. For example, the rule for changing the gender on a driver's license in New York is the not the same as the rule for changing the gender on a birth certificate in New York. The rule for changing the gender on a birth certificate if the person was born in New York is not the same as the rule for changing the gender on the birth certificate if the person was born in New Jersey. The rule for changing the gender on a birth certificate in New York today is also not the same as the rule for the same thing just a couple of years ago. Many TGNC people have their gender listed in one way on some identity documents, and in another way on others (Grant et al., 2011).

Sometimes people think that gender change and name change are the same thing, but they are usually separate processes. Usually, people can change their name without any documentation from an MHP or other professional (*In re Powell*, 2012; *In re McIntyre*, 1998). Also, the gender on a person's identity documents does not necessarily dictate how a government agency or court will treat that person for a particular purpose. A TGNC person with female-indicated identity document might get placed in a men's jail (*Shaw v. D.C.*, 2013). Some courts have treated TGNC people who changed their gender designation on all identity documents, including their birth certificates, as the sex assigned to them at birth for purposes of determining whether they had entered into a valid heterosexual marriage (*Kantaras v. Kantaras*, 2004). Thus, although it is vital to assist TGNC people in changing the gender on their identity documents in accordance with their wishes, it is worth keeping in mind that these changes will not necessarily guarantee treatment according to the gender designation in all circumstances.

TGNC people and allies have worked hard on access to identity documents over the past few decades, creating ways to change gender on these documents and making those ways more accessible to people. As a result, federal government agencies and many state agencies no longer require proof of surgery to change gender in their records (National Center for Transgender Equality [NCTE], n.d.). The unfortunate news is that not all agencies have changed their rules yet, and even the better policies still have substantial problems. Virtually all policies require some form of documentation from a medical or MHP to support a gender change on identity documents. The policies vary in three main ways: (a) in terms of who can provide the documentation, (b) in terms of the form the documentation must take, and (c) in terms of what the documentation must state.

Who Can Provide Letters of Support

Federal agencies, including those that issue passports, Social Security cards, and immigration documents, insist on documentation from an MD or DO. As of this writing, letters from MHPs *will not* be accepted for these purposes, although we hope that will change. State policies regarding who may provide documentation are often (but not always) broader, permitting MHPs to fill this role. Most policies require the person who provides the documentation either to have treated the person or to have reviewed relevant records.

Form of Documentation

Some agencies require a signed letter on the medical or MHP's letterhead and some require professionals to fill out a particular form. Some agencies, particularly for birth certificates, require a court order and courts in turn often require notarized statements from professionals.

When agencies have their own form, such as the departments of motor vehicles in Delaware, Hawaii, Virginia, and Washington, it is usually straightforward and easy to complete.

Content of Documentation

The last area of variation is in the content of the documentation. Unfortunately, on one end of the spectrum, some agencies still require evidence of gender-affirming surgery[2]. Most, however, do not specify the type of surgery; any gender-affirming surgery is sufficient. These policies are most common for changes to birth certificates and are becoming less common all the time. At the other end of the spectrum, some agencies do not require comment on diagnosis or treatment whatsoever, they merely seek a statement that confirms the person's identity. In the middle of the spectrum, agencies may require some statement about the person having completed transition or received appropriate clinical gender transition treatment. These policies are intentionally broad. The agencies wrote them to encompass any form of treatment, including counseling, change in gender expression, hormones, surgery, or other treatment.

One of the most important aspects of writing appropriate letters or notarized statements in these contexts is knowing what not to write. These letters are not psychosocial evaluations, case studies, or even referrals for surgery. They are intended for government agencies and will often become public records. Sometimes they will be shared with other government agencies without the record holder's consent. They do not require, and should not contain, most of the detail one would provide in writing about clients in other contexts (APA, 2010, Standard 4.05a).

For example, when writing for an agency that does not require documentation of surgery, it is best not to mention surgery at all; unless, of course, the client or client's lawyer requests otherwise. If the MHP says that the patient has not had surgery, or plans to get surgery in the future, it could confuse officials who are not well-trained on their policy and lead to a wrongful denial of a gender change on that person's identity documents. If the client has had surgery, sharing that information will probably not result in a wrongful denial, but it would result in the public disclosure of personal medical information without a good reason. Similarly, it does not make sense to include in these letters information about a client's support network, diagnoses, sexuality, history

---

[2]A few states and territories, as well as some other countries, do not permit gender changes on certain documents (usually birth certificates) under any circumstances. Fortunately, a strong majority of U.S. jurisdictions permit such changes.

of significant life events, or financial situation. At worst, including the information leads to inappropriate denials of people's requests; at best, it needlessly reveals personal information. Even information that may seem relevant, such as the way that the client has thought about gender over time and arrived at a stable identity, may cause more harm than good. The vast majority of time there is no reason to provide that level of detail. Instead, it is best to retain only what is required. It is ideal if the relevant agency requirements are known. If the requirements are not known, the following is some broad language that works to satisfy most current policies:

> I am licensed to practice in [jurisdiction]. My license number is [number].
> I have treated [client name] in relation to gender transition. [If the client hasn't been treated in relation to gender transition, instead state that the client's treatment records have been reviewed.] I have a doctor/patient [or MHP/patient, if more appropriate] relationship with [client name].
> [Client name] has had appropriate clinical treatment for gender transition to [male/female]. In my professional opinion, [client name]'s current gender identity is [male/female].
> I affirm, under the penalty of perjury, that all of the information contained herein is the truth.

The letter should be printed on letterhead with the MHP's address and phone number, and should be signed by the MHP.

It is understandable that many MHPs feel uncomfortable with language that some of these policies require. They do not think of their client's gender or transition in quite these terms. Few professionals make a determination of whether one sex "predominates" over another, or even understand that as a particularly sensible question to ask—but that, for example, is the language required to change one's gender designation on a New York driver's license or state ID. Also, many TGNC people have identities that do not fall neatly into a male or female binary, a reality that current government policies do not reflect.

Part of what is happening, of course, is political compromise and discomfort among government officials in determining the listed sex of individuals. They typically have decided to defer to mental health and medical professionals. Although the language these agencies use may be awkward, frequently the politicians and bureaucrats have accepted the idea that people do not need any particular sort of medical, surgical, or mental health care to have transitioned. Officials have concluded that the right time to call a transition complete for purpose of changing one's gender on identity documents is a decision best left to an individual and a medical professional or MHP working with that individual.

A final note is that some professionals attempt to write letters that will work for a gender change on identity documents and for a recommendation for surgery or other treatment. However, because the letters have different audiences and goals, it is usually best to keep them separate. The primary audience for a letter about identity documents is a court or government agency. The primary audience for a letter supporting medical or surgical treatment is the medical professional who may provide such treatment.

ASYLUM

Many TGNC immigrants need to seek asylum in the United States. In fact, although there is no solid data, many advocates believe that asylum is more important to TGNC immigrants than other immigrants (Gehi, 2009). Partly, this is because TGNC people often get persecuted for being TGNC, which can mean that an asylum claim is available to them, and that returning to a country of origin could endanger them by virtue of their TGNC status. Partly, that is because asylum is often the only possible way for TGNC immigrants to get access to lawful immigration status. The restrictive immigration laws that harm all immigrants have a particularly harsh impact on TGNC people. Immigration law recognizes only narrow definitions of family, and many TGNC people face rejection from their families of origin. Thus, family-based immigration status is less accessible for TGNC people. Because of widespread discrimination in employment and education against TGNC people in the United States and elsewhere, employment-based paths to immigration status are even more rarely accessible to TGNC immigrants.

Support from MHPs can make successful asylum claims possible in at least three ways. First, the process of applying for asylum is often intensely painful for people who have experienced rape, torture, arrest, or other forms of persecution (Foster, 2001). Asylum applicants must retell their stories, in detail, and at times to an unfriendly audience. This also takes place in a stressful context; the applicant does not know whether they might be detained and forcibly removed to the exact same place where these forms of abuse occurred. For those reasons, many lawyers encourage asylum seekers to take advantage of professional mental health services to help cope with the application process itself. MHPs can help by providing nonjudgmental services.

Second, even with no specific reason to believe a client is an immigrant, screening all clients routinely for posttraumatic stress disorder (PTSD) and related conditions can help not only with providing appropriate services, but with clients' legal cases (see Chapter 9, this volume, for a full discussion of trauma). For example, to bring a successful asylum claim, immigrants must file within 1 year of arriving in the United States. Many people miss that deadline. With a documented record of

PTSD, immigrants and their lawyers can sometimes successfully advocate for an exception to the 1-year deadline (*Munoz v. Holder*, 2010). If
the treating MHP missed the PTSD diagnosis, though, it will be much
harder, and perhaps impossible, for an immigrant to get asylum after
spending a year or more in the United States.

Finally, thorough documentation of conditions, and their impact on
clients, can help not only with asylum cases but also with other legal
claims. For example, especially given the high rates of poverty in TGNC
communities (Grant et al., 2011), access to supplemental security income
and Social Security disability benefits can save lives. The extensive amount
of documentation required to obtain access to those benefits can be overwhelming. Keeping thorough notes makes these cases possible to win.
Many legal professionals and MHPs quite appropriately want to avoid
excessively pathologizing anyone, particularly TGNC people. It can be
difficult to figure out how to strike that balance when dealing with legal
systems that have narrow understandings of human experience and
pain. It should be possible to work together to find ways to engage with
people holistically, rather than reducing them to diagnostic labels, while
still using those diagnostic labels when they help.

ACCESS TO GENDER-AFFIRMING CARE

Laws have started changing in positive ways for access to care. Medicare
no longer excludes gender-affirming health care for TGNC people from
coverage, and a handful of states have also removed the discriminatory
provisions from their Medicaid programs (NCTE, 2015a). Some jurisdictions have also insisted that private insurance begin providing coverage for this care. The U.S. Department of Health and Human Services
has proposed a rule that would make it illegal to discriminate against
TGNC people in making insurance determinations (NCTE, 2015c). This
progress would not have been possible without extensive work and
collaborations among TGNC people and allies, including MHPs, medical
professionals, community organizers, and lawyers.

This is good news, but it does not mean the struggle is over. Also,
we have not seen the same level of positive changes in institutions such
as foster care, juvenile justice, nursing homes, prisons, jails, and psychiatric hospitals. This puts MHPs in the perhaps all-too-familiar role of
advocate with insurance companies and other institutions. There are at
least four different ways that MHPs can assist TGNC people in getting
the care they need.

First, document the need for the care, and make the phone calls
to advocate for coverage. Some insurance companies are particularly
reluctant to cover facial feminization surgeries and breast augmentation surgery because of a perception that these procedures are purely
cosmetic even if hormones and other gender-affirming surgery are not.

Help insurance companies understand why TGNC clients need this care, why it is medically necessary. It often takes multiple appeals to get approval for care.

Second, accept Medicaid and Medicare, set reasonable rates, and be willing to work with people who are institutionalized. All of the tremendous effort TGNC people, allies, and advocates have put into making change in the law will come to nothing if professionals refuse to treat TGNC people who now ought to have access to services. TGNC people are far more likely to be poor and/or incarcerated than cisgender people (Grant et al., 2011). If MHPs do not accept Medicaid and Medicare and do not work with people who are imprisoned, only a few of the most privileged TGNC people will get help. An entire practice need not involve working with prisoners or youth in foster care. Exorbitantly high rates threaten to roll back some of the successes TGNC people and allies have achieved. One of the biggest counterarguments to providing gender-affirming care is that it will cost taxpayers or insurance purchasers too much money. So far, advocates have been able to break down that myth, but if mental health and medical professionals hike their rates beyond the ordinary rate of inflation, it will not only decrease access for people without insurance but also make ending discriminatory policies less politically palatable.

Third, educate clients about their rights. Some clients will already know, in more detail than the professional, the rules for various types of insurance coverage. Others, though, may still assume that it is impossible for them to get the care they need through insurance, even in a state that has made significant changes. Help clients understand their options.

Finally, educate colleagues about rules and laws relevant to their jurisdiction. Sometimes institutions make sudden changes to comply with a new law, court order, or demands made through actual or threatened direct action, political pressure, litigation, or publicity. In some situations, MHPs and others who were told in the past they absolutely may not provide gender-affirming services of any kind suddenly get instructions that they not only can but must provide services to TGNC people. Of course, those professionals might not have the competence to offer these services and so they may seek consultation or continuing education. Experienced MHPs may be able to help a great deal by sharing their knowledge and expertise, partnering with community groups offering trainings in these institutions, or referring other professionals to appropriate resources for learning more.

Of course, there are many other legal issues that confront TGNC people, and many other ways for MHPs to play an important role. MHPs can serve as expert witnesses in civil rights cases on behalf of TGNC people; help avoid or resolve custody and visitation conflicts, conflicts with schools, and other conflicts involving TGNC youth and parents;

help lawyers learn how to overcome communication barriers with their clients who have mental disabilities; and prevent inappropriate or unlawful commitment of TGNC people for involuntary treatment. Do not hesitate to reach out to local or national TGNC-affirming legal professionals for information and support.

PROTECTION FROM LIABILITY

Generally, working with TGNC people presents no special exposure to professional discipline, civil liability, or criminal liability. In fact, there are very few reported cases where MHPs faced any form of liability or discipline related to TGNC clients. Of course, the usual rules apply. For example, in one New York case, a psychiatrist faced revocation of his license to practice medicine because of a pattern of inappropriate sexual relationships with patients, including one patient with a diagnosis of gender identity disorder (*In re Earle F. Alexander*, 1995). The alleged conduct was unethical regardless of the gender or diagnosis of the clients involved (New York State Education Law, 2008). It is useful to review a few applicable legal frameworks that may be of special concern.

Antidiscrimination Law

In some jurisdictions, it is against the law to discriminate against TGNC people in employment, housing, or public accommodations. These laws apply to hospitals, drug treatment programs, clinics, and professionals' offices. Some states and municipalities have protections in place that explicitly prohibit discrimination against TGNC people (NCTE, 2015b). Even in those areas without such explicit protections, laws prohibit discrimination on the basis of sex and disability. Many courts and agencies, including at the federal level, have ruled that discrimination on the basis of sex includes discrimination against TGNC people (*Glenn v. Brumby*, 2011). Although the federal Americans With Disabilities Act excludes TGNC people from protection, in some states discrimination on the basis of disability includes discrimination against people who have, or who are perceived as having, gender dysphoria (*Doe v. Bell*, 2003). It is also against the law, throughout the United States, for a hospital with an emergency room to turn *anyone* away without first providing screening and necessary stabilizing treatment for medical emergencies (Examination and Treatment for Emergency Medical Conditions, 2014). Discrimination against TGNC people is illegal.

In one case, a court ruled that a TGNC woman had a valid legal basis for her discrimination claim against a drug treatment program and its director. She alleged that the program refused to allow her to wear a wig or high heels, even though cisgender women could; refused to allow her to participate in a women's support group; forced her to use men's sleeping and bathing facilities; and ultimately decided to expel her from the facility purportedly because it could not accommodate her "special needs" as a TGNC woman (*Wilson v. Phoenix House*, 2013).

To avoid possible liability for discrimination against TGNC people MHPs should avoid turning away TGNC people for services if they would not turn away cisgender people in the same circumstances. Claiming inadequate experience in TGNC issues in such circumstances is not an adequate defense, particularly if the TGNC person seeks ordinarily provided treatment. For example, if an MHP generally treats attention deficits, then that professional should not refuse to treat a TGNC person for an attention deficit. The best remedy for a lack of expertise in TGNC issues is collaborating with colleagues, acquiring appropriate training, and reading relevant literature (see Chapters 3 and 8, this volume, for more information on training and collaboration). MHPs should support TGNC clients in accessing any gender-segregated facilities or services in accordance with their gender identity (not their sex as assigned at birth), and should always permit TGNC people to express their gender through clothing and other means.

Fraud

Some professionals fear writing letters to support TGNC people changing their gender in government ID and records because they think that doing so may constitute fraud. The relevant federal definition of fraud includes "knowingly and willfully [making a] materially false . . . statement [in a matter] within the jurisdiction of the United States" (False Statements Act, 2014). Most state laws use similar definitions. In other words, if individuals deliberately lie about anything that matters to a government agency, including government agencies that can grant gender designation changes to TGNC people, they have committed a crime.

Note that individuals must deliberately lie to commit this crime. Stating a genuine opinion is not fraud, even if not everyone else shares the opinion. Miswriting something accidentally is not fraud. Writing an honest letter for someone who may not qualify for a gender designation change with a particular agency is not fraud either. The legal obligation is to avoid deliberately lying in a statement.

We are not aware of any reported cases in which an MHP was charged with fraud for writing a letter supporting a TGNC person's application to change gender designation with a government agency, nor are we aware of any reports of anecdotal situations where MHPs were investigated for fraud in such circumstances. This absence suggests that such investigations and prosecutions have been rare, if they have occurred at all. To protect oneself from liability for fraud, one should avoid lying in any document going to a government agency. For example, an MHP should not state that someone has had surgery if the person has not had surgery. Put simply, an MHP should never write or state an opinion that is known to be false.

ACCESS TO GENDER-AFFIRMING CARE IN INSTITUTIONAL SETTINGS

Legal issues may also arise when TGNC people seek support from MHPs in accessing gender-affirming treatment. TGNC people often seek access to gender-affirming treatment they need while in government institutions that have an obligation to provide adequate medical care, such as psychiatric hospitals, prisons, foster care, nursing homes, and jails. Unfortunately, those institutions often do not provide adequate treatment, despite clear legal requirements to do so. The most common legal actions against MHPs with regard to TGNC clients arise in this context. TGNC people sue those individuals responsible for their care, including at times MHPs, if those people refuse them access to gender-affirming treatment.

In one example of a case from this context, a court ruled in favor of a TGNC woman held in the psychiatric unit of a state prison. She sued her facility and various people responsible for denying her care, including MHPs, because she could not get access to estrogen treatment. The denial of hormone treatment persisted even after she had completed self-surgery, removing her own testicles. The court ordered the people responsible for her care to begin providing hormone treatment (*Gammett v. Idaho State Bd. of Corr.*, 2007).

Sometimes MHPs have little choice in these circumstances as some administrative policy has tied their hands. They may want the person who is suing them to win, so that they can provide the care they know is appropriate. Other times, unfortunately, the MHP has played an active role in the denial. Unless the MHP was acting outside the scope of employment, usually the government will indemnify the MHP in these sorts of situations. That means that the government will provide the lawyer to defend the case, and will pay any damages the professional is ordered to pay.

MHPs also sometimes worry about potential liability for recommending that a TGNC person receive gender-affirming treatment. Once, a court sustained the suspension of psychiatrist's license to practice because his evaluations of TGNC people he recommended for gender-affirming surgery were inadequate. The case may have come to attention of the professional board because one of the doctor's patients died by suicide, but neither the board nor the court held the doctor responsible for the suicide. Instead, the suspension was on the basis of a finding that his

> psychiatric examinations failed to meet acceptable medical standards in that his histories failed to refer to the patients' emotional and behavioral needs, failed to document the patients' emotional states and previous psychological problems, and failed to describe their personality makeup. (*Reisner v. Bd. of Regents of State of N.Y.*, 1988)

Unlike cases where people have been denied access to care, this case appears to be something of an anomaly as it was decided almost 30 years ago, and there are no similar cases before or since.

CONVERSION THERAPY

Some states, such as California and New Jersey, have passed laws prohibiting MHPs and others from conducting "conversion therapy" or "sexual orientation change efforts" designed to change a young person's sexual orientation or gender identity (California Sexual Orientation Change Efforts, 2015; New Jersey Sexual Orientation Change Efforts, 2013). So far, courts have said that these laws are constitutional (*King v. Governor of the State of New Jersey*, 2014). That is, courts have said that these laws do not infringe on an MHP's free speech rights and states may enforce them. To avoid liability under these laws, MHPs should never try to get someone under the age of 18 to stop identifying or acting trans, gender nonconforming, gay, lesbian, bisexual, or another gender identity or sexual orientation.

TAKE HOME MESSAGES: DR. B.

As we examine the scenario from the beginning of this chapter about the well-intentioned but ill prepared Dr. B., important considerations emerge:

- Expansion of scope of practice without careful attendance to standards of practice can result in drift from competency to incompetency without the MHP's awareness.
- Generalization across diversity identities may recognize the importance of services and advocacy for marginalized groups but fails to respect the individual needs and characteristics of specific identity groups and persons.
- Self-assessment for competence, understanding the experience of the client, and engagement with the environment of the client are

all essential in working with TGNC individuals and in this developmental order.

Chapter Summary

The ethical and legal aspects of working with TGNC populations for psychologists and other MHPs require a distinct competence, a willingness to understand and apply unique legal aspects to the work, and the commitment to integrate these critical components into their services. Other client populations also require distinctiveness in competence and other therapeutic features. However, MHPs claim to be less familiar in working with TGNC concerns and may also be less competent. The adoption of guidelines, the application of these guidelines to the Ethics Code, and the identification of key legal components cited in this chapter are intended to facilitate the steps toward greater understanding and capability in providing this important service.

References

American Psychological Association. (2010). *Ethical principles of psychologists and code of conduct* (2002, amended June 1, 2010). Retrieved from http://www.apa.org/ethics/code/index.aspx

American Psychological Association. (2012). Guidelines for psychological practice with lesbian, gay, and bisexual clients. *American Psychologist, 67,* 10–42. http://dx.doi.org/10.1037/a0024659

American Psychological Association. (2015). Guidelines for psychological practice with transgender and gender nonconforming people. *American Psychologist, 70,* 832–864. http://dx.doi.org/10.1037/a0039906

American Psychological Association Task Force on Gender Identity and Gender Variance. (2009). *Report of the task force on gender identity and gender variance.* Retrieved from http://www.apa.org/pi/lgbt/resources/policy/gender-identity-report.pdf

Bess, J. A., & Stabb, S. D. (2009). The experiences of transgendered persons in psychotherapy: Voices and recommendations. *Journal of Mental Health Counseling, 31,* 264–282. http://dx.doi.org/10.17744/mehc.31.3.f624154681133w50

Borden, K. A. (2015). Introduction to the special section transgender and gender nonconforming individuals: Issues for professional psychologists. *Professional Psychology: Research and Practice, 46,* 1–2. http://dx.doi.org/10.1037/a0038847

Budge, S. L., Adelson, J. L., & Howard, K. A. (2013). Anxiety and depression in transgender individuals: The roles of transition status, loss, social support, and coping. *Journal of Consulting and Clinical Psychology, 81*, 545–557. http://dx.doi.org/10.1037/a0031774

Buehler, S. (2014). *What every mental health professional needs to know about sex.* New York, NY: Springer.

California Sexual Orientation Change Efforts, Cal. Bus. & Prof. Code § 865.1 (West 2015).

Campbell, L., Vasquez, M. T., Behnke, S. H., & Kinscherff, R. (2010). *APA Ethics Code commentary and case illustrations.* Washington, DC: American Psychological Association.

Doe v. Bell, 194 Misc. 2d 774 (Sup. Ct. 2003).

Examination and Treatment for Emergency Medical Conditions, 42 U.S.C.A. § 1395dd (2014).

False Statements Act, 18 U.S.C.A. § 1001 (2014).

Foster, R. P. (2001). When immigration is trauma: Guidelines for the individual and family clinician. *American Journal of Orthopsychiatry, 71*, 153–170. http://dx.doi.org/10.1037/0002-9432.71.2.153

Gammett v. Idaho State Bd. of Corr., No. CV05-257-S-MHW (D. Idaho July 27, 2007).

Gehi, P. (2009). Struggles from the margins: Anti-immigrant legislation and the impact on low-income transgender people of color. *Women's Rights Law Reporter, 30*, 315–346.

Glenn v. Brumby, 663 F.3d 1312, 1318 (11th Cir. 2011).

Grant, J. M., Mottet, L. A., Tanis, J., Harrison, J., Herman, J. L., & Keisling, M. (2011). *Injustice at every turn: A report of the national transgender discrimination survey.* Washington, DC: National Center for Transgender Equality and National Gay and Lesbian Task Force.

Hendricks, M. L., & Testa, R. J. (2012). A conceptual framework for clinical work and with transgender and gender nonconforming clients: An adaptation of the minority stress model. *Professional Psychology: Research and Practice, 43*, 460–467. http://dx.doi.org/10.1037/a0029597

In re Earle F. Alexander, M.D., BPMC 95-45, 1995 WL 17785020 (Mar. 2, 1995).

In re Powell, 95 A.D.3d 1631 (N.Y. App. Div. 2012).

In re McIntyre, 552 Pa. 324 (1998).

Institute of Medicine. (2011). *The health of lesbian, gay, bisexual, and transgender people: Building a foundation for better understanding.* Washington, DC: National Academy of Sciences.

Kantaras v. Kantaras, 884 So. 2d 155 (Fla. Dist. Ct. App. 2004).

King v. Governor of the State of New Jersey, 767 F.3d 216, 220 (3d Cir. 2014).

Koocher, G. P., & Campbell, L. F. (2016). Professional ethics in the United States. In J. Norcross, G. VandenBos, & D. Freedheim (Eds.), *Handbook of clinical psychology* (Vol. 5, pp. 301–337). Washington, DC: American Psychological Association.

Lev, A. I. (2009). The ten tasks of the mental health provider: Recommendations for revision of the World Professional Association for Transgender Health's Standards of Care. *International Journal of Transgenderism, 11*, 74–99. http://dx.doi.org/10.1080/15532730903008032

Munoz v. Holder, 407 F. App'x 185 (9th Cir. 2010).

Nadal, K. L. (2013). *That's so gay! Microagressions and the lesbian, gay, bisexual, and transgender community.* Washington, DC: American Psychological Association. http://dx.doi.org/10.1037/14093-000

National Center for Transgender Equality. (2015a). *Map: State health insurance rules.* Retrieved from http://transequality.org/issues/resources/map-state-health-insurance-rules

National Center for Transgender Equality. (2015b). *Map: State nondiscrimination laws.* Retrieved from http://transequality.org/issues/resources/map-state-transgender-non-discrimination-laws

National Center for Transgender Equality. (2015c). *New proposed federal rules will help end health insurance discrimination.* Retrieved from http://transequality.org/blog/new-proposed-federal-rules-will-help-end-health-insurance-discrimination

National Center for Transgender Equality. (n.d.). *Issues: Identity documents and privacy.* Retrieved from http://transequality.org/issues/identity-documents-privacy

New Jersey Sexual Orientation Change Efforts, N.J. Stat. Ann. § 45:1-55 (West 2013).

New York State Education Law § 6530 (2008).

Raj, R. (2002). Towards a transpositive therapeutic model: Developing clinical sensitivity and cultural competence in the effective support of transsexual and transgendered clients. *The International Journal of Transgenderism, 6.* Retrieved from http://www.iiav.nl/ezines/web/ijt/97-03/numbers/symposion/ijtvo06no02_04.htm

Reisner v. Bd. of Regents of State of N.Y., 535 N.Y.S.2d 197, 199 (1988).

Shaw v. D.C., 944 F. Supp. 2d 43 (D.D.C. 2013), appeal dismissed (Aug. 8, 2014), appeal dismissed sub nom.

Singh, A. A. (2013). Transgender youth of color and resilience: Negotiating oppression, finding support. *Sex Roles, 68*, 690–702. http://dx.doi.org/10.1007/s11199-012-0149-z

Singh, A. A., & Burnes, T. R. (2009). Creating developmentally-appropriate, safe counseling environments for transgender youth: The critical role of school counselors. *Journal of LGBT Issues in Counseling, 3*, 215–234. http://dx.doi.org/10.1080/15538600903379457

Spade, D. (2008). Documenting gender. *The Hastings Law Journal*, *59*, 731–832.

Wilson v. Phoenix House, 42 Misc. 3d 677, 706, 978 N.Y.S.2d 748, 769 (N.Y. Sup. Ct. 2013).

World Professional Association for Transgender Health. (2010, May 26). *Depsychopathologisation statement*. Retrieved from http://www.wpath.org/uploaded_files/140/files/de-psychopathologisation%205-26-10%20on%20letterhead.pdf

Laura Edwards-Leeper

Affirmative Care of TGNC Children and Adolescents

5

Much has been written about the challenges transgender and gender nonconforming (TGNC) youth face and the multitude of risk factors that exist for them (Almeida, Johnson, Corliss, Molnar, & Azrael, 2009; Grossman & D'Augelli, 2006; Spack et al., 2012). However, these youth also show considerable resilience, strength, and courage in their conviction of who they are. The role of mental health providers (MHPs) is to hear the stories of these courageous children and adolescents and advocate on their behalf. It is also the responsibility of MHPs to critically examine the existing research while simultaneously moving the field forward by ensuring that the right questions are asked and methodology is approached with an awareness of assumptions and biases. Additionally, MHPs must recognize the importance of assisting families with the undeniable stress that exists when a child comes out as TGNC, as children are not independent and do not live in a vacuum. Most important, MHPs

---

http://dx.doi.org/10.1037/14957-006
Affirmative Counseling and Psychological Practice With Transgender and Gender Nonconforming Clients, A. A. Singh and l. m. dickey (Editors)

should approach this work in a balanced and affirmative manner, paying close attention to Principle A (Beneficence and Nonmaleficence) from the *Ethical Principles of Psychologists and Code of Conduct* (American Psychological Association [APA], 2010; see also Chapter 4, this volume, for a more detailed discussion of ethical and legal concerns for MHPs working with TGNC clients). The goal of this chapter is to offer an overview of balanced, affirmative care for TGNC children and adolescents, with the hope of encouraging providers to be thoughtful in their care of this unique client population, taking into consideration the complexities that accompany these developmental stages.

History of TGNC Child and Adolescent Treatment in the United States

Gender identity development has long been assumed to follow a standard and predictable trajectory, with the underlying premise that gender is a socially constructed, binary phenomenon (Martin & Ruble, 2010). Scholars have shifted from assuming children are blank slates in terms of gender, with the notion that they can be easily shaped to embrace the gender identity that aligns with their sex assigned at birth, to recognizing gender as something that may be influenced by a multiplicity of factors, including biology (Jones, 2009). Regardless of the etiology, the gender identity trajectory for most children is believed to begin in early childhood and become solidified by adolescence (Steensma, Kreukels, de Vries, & Cohen-Kettenis, 2013). It is also important to note that the impacts of culture and race are generally absent in the literature on gender identity development. For example, the way in which one's racial and ethnic background support or discourage the individual's expression and acceptance of their inherent gender identity is a critical component that has not been adequately examined. Additionally, the research on TGNC youth has primarily included White children of families who had the resources and financial means to seek services. Research is lacking on the experience of racial and ethnic minority groups of TGNC youth as well as on youth from lower socioeconomic backgrounds.

The last decade has been pivotal in increasing awareness among U.S. health care providers and the public about the existence of TGNC children and adolescents (Edwards-Leeper & Spack, 2012; Hidalgo et al., 2013; Pleak, 1999). In 2007, the first U.S. pediatric hospital-based interdisciplinary clinic was formed to offer psychological evaluation and medical services to TGNC adolescents because it was apparent, at that time, that the numbers of youth presenting with issues related to gender identity were increasing around the globe (Tishelman et al., 2015). Following the lead of a world-renowned clinic in The Netherlands, Boston Children's Hospital started the Gender Management Service (GeMS), a program that serves pediatric patients with disorders of sexual development and TGNC adolescents. The number of TGNC client referrals to the GeMS program within the first couple of years exceeded expectations as youth and their parents from across the United States and overseas desperately sought services.

Prior to the development of the GeMS program, child and adolescent clients with issues related to gender who were courageous enough to come forward, and whose parents recognized the need to receive help, were likely seen by their pediatricians and MHPs in their community. The therapeutic approach used may or may not have been supportive and affirming, and many providers were not prepared to work with this client population. TGNC youth who did not have a supportive family likely fared much worse, at times possibly becoming homeless and/or turning to substances (Cochran, Stewart, Ginzler, & Cauce, 2002).

The initial reaction to this landmark program offering medical services to TGNC adolescents, despite being housed within one of the country's elite children's hospitals, was skepticism and concern from medical and MHPs. Skeptics questioned whether adolescents could be trusted to truly know their gender identity and to be capable of making decisions related to altering their bodies and identities. The first few years of the GeMS program involved many discussions with health care providers, educators, community groups, parents, and media outlets about the numerous reasons why medical interventions were justified and medically and psychologically necessary for these youth. The GeMS protocol, which initially included 6 months of supportive therapy with a gender specialist in the community, followed by a 4-hour comprehensive psychological readiness evaluation, was seen by many as insufficient when considering the magnitude of the decisions being made in collaboration with these young clients. Most medical providers did not feel comfortable providing medical treatment (e.g., puberty-blocking medication and hormone treatment) to these clients, and the majority of MHPs viewed the issue as a psychiatric one. Throughout most of the United States at that time, the standard treatment approach was to urge the child or adolescent to accept their given body and identity, many times by encouraging the stereotypical toys, activities, clothes, and playmates of the assigned gender and simultaneously not permitting the child or adolescent to pursue their identified gender interests (Zucker, Wood, Singh, & Bradley, 2012).

Since the GeMS program opened its doors, much has shifted in the care of TGNC youth in the United States. With the help of the media, educational efforts by various health care fields, and the development of professional guidelines and standards of care (Coleman et al., 2012; Hembree et al., 2009), the number of youth seeking services continues to skyrocket, and health care providers have responded more quickly than might have been predicted given the initial reticence. An article published in 2014 reported the number of interdisciplinary clinics serving TGNC youth in the United States to have exceeded 35 (Hsieh & Leininger, 2014), and this number is steadily increasing. Despite the growing number of clinics, the demand continues to exceed the supply, leaving many well-intentioned clinic directors in a position of quickly drafting protocols and pulling together interdisciplinary teams without adequate time or support to develop thorough programs grounded in research and expertise. Out of necessity and lack of providers, these teams often consist of individuals who have not been trained to complete the recommended evaluations with these youths and are unfamiliar with the current standards of care, the research on best practices, and the important role of advocacy in this work.

In the midst of this surge of TGNC youth seeking services, the slowly decreasing stigma around TGNC people, and the willingness of health care providers to offer services, there has been a shift to approaching care in a nonpathologizing and affirming manner. This shift has occurred simultaneously in the care of adult TGNC individuals, with the movement toward an informed consent model of care (Coleman et al., 2012), one that does not require the multiple barriers and hurdles that TGNC adults have had to face historically (e.g., undergoing a "real-life experience," obtaining letters of support from multiple MHPs). Interestingly, in the care of TGNC adolescents, in less than a decade, the pendulum has shifted so much that the protocol developed by the GeMS program described previously (e.g., required supportive therapy, psychological evaluation) is no longer considered progressive or too lenient by many but is now criticized by some as being too conservative and not affirming enough.

Given the rapid and drastic shift in views regarding how to best work with this population, it is an ideal time to take a step back and thoughtfully consider the construct of affirmative care for TGNC youth. This is also an appropriate time to move this conversation forward as more and more pediatric clinics open and strive to provide optimal care to their TGNC clients. Although there are aspects of providing affirmative care to children and adolescents that overlap, these two developmental groups are unique and each worthy of deeper discussion than can be offered here (Edwards-Leeper, Leibowitz, & Sangganjanavanich, 2016).

Defining Affirmative Care
With TGNC Youth

The term *affirmative care* has been used with increased frequency in the past couple of years to describe an approach to working with TGNC individuals that is nonpathologizing (APA, 2010). A recent paper on this philosophy of working with TGNC youth served to open the conversation among researchers and pediatric health care providers (Hidalgo et al., 2013). Hidalgo et al. (2013) described *affirmative care* as "a child's opportunity to live in the gender that feels most real or comfortable to that child and to express that gender with freedom from restriction, aspersion, or rejection" (p. 286). They emphasized that gender development involves biological, developmental, and cultural influences, is not pathological, and is nonbinary. Although this is a good start to describing this model of care, given the short and rapidly shifting history of approaches used for treating TGNC youth, it is important to expand on this initial discussion, taking into consideration the historical context.

One reason the pendulum of care for TGNC youth has likely shifted so drastically in such a short period of time may be related to well-intentioned health care providers eager to offer supportive services to younger generations of TGNC individuals and, as a result, simply applying models of affirmative care appropriate for TGNC adults to their younger clients. Albeit well-meaning, this may be a risky leap, as it is well understood that childhood, adolescence, and adulthood are unique developmental stages, each bringing its own challenges and complexity.

There are several assumptions that underlie affirmative care of TGNC individuals, regardless of the client's age or developmental level. For example, affirmative care trusts that the individual knows themselves. Additionally, affirmative care values one's long-term psychological health and quality of life over maintaining the status quo as it relates to gender. This type of care also offers support to the individual (and family) to make decisions and take steps that allow the individual to be as true to themselves as possible. Finally, affirmative care does not perceive gender on a binary and supports those who do not identify on the binary. The reality remains, however, that our society places gender into two categories: male and female. Society may be shifting in this regard, individuals often need support in living under the current circumstances.

Although there are some similarities, affirmative care of TGNC youth is not identical to that of adults. First, the developmental stages of childhood and adolescents are significantly different than the various stages of adulthood. Socially, emotionally, cognitively, biologically, and neurologically, children and adolescents move through stages of development at somewhat predictable but also very individualized speeds (Martin &

Ruble, 2010). The shift from concrete to abstract cognitive processes; the movement toward mastery of regulating emotional states; the progression from developing early attachment through various stages of independence and autonomy; the changes in physical development, particularly during puberty; and the drastic neurological shifts during childhood and adolescence are some of the very real and important ways the age span from birth to the early 20s has developed into its own area of specialization in the mental health, medical health, and education fields (e.g., Steinberg, 2009). The developmental psychopathology model emphasizes a multifactorial, dynamic perspective through understanding that children and adolescents constantly adapt to the numerous environments in which they are raised in a more profound way than do adults (Wakefield, 1997).

Second, there is research on the typical trajectories of gender dysphoric children, which can, and should, be used as a part of clinical decision making. Although this research is limited in quantity, and some of the studies' results have been questioned because of potential methodological issues (APA, 2015; Rapier, 2015), the general finding is consistent across studies and indicates that most gender dysphoric *young* children will not persist in their TGNC identity or experience of gender dysphoria (Drummond, Bradley, Peterson-Badali, & Zucker, 2008; Steensma, McGuire, Kreukels, Beekman, & Cohen-Kettenis, 2013; Wallien & Cohen-Kettenis, 2008). Although there are clearly children who do persist, it would be irresponsible to not inform parents of young children about the existing research (including the flaws) and the various ways in which their individual child's gender identity may develop. Informing parents that it is impossible to definitively predict the specific course and/or outcome for any individual child is an important part of the conversation in an affirmative approach. Keeping this reality in mind when working with TGNC children, and encouraging parents to do the same, regardless of what social and/or physical transitions take place, is essential. An affirmative approach places significant value and belief in a child or adolescent's stated gender identity; however, the appreciation for a given child's declaration about their gender must be balanced with an understanding and incorporation of theories of child development. Assuming that what a young child tells an MHP about their gender identity at one moment in time is solidified and can accurately predict their future gender identity, ignores the solid research on the evolving nature of child and adolescent development described previously (Steinberg, 2009), as well as the research on gender identity development in TGNC children specifically. Dismissing this research and making firm decisions about a child's gender, without recognizing that this could be fluid and still forming, and as a result not providing space for growth and change, risks boxing the child into a gender with which they may not ultimately identify. One might argue that this would in fact be an unaffirming and unethical approach to caring for these children.

Third, many TGNC adolescents are also still evolving in their gender identity development. Given the multiple factors that make adolescence one of the most challenging periods across the lifespan (because of pubertal changes, cognitive development, social-emotional maturity, etc.), it is not surprising that many adolescents are overwhelmed with the numerous aspects of their identity that are being solidified at this developmental juncture. Gender identity, sexual orientation, religious/spiritual identity, racial/ethnic identities, and family-of-origin issues (particularly of adopted children, those with separated parents, and/or those who have lost a parent) are a few of the many identity-development factors that adolescents face (Lerner & Steinberg, 2009). An additional burden children and adolescents cannot escape is the experience of *adultism*, which involves having limited power and autonomy over one's life and decisions. Being controlled by adults in power (i.e., parents, teachers, health care providers) may result in increased psychological distress and despair for youth who are struggling to understand and embrace an identity that is not considered traditional (Singh & Jackson, 2012).

With the increased media attention and easy access to social networking sites by teenagers, today's youth who are questioning their gender identity have more freedom to explore this aspect of their developing self than past generations. Possibly because of this, clinicians working with TGNC adolescents are recognizing an increased number of youth rejecting the gender binary and working to find their place somewhere along the gender continuum, but not on either extreme. This, too, is an evolving process and should be supported in a careful and thoughtful way, so as to avoid pushing an adolescent in any one particular direction. Because of the complex nature of adolescent development and the myriad issues with which most are grappling, applying models of care used with TGNC adults to most adolescents may not be in their best interest.

Application of Affirmative Care in Work With TGNC Children and Adolescents

Given the complexity of working with children and adolescents, one may wonder what affirmative care actually looks like in practice. Although there are some aspects of this care that are specific to children or adolescents, there are some areas of overlap. For example, affirmative care with all youth typically involves helping the individual recognize various ways of experiencing gender—as male, female, or somewhere in between/something else. Supporting youth who do not fit the mold of being either male or female is affirmative; however, this support must include helping the individual figure out how to navigate a world that still applies a gender binary to many aspects of life. Youth and their parents may also be assisted with how to respond to friends, classmates, family members, neighbors, and coworkers who question the child or adolescent's gender. Developing tools for dealing with teasing and bullying is another important part of this work, while simultaneously advocating to change the hostile and unsafe environment in which the child may live. For TGNC children and adolescents, providing resources in the way of groups and other LGBTQ friendly organizations may be critical if they attend a less tolerant school and have not found such support on their own. For youth at any developmental level, affirmative care helps build resilience and inner strength.

Although some youth view their gender as more fluid, other children and adolescents hold a very narrow view about what it means to be a boy or a girl. Influences from familial, cultural, or religious beliefs that adhere to more traditional notions of gender roles, behaviors, and sexuality (e.g., heterosexism) may leave some youth believing that the only way to engage in activities they want to do, wear clothes they want to wear, or be in sexual/romantic relationships with those to whom they are attracted, means living as a different gender than they were assigned at birth. For example, a Mexican American TGNC child who identifies as female and has a family that adheres to traditional gender roles may experience the added stress of disappointing a father who is unable to accept his birth-sex-assigned son as his daughter. Children whose families belong to religious organizations that adhere to traditional notions of gender may feel responsible for ostracism by the church if the child's parents support them in their identity.

SOCIAL TRANSITION IN CHILDREN

Specific to the affirmative care of children is the topic of social transition. There has been considerable dialogue around this topic for many reasons. Those who support early social transition point out that this allows TGNC children to begin living as their true self as early in life as possible (Ehrensaft, 2012). Given that some TGNC adolescents report feeling as if their childhood was wasted due to not being able to live as their "true" gender, it makes sense that many would see early social transition as being beneficial. Similarly, early social transition is supported by the reports of providers who observe a decrease in emotional and behavioral problems among TGNC children once they make this transition.

Those who recommend using caution in considering early social transition point to concerns related to the research that indicates only 12% to 50% of gender dysphoric children will persist, and for some of these children, their long-term trajectory may be related to sexual orientation rather than gender identity (Drummond et al., 2008; Steensma, McGuire, et al., 2013; Wallien & Cohen-Kettenis, 2008). Additionally, there is one small, qualitative study that reports psychological distress among a portion of the early social transitioned participants who decided to return to their assigned gender (Steensma, Biemond, de Boer, & Cohen-Kettenis, 2011). These factors, along with the reality that children are constantly growing and evolving in multiple ways, result in some providers' hesitancy to quickly support early social transitioning for all TGNC children.

Historically, one additional reason that this intervention was not supported was the belief that living as TGNC was far more difficult than living as one's gender assigned at birth and would likely result in a host of psychological, social, and medical challenges. This belief was based on research that discussed the challenges many TGNC adults have faced in our society (APA, 2015). Thus, it was not purely a bias of those researching or questioning the benefits of early social transition but was based on findings from early TGNC adult research. Given the newly available medical interventions for young adolescents (e.g., puberty-suppressing medication), which have shown promise in allowing those treated with this intervention to "pass" as their affirmed gender more easily in adulthood (de Vries et al., 2014), the previous concerns about long-term quality of life are likely less relevant to the discussion than they were previously.

It seems that affirmatively approaching this particularly "hot topic" in the care of TGNC children needs to be more balanced; it is important to consider both sides of the dialogue. Thus, to appropriately consider the recommendation to support early social transition, one must acknowledge that some children will persist in a gender different from that which they were assigned at birth and recognize that to permit an early social transition is likely in their best interest. Additionally, there is not sufficient research to claim that most children who make an early social transition and then change their mind will actually suffer psychologically from these gender transitions.

Additionally, when considering the recommendation to support an early social transition, we must acknowledge that children do not live and grow in isolation but are supported and influenced by their environments and by their parents in particular. As Lev (2004) discussed, parents of TGNC children experience a grief and loss process of their own. Many parents move through this process and ultimately become supportive of their TGNC child. Although this is very encouraging, some parents may struggle to accept the possibility that their child,

whom they have worked hard to accept in a different gender, may ultimately change again. In some cases, parents go to great lengths to support their TGNC child, such as finding a new school, quitting their job to
home-school their TGNC child, moving the family to a new, more progressive city, not to mention facing the challenge of informing friends,
relatives, and coworkers. Families of cultural or religious backgrounds
that hold more traditional beliefs regarding gender may experience an
even greater struggle to understand and accept their TGNC child.

Moreover, children may be more comfortable in a fluid gender than
what their parents are able to tolerate. It is easy to see how some TGNC
children may come to feel trapped in the gender they affirmed as a young
child. Being aware of the possibility that their gender may change again,
and encouraging continued, periodic check-in appointments with a
knowledgeable MHP to explore the child's evolving gender identity and
address parental concerns if they arise, are important parts of affirmative
care. In essence, affirmative work with TGNC children approaches the
option of socially transitioning on a case-by-case basis, weighing the pros
and cons of doing so in each case, recognizing the existing research, and
always putting considerable weight on the child's identified gender at
that point in time.

MEDICAL INTERVENTION
FOR TGNC ADOLESCENTS

Another current topic of discussion in the care of TGNC youth is the use
of medical interventions for adolescents. The use of puberty-blocking
medication for young TGNC adolescents has become increasingly popular
and hormone treatment (e.g., testosterone, estrogen) is frequently used
with older adolescents (Tishelman et al., 2015). In some cases, gender-
affirming surgeries are also approved for older adolescents. Some of the
current questions related to these interventions include the following:

- Are there any psychological or physical risks to using puberty-
  blocking medications with TGNC youth?
- Does blocking hormones at puberty (i.e., initiating puberty-
  suppressing medication) somehow interfere with a growing individual's gender identity development?
- Is the involvement of an MHP a necessary part of treatment for
  TGNC youth seeking puberty-blocking medication? What about
  when considering hormone treatment?
- Should a formal psychological/readiness evaluation be completed
  prior to initiating medical interventions with TGNC youth?
- Should an informed consent model be used with TGNC youth in
  making decisions regarding medical interventions?

- At what age should TGNC youth be considered eligible for less reversible hormone treatments?
- What are the pros and cons of starting hormone treatment prior to the recommended age of "around" 16 years old?
- Are TGNC adolescents able to accurately predict their future feelings and plans regarding fertility so as to make a fully informed decision related to medical interventions?
- In what way should we approach care for TGNC adolescents who report no childhood history of gender dysphoria (i.e., late-onset cases)?
- How should medical interventions be approached with TGNC adolescents who do not fall on the gender binary and who are only seeking moderate physical feminizing or masculinizing changes?
- How can parents be supported and their perceptions be heard and included in clinical decision making, particularly when evaluating late-onset TGNC adolescents and those who may have cognitive deficits and/or cooccurring mental health concerns?
- What role do cultural factors play in an adolescent's freedom to express their gender identity and their parents' ability to support their child?

These questions point to the complexity of working with TGNC adolescents, and covering each point in depth goes beyond the scope of this chapter. However, it is worth addressing several of these questions as they relate to the affirmative care of TGNC adolescents.

Pubertal Suppression

Current standards of care recommend the use of puberty-suppressing medication for appropriately screened TGNC adolescents, and many providers are comfortable with this intervention; thus, this is considered an affirmative aspect of treatment (Coleman et al., 2012). Although research does not currently exist to shed light on the degree to which hormones influence one's gender identity development through the adolescent years, most providers working with TGNC youth feel that the benefits of "buying time" for the adolescent to continue sorting out their gender identity without the added stress of their body changing in a way that is highly distressing, outweighs the risks of altering the body's natural progression (i.e., with the absence of puberty blockers; Edwards-Leeper & Spack, 2012). It is important to note, however, that these standards of care are based on the empirical research to date, which suggests that appropriately evaluated TGNC youth who are identified as a good candidate for puberty-blocking medication do well with this course of treatment (de Vries et al., 2014). Unfortunately, for a variety of reasons, newer clinics serving this adolescent population may not adhere to this critical piece—perhaps the most critical piece—that forms the basis for this recommended treatment. In an effort to support the adolescent and provide services quickly, providers may ignore the research and focus only on the medical intervention. It is important for MHPs to know that affirmative care often supports the use of puberty-suppressing medication for TGNC adolescents who have been appropriately evaluated by a trained MHP.

Hormone Treatment

In a similar effort to be affirming, some providers interpret the recommendation to initiate hormone treatment "around" 16 years of age, as outlined in the Endocrine Society Clinical Practice Guidelines (Hembree et al., 2009), to apply to children as young as age 11 or 12 years old, arguing that to be affirming of TGNC youth, we should support them in progressing through puberty at the same age and pace as their peers. The concern is that not to allow this, the TGNC youth will experience psychological distress. Although there is likely some truth in this expressed concern for some TGNC youth, and there are certainly cases in which initiating hormones prior to age 16 is beneficial to an individual teenager, assuming that all TGNC adolescents would be best served by initiating hormone treatment in early adolescence fails to take into account the multiplicity of ways in which adolescents are different from adults. Specifically, one cannot ignore where most adolescents fall in terms of their identity development, susceptibility to influence, cognitive maturity, and neurological development (e.g., underdeveloped areas of the brain responsible for decision making and risk taking). These factors must be taken into consideration when making medical decisions.

There is no existing research to support starting TGNC youth on irreversible medical intervention prior to age 16; thus, by doing so, providers may be taking substantial risks related to individual client's physical, psychological, and cognitive development and long-term satisfaction with the intervention. Applying this universally risks backlash by the public and skeptics in the medical and mental health communities if the outcomes are undesirable (e.g., if large numbers of individuals treated with less reversible interventions at a young age later regret this decision). This backlash could compromise the future care of TGNC youth who would benefit from medical interventions. At the same time, applying a universal protocol to all TGNC adolescents that includes a strict age requirement for starting medically necessary treatment also carries significant risks for individual TGNC adolescents, such as increased dysphoria and mental health concerns. Therefore, the affirmative care of TGNC adolescents may involve offering hormone treatment around the age of 16, after evaluation by a trained MHP. Although lowering the age requirement is being increasingly and appropriately recommended in some cases, this medical decision should be approached with caution, and is best done with the involvement of a trained and knowledgeable MHP.

PARENT INVOLVEMENT IN THE EVALUATION

Approaching the care of TGNC adolescents from an affirmative stance may involve going against the wishes of parents. One can imagine situations in which parents are unable to accept their child's affirmed gender identity and as a result try to control their child's ability to receive care that may be in the best interest of the child. This situation often occurs in families with more traditional gender roles or with late-onset adolescents because, from the parents' perspective, the gender dysphoria appears to come out of nowhere. Although parental skepticism exists for many TGNC youth, assuming that this is the case for all TGNC adolescents seeking services and dismissing the parents' perspective on the situation is ill advised. Given how persuadable some adolescents are, failing to consider the parents' perspectives on their child's experience may result in the loss of important information for conceptualizing the case and ignore the opportunity to enhance the possibility for the positive long-term outcomes that can occur when parents are involved and supportive.

Affirmative care with TGNC adolescents should involve the parents whenever possible for several reasons. First, it is important to obtain a comprehensive history from parents, including gender identity development; psychological/emotional development; and family, social, academic, and medical history. Second, obtaining parents' perceptions of their adolescent's development and current struggles creates a more holistic picture from which the clinician can more accurately and comprehensively conceptualize the case and make appropriate recommendations. Finally, involving the parents in the evaluation process provides an opportunity for them to be educated, validated, and heard regarding their fears and concerns, all in an effort to encourage support of their child in whatever direction is ultimately recommended. Given that most TGNC youth do best when they have the support of their parents, an affirmative approach should make every effort to involve parents in the evaluation and treatment processes.

REPRODUCTIVE CONSIDERATIONS

Some providers who are hesitant to initiate medical interventions with TGNC adolescents cite potential fertility implications as a concern. Those who regularly offer puberty-blocking interventions with young

TGNC adolescents point out that this intervention is completely reversible; discontinuing the medication at any time will result in an adolescent's biologically determined puberty resuming at whatever point it was halted and in no way impacts fertility (Carel, Eugster, Rogol, Ghizzoni, & Palmert, 2009).

Given these considerations, some providers may not see the relevance of having a formal psychological evaluation prior to starting puberty-blocking medication for all TGNC adolescents, which ideally includes a discussion about fertility. Although circumventing a "readiness" evaluation by an MHP may appear safe and appropriate at first glance, perhaps even seeming more affirmative because it eliminates a hurdle to starting medical intervention, when considering the broader picture, it becomes apparent that an affirmative approach should include evaluation and conversations about fertility. Specifically, along with determining if the youth experiences severe enough gender dysphoria and/or gender confusion to recommend the use of puberty-suppressing medication, there are other important factors to consider when making this clinical decision. For example, assessing who is influencing the desire for the medical intervention is critical to ensuring that the adolescent—not just their parent(s)—truly desires, understands, and assents to the intervention. Additionally, using this as an opportunity to emphasize the purpose of the puberty-suppressing medication—to buy time for the adolescent to continue sorting out their gender identity—to the adolescent and parents alike is imperative. This critical message is necessary to prevent adolescents from feeling stuck on a "runaway gender train" that they cannot get off. Despite the importance of relaying this message as clearly as possible, the reality is that in many cases the use of puberty-blocking medication will be perceived by the adolescent and/or parents—and possibly described by the providers involved in the adolescent's care—as the first step in a sequence of medical interventions, including hormones and surgeries. For this reason, discussing fertility issues with adolescents and parents prior to initiating any medical intervention is advised.

Given that hormone treatment (i.e., estrogen or testosterone) is more likely to have implications for fertility, most do not question that a similar conversation should occur with adolescents prior to initiating this intervention. Given the importance of parental support through this process, it is recommended that parents be included in this discussion whenever possible. Because of the magnitude of this decision for an adolescent, it is critical for an MHP to be involved by helping the youth explore long-term desires related to having biological children, assessing the adolescent's understanding of the possible implications of hormones on fertility, and determining whether they are able to fully consent to treatment. This conversation and assessment can be best accomplished within the context of a supportive relationship with an MHP as well as through a more formal, comprehensive psychological/readiness evaluation. Younger adolescents in particular may struggle to predict their future desires related to fertility; thus, the use of less reversible medical interventions (e.g., hormones and surgeries) should only be considered for these younger adolescents in straightforward cases with ongoing mental health support, including an evaluation to determine readiness. In sum, affirmative care of adolescents often includes the use of medical interventions, but these should be considered after a comprehensive psychological/readiness evaluation, including a discussion about possible implications for fertility. Additionally, the involvement of parents should occur whenever possible, and the ongoing involvement of a supportive and knowledgeable MHP is strongly recommended.

INTERDISCIPLINARY TEAM APPROACH

The other key aspect of affirmative care of TGNC youth involves collaboration with an interdisciplinary team of providers. (See Chapter 3, this volume, for a more in-depth discussion about the importance of consulting with other providers in the care of TGNC individuals.) Although this is recommended in the care of TGNC adults as well (Coleman et al., 2012; Hembree et al., 2009), because of the complexities outlined in this chapter, involving providers from a variety of disciplines is especially recommended when working with adolescents. These interdisciplinary teams typically involve a medical provider (e.g., pediatric endocrinologist, adolescent medicine doctor) and one or more MHPs. Typically, social workers, psychologists, psychiatrists, and other licensed counselors may be involved in providing ongoing supportive therapy on an individual level or level or within a supportive group environment. The focus of this treatment often involves one or more of the following aspects, with thoughtful consideration of the impact of the youth's and family's various intersecting identities:

- assisting the youth in clarifying their gender and gaining certainty about what, if any, medical interventions they desire;
- providing support related to challenging family dynamics and/or lack of support within the family;
- assisting with difficulties in peer relationships and in navigating romantic relationships;
- assessing and addressing any co-occurring mental health issues (e.g., depression, anxiety, eating disorders, behavioral problems, substance use, autism spectrum disorders, thought disorders) and concerns related to safety (e.g., suicidal ideation, self-injurious behaviors, reports of abuse, trauma, bullying);
- assisting parents with their emotional reactions to their TGNC child's gender identity development (e.g., grief and loss), and

providing education and support in an effort to help them better understand and accept their TGNC child;

- advocating for the youth in the various environments in which they live (e.g., school, community, immediate and extended family, religious organization); and
- assisting youth in addressing discrimination, including the experience of dealing with multiple minority identities (e.g., a person of color and gender fluid).

The other important role that MHPs play in an affirmative, interdisciplinary approach to working with TGNC youth is providing comprehensive psychological/readiness evaluations to help determine whether moving forward with a medical intervention is recommended for a particular TGNC youth. By incorporating such an evaluation in an affirmative care protocol (including a comprehensive semistructured clinical interview with the adolescent and parent, in conjunction with a battery of psychological and gender measures), adolescents, parents, and medical providers can feel more confident in their decisions about intervening medically. Additionally, because this multimethod approach is based on research, parents may feel more assured that when these interventions are recommended, they will likely result in long-term improvements in quality of life and psychological functioning. By approaching this evaluation as a second opinion and a part of a comprehensive protocol of care for TGNC youth, clinics will be following the empirically supported standards developed by the Dutch (de Vries & Cohen-Kettenis, 2012). This approach is consistent with other psychological/readiness evaluations used for clients seeking other types of medical interventions that have a behavioral health component, such as bariatric surgery and organ transplants. Most of the current research that supports the use of medical interventions for TGNC adolescents incorporates this protocol. Moreover, the importance of this interdisciplinary approach cannot be overstated. In sum, because of the complexities that exist in the care of TGNC adolescents, affirmative treatment is best performed by an interdisciplinary team, which includes MHPs who provide supportive therapy and offer comprehensive readiness evaluations.

Case Vignettes

In an effort to highlight the varied ways in which affirmative care can be implemented, several brief case vignettes are provided. Although they certainly do not offer an exhaustive view of how TGNC youth present, the case vignettes highlight common youth presentations and briefly describe how an affirmative model would be used in each case.

KARA

Kara, an 11-year-old European American who was assigned male at birth and who identifies as female, presented for a readiness evaluation for consideration of puberty-suppressing medication. Kara's biological mother and father accompanied her to the appointment. Kara and her parents reported that she has identified strongly as female since she began to talk. Kara insisted from a young age that "God made a mistake" and that she was given the "wrong body." Kara always asked to wear female clothing, and her favorite color is pink. She enjoyed playing with dolls and playing "house" when she was younger, in which she always role-played as the mother. Kara's parents decided to allow her to socially transition in regard to her gender expression (clothing, hairstyle) and her desired name and pronouns in the second grade. Kara's school has been supportive of her female identity, as have her friends and extended family members. Kara and her parents reported that her gender dysphoria persisted and intensified as she neared puberty. She was "terrified" of masculinizing and felt "100% sure" that she wanted puberty blockers. Kara and her parents reported that she was very well-adjusted psychologically, socially, and academically. She experienced some anxiety related to schoolwork at times, but this was not impacting her functioning. Kara has an MHP with whom she has met periodically since age 6, and part of their work has been exploring her gender. Kara was happy to continue meeting with her therapist monthly while on blockers.

Affirmative Care Recommendation

Given the relatively straightforward nature of this case (gender identity history typical of many TGNC youth, increased dysphoria at puberty, expressed desire for and a developmentally appropriate understanding of puberty-blocking medication, support of friends and family, no significant mental health concerns, connection with a knowledgeable and supportive MHP), Kara is likely a good candidate for puberty-blocking medication from an affirmative care perspective. The expectation is that Kara will continue meeting with her MHP as often as she, her parents, and the members of the interdisciplinary team evaluating her feel will be most beneficial for her. The focus of this aspect of Kara's care will be to assist her in continuing to explore her gender identity as she moves through adolescence in an effort to help her figure out where she feels most comfortable on the gender spectrum and decide whether she ultimately desires additional medical interventions. The MHP will also assist with other issues that come up related to her overall psychological and social functioning.

KEITH

Keith, a 16-year-old African American who was assigned female at birth and who identifies as male, presented to his pediatrician asking for testosterone. Keith's parents accompanied him to the appointment and informed the pediatrician that they were very concerned and skeptical about Keith's identification as male because this was an announcement he made 6 weeks ago and there had been no history of gender dysphoria or identification with a different gender throughout his childhood. They were further concerned because Keith was diagnosed with an autism spectrum disorder and attention-deficit/hyperactivity disorder. They reported that since childhood he had become "obsessed" with various interests for periods of time, and they believed that his current identification as male was just another one of these obsessions. Keith's parents further expressed their worry about Keith's increased time spent online, where he had found other youth who identify as TGNC and were supporting him in this identity. His parents were worried that his online friends were influencing his stated gender identity. When Keith met with the pediatrician alone, he was adamant that he was truly a male and was angry when the pediatrician discussed the importance of meeting with an MHP to explore this further. Keith argued that his online TGNC friends were not required to see a "shrink" and that if the pediatrician and parents were not willing to give him testosterone, he would find another way to get it.

Affirmative Care Recommendation

The complexities described in this case are common and highlight the advantages of following an established protocol within an interdisciplinary team, which can take pressure off individual providers striving to provide optimal patient care. In Keith's case, the most affirmative approach to care was to educate Keith and his parents about the recommended protocols for providing affirmative care to TGNC youth, which included referring Keith to a knowledgeable MHP and an interdisciplinary clinic that could provide further evaluation and recommendations. After some time exploring his gender identity with an MHP, which included helping Keith's parents understand his gender identity and making referrals for their own supportive therapy if necessary, Keith was referred for a readiness evaluation prior to starting any medical interventions. Completed in an affirming manner, this evaluation provided Keith further opportunity to talk with a provider who was trained specifically to evaluate TGNC youth, with the goal of discussing his gender, assessing any mental health concerns, and ensuring that Keith was able to fully understand and consent to the medical interventions he was seeking.

MAX

Max, a 5-year-old Mexican American who was assigned male at birth, was brought by his divorced biological parents to see a psychologist due to their concern about his gender identity. Max's parents reported that Max has preferred more feminine things since age 3, including wearing his older sister's princess dresses around the house, painting his nails, and wanting to grow his hair long. On some days, Max stated that he wanted to be called Mary, but he did not insist that he was a girl and had not asked his parents to use female pronouns. He would be starting kindergarten in 4 months, and his mother, with whom he lives during the week, felt they should socially transition Max when he starts kindergarten because, based on what she had read, this would be affirming and supportive. Max's father also wanted to be supportive, but he questioned whether this was the best decision, given that Max had not asked for this and seems more fluid in his gender. Max's father also acknowledged that he was struggling with his own traditional notions of gender, particularly because it was his son who was expressing an interest in "female things."

Affirmative Care Recommendation

In this case, an affirmative care approach would likely not encourage Max and his family to make a social transition at school at the present time. Consistent with Max's father's concern, it is unclear whether Max identifies as female or is simply exploring his gender. There is no reason to push Max into one gender identity or another if he is functioning well being more fluid and nonbinary. A recommendation in this case is for Max's parents to continue monitoring Max's gender identity development, as well as changes in behavior and emotional functioning. As time progresses, if Max reports identifying as female more clearly and consistently, perhaps wishing to be called Mary with female pronouns all of the time, and/or if significant changes to Max's behavior and/or emotional functioning occur, further evaluation would be important. This evaluation could assist the family in deciding whether to pursue a more formal social transition for Max. The other important piece of an affirmative approach in Max's case is to work with Max's parents to help them feel more comfortable in having a child who does not, and may never, clearly identify as male or female. Along those same lines, exploring Max's parents' feelings around the possibility of Max identifying as something other than heterosexual in regard to his future sexual orientation is an important aspect of treatment. Supporting Max's parents in their feelings around this, taking into consideration and being respectful of their cultural background, and encouraging them to expand their views about gender norms may be the most important and affirmative work with Max at the present time.

Chapter Summary

MHPs are in the early stages of an exciting and critical time in the care of TGNC children and adolescents. The movement toward a more affirmative approach will, hopefully, result in a decrease in psychological problems found among TGNC youth and an increase in acceptance of this population among society in general. Now is the time to take a moment to step back, assess the history of the approach to care of TGNC youth in the last decade, review the existing research, and create protocols that are thoughtful, balanced, and affirming. If this approach is taken, the care of TGNC children and adolescents will be improved for generations to come.

References

Almeida, J., Johnson, R. M., Corliss, H. L., Molnar, B. E., & Azrael, D. (2009). Emotional distress among LGBT youth: The influence of perceived discrimination based on sexual orientation. *Journal of Youth and Adolescence, 38,* 1001–1014. http://dx.doi.org/10.1007/s10964-009-9397-9

American Psychological Association. (2010). *Ethical principles of psychologists and code of conduct* (2002, Amended June 1, 2010). Retrieved from http://www.apa.org/ethics/code/index.aspx

American Psychological Association. (2015). Guidelines for psychological practice with transgender and gender nonconforming people. *American Psychologist, 70,* 832–864. http://dx.doi.org/10.1037/a0039906

Carel, J. C., Eugster, E. A., Rogol, A., Ghizzoni, L., & Palmert, M. R. (2009). Consensus statement on the use of gonadotropin-releasing hormone analogs in children. *Pediatrics, 123,* e752–e762. http://dx.doi.org/10.1542/peds.2008-1783

Cochran, B. N., Stewart, A. J., Ginzler, J. A., & Cauce, A. M. (2002). Challenges faced by homeless sexual minorities: Comparison of gay, lesbian, bisexual, and transgender homeless adolescents with their heterosexual counterparts. *American Journal of Public Health, 92,* 773–777. http://dx.doi.org/10.2105/AJPH.92.5.773

Coleman, E., Bockting, W., Botzer, M., Cohen-Kettenis, P., DeCuypere, G., Feldman, J., . . . Zucker, K. (2012). Standards of care for the health of transsexual, transgender, and gender-nonconforming people, 7th version. *International Journal of Transgenderism, 13,* 165–232. http://dx.doi.org/10.1080/15532739.2011.700873

de Vries, A. L. C., & Cohen-Kettenis, P. T. (2012). Clinical management of gender dysphoria in children and adolescents: The Dutch approach. *Journal of Homosexuality, 59*, 301–320. http://dx.doi.org/10.1080/00918369.2012.653300

de Vries, A. L. C., McGuire, J. K., Steensma, T. D., Wagenaar, E. C. F., Doreleijers, T. A. H., & Cohen-Kettenis, P. T. (2014). Young adult psychological outcome after puberty suppression and gender reassignment. *Pediatrics, 134*, 696–704. http://dx.doi.org/10.1542/peds.2013-2958

Drummond, K. D., Bradley, S. J., Peterson-Badali, M., & Zucker, K. J. (2008). A follow-up study of girls with gender identity disorder. *Developmental Psychology, 44*, 34–45. http://dx.doi.org/10.1037/0012-1649.44.1.34

Edwards-Leeper, L., Leibowitz, S., & Sangganjanavanich, F. (2016). Affirmative practice with transgender and gender nonconforming youth: Expanding the model. *Psychology of Sexual Orientation and Gender Diversity, 3*, 165–172. http://dx.doi.org/10.1037/sgd0000167

Edwards-Leeper, L., & Spack, N. P. (2012). Psychological evaluation and medical treatment of transgender youth in an interdisciplinary "Gender Management Service" (GeMS) in a major pediatric center. *Journal of Homosexuality, 59*, 321–336. http://dx.doi.org/10.1080/00918369.2012.653302

Ehrensaft, D. (2012). From gender identity disorder to gender identity creativity: True gender self child therapy. *Journal of Homosexuality, 59*, 337–356. http://dx.doi.org/10.1080/00918369.2012.653303

Grossman, A. H., & D'Augelli, A. R. (2006). Transgender youth: Invisible and vulnerable. *Journal of Homosexuality, 51*, 111–128. http://dx.doi.org/10.1300/J082v51n01_06

Hembree, W. C., Cohen-Kettenis, P., Delemarre-van de Waal, H. A., Gooren, L. J., Meyer, W. J., III, Spack, N. P., . . . Montori, V. M., & the Endocrine Society. (2009). Endocrine treatment of transsexual persons: An Endocrine Society clinical practice guideline. *The Journal of Clinical Endocrinology and Metabolism, 94*, 3132–3154. http://dx.doi.org/10.1210/jc.2009-0345

Hidalgo, M. A., Ehrensaft, D., Tishelman, A. C., Clark, L. F., Garofalo, R., Rosenthal, S. M., . . . Olson, J. (2013). The gender affirmative model: What we know and what we aim to learn. *Human Development, 56*, 285–290. http://dx.doi.org/10.1159/000355235

Hsieh, S., & Leininger, J. (2014). Resource list: Clinical care programs for gender-nonconforming children and adolescents. *Pediatric Annals, 43*, 238–244. http://dx.doi.org/10.3928/00904481-20140522-11

Jones, L. (2009). The third sex: Gender identity development of intersex persons. *Graduate Journal of Counseling Psychology, 1*, 9–16.

Lerner, R. M., & Steinberg, L. (Eds.). (2009). *Handbook of adolescent psychology, individual basis of adolescent development: Volume 1*. Hoboken, NJ: John Wiley & Sons.

Lev, A. I. (2004). *Transgender emergence: Therapeutic guidelines for working with gender-variant people and their families.* New York, NY: Haworth Clinical Practice.

Martin, C. L., & Ruble, D. N. (2010). Patterns of gender development. *Annual Review of Psychology, 61,* 353–381. http://dx.doi.org/10.1146/annurev.psych.093008.100511

Pleak, R. R. (1999). Ethical issues in diagnosing and treating gender-dysphoric children and adolescents. In M. Rottnek (Ed.), *Sissies and tomboys: Gender nonconformity and homosexual childhood* (pp. 34–51). New York, NY: New York University Press.

Rapier, D. (2015). *Redefining trans* persistence and desistence toward a more inclusive account of trans* populations.* (Unpublished doctoral dissertation). Pacific University, Forest Grove, OR.

Singh, A. A., & Jackson, K. (2012). Queer and transgender youth: Education and liberation in our schools. In T. Quinn & E. R. Meiners (Eds.), *Sexualities in education: A reader* (pp. 175–186). New York, NY: Peter Lang.

Spack, N. P., Edwards-Leeper, L., Feldman, H. A., Leibowitz, S., Mandel, F., Diamond, D. A., & Vance, S. R. (2012). Children and adolescents with gender identity disorder referred to a pediatric medical center. *Pediatrics, 129,* 418–425. http://dx.doi.org/10.1542/peds.2011-0907

Steensma, T. D., Biemond, R., de Boer, F., & Cohen-Kettenis, P. T. (2011). Desisting and persisting gender dysphoria after childhood: A qualitative follow-up study. *Clinical Child Psychology and Psychiatry, 16,* 499–516. http://dx.doi.org/10.1177/1359104510378303

Steensma, T. D., Kreukels, B. P. C., de Vries, A. L. C., & Cohen-Kettenis, P. T. (2013). Gender identity development in adolescence. *Hormones and Behavior, 64,* 288–297.

Steensma, T. D., McGuire, J. K., Kreukels, B. P., Beekman, A. J., & Cohen-Kettenis, P. T. (2013). Factors associated with desistence and persistence of childhood gender dysphoria: A quantitative follow-up study. *Journal of the American Academy of Child & Adolescent Psychiatry, 52,* 582–590. http://dx.doi.org/10.1016/j.jaac.2013.03.016

Steinberg, L. (2009). Should the science of adolescent brain development inform public policy? *American Psychologist, 64,* 739–750. http://dx.doi.org/10.1037/0003-066X.64.8.739

Tishelman, A. C., Kaufman, R., Edwards-Leeper, L., Mandel, F. H., Shumer, D. E., & Spack, N. P. (2015). Serving transgender youth: Challenges, dilemmas, and clinical examples. *Professional Psychology: Research and Practice, 46,* 37–45. http://dx.doi.org/10.1037/a0037490

Wakefield, J. C. (1997). When is development disordered? Developmental psychopathology and the harmful dysfunction analysis of mental disorder. *Development and Psychopathology, 9,* 269–290. http://dx.doi.org/10.1017/S0954579497002058

Wallien, M. S., & Cohen-Kettenis, P. T. (2008). Psychosexual outcome of gender-dysphoric children. *Journal of the American Academy of Child & Adolescent Psychiatry, 47*, 1413–1423. http://dx.doi.org/10.1097/CHI.0b013e31818956b9

Zucker, K. J., Wood, H., Singh, D., & Bradley, S. J. (2012). A developmental, biopsychosocial model for the treatment of children with gender identity disorder. *Journal of Homosexuality, 59*, 369–397. http://dx.doi.org/10.1080/00918369.2012.653309

Sand C. Chang, Jessie R. Cohen, and Anneliese A. Singh

Working With TGNC Primary Caregivers and Family Concerns Across the Lifespan

6

P arenting and family building can take on a variety of forms within the transgender and gender nonconforming (TGNC) community (Polly & Polly, 2014). In this chapter, we use the term *primary caregiver* as an umbrella term for any person playing a central role in the upbringing of a child, adolescent, or young adult. Primary caregivers may include biologically related, adoptive, or foster parents, as well as legal guardians, extended family, and other significant adults in a young person's life. Survey research suggested that 38% of TGNC people are parents as compared with 64% in the general public (Grant et al., 2011). In addition, a survey of TGNC caregivers in Canada reported that 66% of TGNC parents were male-to-female and over 73% were over 35 years old at the time of the survey (Pyne, Bauer, & Bradley, 2015). It can be argued that similar to studies finding no difference in a child's adjustment in the home of lesbian, gay, and bisexual (LGB) caregivers (Goldberg, 2010; Lofquist, 2011), a caregiver's TGNC status may not have a significant impact on the emotional health

http://dx.doi.org/10.1037/14957-007
Affirmative Counseling and Psychological Practice With Transgender and Gender Nonconforming Clients, A. A. Singh and l. m. dickey (Editors)

of a child (White & Ettner, 2004, 2007). Because much of the academic literature on TGNC primary caregivers is centered on TGNC people and families in Western cultures, it is important for mental health providers (MHPs) to understand that family building may vary significantly according to culture and context. In this chapter, we address concerns related to counseling TGNC people who play or wish to play a role in raising a young person. Although this chapter centers on the experiences of TGNC people who choose to disclose their TGNC status in some context, MHPs should be aware that some caregivers opt not to disclose TGNC status and choose to form social communities primarily with heterosexual, cisgender people. Concerns regarding reproductive options and navigating the associated health care systems are also discussed, as well as TGNC people's engagement in family building through fostering or adoption.

General TGNC Primary Caregiver Concerns

In some respects, TGNC primary caregivers may have experiences similar to those of cisgender primary caregivers in navigating normative developmental concerns (Lev, 2004). Examples of this may include introducing the birth of a younger sibling or dealing with separation or divorce. TGNC people may also have unique concerns related to becoming primary caregivers. The ways in which TGNC people approach concerns related to caregiving may vary on the basis of a number of factors, as described in the following sections.

GENDER IDENTITY AND/OR EXPRESSION

Gender identity and/or expression is often a central factor in determining the family building options that TGNC people can access. Some means of family building may or may not feel congruent with a person's gender identity. For example, a TGNC woman may choose to bank sperm to preserve the option of having genetically related offspring, whereas another may not feel comfortable contributing her own genetic material because she associates it with parts of her body that do not feel congruent with her gender identity. Some TGNC men feel that undergoing pregnancy is counter to a masculine gender expression, whereas others embrace pregnancy as a viable option that does not create gender role conflict. MHPs can explore which possibilities feel in line with gender identity and/or expression for TGNC people considering family building.

CULTURAL BACKGROUND

There are different cultural norms for the roles that primary caregivers take in relationship to children or other caregivers (e.g., division of labor by gender with respect to child care). MHPs can help TGNC people identify the prescribed gender roles they were socialized with and to what extent an endorsement (or rejection) of these norms influences their decision-making process regarding primary caregiver roles or behaviors. For clients with nonbinary gender identities, MHPs can aid in exploring parental roles that feel authentic with respect to clients' cultural or gender identity. Cultural background may also shape norms with respect to how single or solo parenting and collective caregiving may occur in particular clients' given culture.

DESIRED METHOD OF BECOMING A PRIMARY CAREGIVER

As with cisgender people, there are differences in the ways in which TGNC people's desire to become primary caregivers. In some cases, this may involve assisted reproductive techniques. Others may prefer fostering or adoption. Some may want to parent with a partner, whereas others may prefer to be solo parents.

TIMING OF DISCLOSURE OF TGNC IDENTITY

A family's process of navigating a TGNC member's transition may vary widely based on the timing of becoming a primary caregiver in relation to TGNC identification or disclosure. In one urban clinic providing services for TGNC people between 1989 and 1997, about 30% of clients were parents (Valentine, 1998). A TGNC person who has identified as one parental role (a "father") to a child from birth will often face concurrent gender transition and family role transition (e.g., now identifying as another parental role [a "mother"]). However, a TGNC person who already lives in their affirmed identity preceding a child's birth may not have to shift in parental role but may have to balance reproductive timing and method with the trajectory and timing of medical transition options. The age or developmental stage of children may affect whether and how a TGNC person may choose to disclose TGNC status or experience to children. Some TGNC primary caregivers may wait to transition out of concern that it will harm their children (Lev, 2004).

SOCIOECONOMIC CONCERNS

Not all TGNC people desire to become primary caregivers, and those who do may not be able to access the necessary resources to achieve this goal (e.g., health care). Medical and legal costs related to all methods (e.g., reproduction, adoption) can be prohibitive. Because of workplace discrimination, many TGNC people face economic conditions that make supporting an existing child challenging and the prospect of having a child unfeasible. Being mindful of the socioeconomic barriers that many TGNC people face, MHPs can aid them in exploring feelings about the options available to them.

LANGUAGE AND GENDER CREATIVITY

TGNC people often find ways to creatively express themselves with regard to gender identity and gender role. TGNC primary caregivers who do not feel that labels such as *mother* or *father* fit for them may come up with alternatives that are more inclusive of their identities. For example, TGNC primary caregivers may come up with hybrid terms like *ma-pa* (combining *mama* and *papa*), abbreviations like *par* (short for *parent*), or other terms that are based in ethnic heritage or another language. MHPs can support TGNC people in finding language that feels affirming and authentic with regard to gender identity, gender role, and their specific relationships to the children in their lives.

TGNC Primary Caregivers of Young Children

Parenting for infants, latency, and preteenage children (ages 0–12 years) is focused in development, attachment, and schooling (Landry, Smith, & Swank, 2006; Waters & Cummings, 2000). Children form their sense of safety and security in the world and learn to see their caregiver not only as a resource but also a source of survival (Main, 2000). The stronger the TGNC caregiver's support system, the better all family members will do in navigating family life (Gates, 2013; Hopkins, Gouze, & Lavigne, 2013). MHPs can aid TGNC caregivers in increasing support and reducing the sense of isolation that can occur when caring for an infant along with the additional stressors that TGNC people face.

MHPs should consider the developmental stages of all family members when working with TGNC primary caregivers of young children. Although children often have more flexible notions about gender than adults (Hill & Lynch, 1983), children at different stages may experience upset about a caregiver's disclosure, gender status, or transition. Elementary age children, for example, may have a range of emotional reactions—from becoming angry with the caregiver to feeling confusion or fear. Younger children often seek out facts, reassurance, and clarity in simple, concrete terms (Fischer, 1980). If a child is at a concrete language stage, for example, they might have more trouble holding the nuance and sophistication of a nonbinary gender identity. A more mature child may hold the developmental capacity for complex language and ideas yet may be embarking on their own identity questions. TGNC caregivers may need help understanding the emotional and psychological life of a child, as well as the cognitive and brain development. MHPs can assess how to best support family members through various stages of grief and social and medical transitions in extended family, school, and community settings and determine whether referrals for family or couples counseling are necessary. Counseling interventions should take into account the developmental stages of each family member, facilitating communication, providing psychoeducation, and connecting families to TGNC-affirmative community resources.

Children who are accepting of their TGNC primary caregiver's identity may not be aware of anti-TGNC prejudice, and this may influence whether and how they choose to talk to their peers about their primary caregiver being TGNC. MHPs can assist TGNC primary caregivers in developing age-appropriate ways to have discussions with their children and determine when and to whom they want to disclose TGNC status to as a family. One useful framework may be to help children understand the difference between what is a secret (often connected with shame) and what is private (appropriate boundaries; Tando, 2015). TGNC primary caregivers may also want to work with teachers or school settings to support their children in navigating these dynamics with peers. Because school-age children are often connected to many communities outside the primary home through schools, camps, sports, or other recreational activities, TGNC caregivers may be more active and visible in the community than those who are not caregivers. They may have to enter spaces for their children that they may otherwise avoid. Family events such as back-to-school nights, play dates, and birthday parties may require discussion at home prior to the event to address out how all family members feel about disclosure. As is true with any issue concerning children, the recommendation is that children have counseling if and when they are distressed or symptomatic—which may or may not be the case related to having a TGNC caregiver. If issues arise within the family as a result of the TGNC caregiver's status, family counseling may be a useful way to support the entire family system.

CASE VIGNETTE

Lilia is a lesbian-identified, Latina, TGNC woman. She has two children, ages 4 and 6, who have known her as "Papi" and a 1-year-old child conceived in her current relationship and birthed by her cisgender female partner, Sonia. Lilia and Sonia have access to some social support through close chosen family members and friends they met through a birthing class; however, they do not know other TGNC parents. Lilia's family of origin invites her to family parties, but they insist on calling her by her birth-assigned name, which is a barrier to Lilia and Sonia feeling comfortable with their involvement with the children. Despite these challenges, the family structure Lilia and Sonia have developed offers love and consistency.

Lilia was terminated from her job as a radiation tech after she transitioned 3 years ago, as her boss told her she "made patients uncomfortable." Her two older children's birth mother has been somewhat supportive yet still wants Lilia to be "a man" for their 6-year-old son, who often asks to see Lilia's penis and wants to talk about bodies. He says things like, "Girls don't have a penis and you do. You are not a girl, Papi. You got confused." Lilia's 4-year-old daughter likes to play dress up in traditionally feminine clothing. This can, at times, be triggering for Lilia in bringing up memories of being punished for trying to dress up in girls' clothes. As her children reach different developmental milestones, which include their own gender identification and expression, Lilia must navigate her own feelings related to reaching these milestones herself prior to transition to her affirmed gender. Lilia and Sonia must decide how to integrate a baby into their lesbian relationship, where the older children were born in a different-gender parental dyad. In addition to navigating issues related to gender and sexual orientation, the family is newly experiencing not only racism but also sexism as the two primary caregivers are women of color.

In this example, Lilia first sought help through individual counseling. However, the MHP recognized that there were many issues to be addressed in the family system. Here, Lilia was able to privately address her employment discrimination, discrimination from her family of origin, and other needs while simultaneously focusing on her role as caregiver within the family counseling. Then, the MHP focused on assisting Lilia and Sonia in communicating to their children about Lilia's transition and how to navigate having a new child in the family. The MHP also provided referrals to a TGNC parent support group. In this example, Lilia and Sonia's family were best served by an MHP who was well trained in working with TGNC parents and skilled in working with family systems, in addition to being well versed in the multicultural (e.g., intersection of gender and racial/ethnic identities) and social justice concerns (e.g., racism, sexism) this family may face.

TGNC Primary Caregivers of Adolescents

Some TGNC primary caregivers may have concerns specific to raising adolescents. Issues of timing of TGNC disclosure and consideration of the developmental level of the adolescent involved are important as children move through the ages of 13 to 24. In addition, because adolescence is a time of great physical and emotional change (Prout & Fedewa, 2015), TGNC parents should be prepared for a range of reactions and understandings that their adolescent may have to their TGNC identity (Polly & Polly, 2014). A major developmental milestone for adolescents in many cultures includes forming a discrete identity as an individual (Meeus, Iedema, Maassen, & Engels, 2005). Therefore, adolescents may feel attached and comfortable with their parents; however, they may also challenge and defy parental boundaries as they explore their own individual identity. Some adolescents may have had extensive exposure to and education about TGNC people, whereas other adolescents may have minimal or incorrect information about TGNC people (Haines, Ajayi, & Boyd, 2014).

A major focus of working with TGNC primary caregivers who are parenting adolescents is to ensure they have education and information on what being an adolescent entails. For example, as adolescents develop their own identities, there is often conflict within the family that can develop. Within Western societies, some level of discord is developmentally appropriate and necessary for successful individuation. However, TGNC primary caregivers may not realize the challenges that adolescents face, for two reasons. First, it typically has been a long time since the TGNC primary caregiver was an adolescent. Second, TGNC primary caregivers—especially those early in their TGNC identity development—are often immersed in self-reflection, due not only to their TGNC identity development but also to needing to navigate societal transnegativity. This focus on the self may occur in tandem with their adolescent moving through a developmental stage of self-reference and learning about the world. With the TGNC primary caregiver and adolescent in parallel developmental stages, clashes can develop between them, making it challenging to understand one another. Family counseling can be a helpful way to address these challenges, as well as working with the TGNC primary caregiver to understand the pressures that their adolescent may be experiencing moving through this developmental stage. The following case vignette explores counseling concerns related to being a TGNC primary caregiver.

CASE VIGNETTE

Minh, an Asian American, TGNC male primary caregiver presented for counseling, describing conflict with his 15-year-old daughter. In his first session, Minh shared that his frustration with his daughter centers on her recent "lack of respect" for him and members of her extended family. He reported that a shift occurred 3 months ago, shortly after he and his husband disclosed his TGNC identity to her. In working with Minh, the MHP explored Minh's cultural background related to his presenting concern, in addition to his TGNC identity development. Minh shared that he is an immigrant from Vietnam and that he helped his mother and brother immigrate to the United States 10 years ago. Minh's mother and brother live in the house with him, his husband, and their daughter. Minh shared that it was most difficult to disclose his TGNC identity to his mother and brother over 20 years ago, and that he expected his daughter to be "OK with it" because she has TGNC peers at her high school. In working with Minh, the MHP explored how cultural values are embedded in his approach to caregiving, while also exploring the relationship between his identity as a TGNC person and as a primary caregiver. In doing so, the MHP shared information about the developmental stage of adolescence and how certain behaviors his daughter is exhibiting may be considered normative for identity individuation in the United States. The MHP then collaboratively identified communication strategies Minh may use with his daughter and address her bicultural experience as an adolescent. The MHP also assessed how much TGNC knowledge Minh's daughter had, the degree of grief and change the daughter and family may be experiencing related to Minh's TGNC identity disclosure, and unmet needs Minh may have about his TGNC identity. The MHP explored the possibility of family counseling and considered referrals to other MHPs with knowledge of TGNC identity and family systems and dynamics.

TGNC Primary Caregivers of Adult Children

Although it may be common for TGNC primary caregivers to experience stress and family rejection when they share their TGNC identity with their families, disclosure to adult children can be especially challenging. Much of this stress may be related to the level of information, exposure, and knowledge children in young adulthood, middle adulthood, or late adulthood may have about the TGNC communities. Media coverage of TGNC people has increased in the 2010s; therefore, many children may have some knowledge about what being TGNC means. However, this media coverage is often stereotyped and does not include TGNC family information, especially for TGNC families of color. These limited representations may lead to stress for adult children as they experience their TGNC primary caregiver's disclosure process.

Veldorale-Griffin (2014) found that TGNC primary caregivers and their adult children experienced stress in the disclosure process; yet, both groups had different needs in terms of managing this stress. TGNC primary caregivers described stress regarding their fear of rejection from their adult children, whereas their adult children described experiencing stress regarding the challenge they had in viewing their TGNC primary caregiver in a different gender and feeling they were an intermediary between family relationships after the TGNC disclosure. Adult children also described stress regarding being harassed for having a TGNC primary caregiver. Counseling TGNC parents of adult children, therefore, should also account for a variety of reactions from adult children and address any fears of familial rejection. Because adult children may feel torn between family members who have differing responses to the TGNC identity disclosure, counseling can also address how to develop empathy in these situations. This empathy can help TGNC primary caregivers of adult children to avoid withdrawing from their parenting role and to support their adult children in moving through the disclosure process in a healthy manner. TGNC-affirming support groups, family counseling, and online resources can be shared with TGNC primary caregivers of adult children (Polly & Polly, 2014). Because custody issues are no longer a concern for TGNC parents of adult children, it can be helpful to remind both parties that they have the ability to make their own decisions. The following case vignette explores being a caregiver for a TGNC person in later adulthood.

CASE VIGNETTE

Melanie is a 64-year-old, White, TGNC woman who has been in counseling for a year to explore her TGNC identity. She had disclosed her TGNC identity to her closest friends and work colleagues; however, she expressed fear in sharing her TGNC identity with her two sons (44 and 42 years old), as she believed that they would reject her. In exploring this potential rejection, the MHP used role-play techniques to identify the range of reactions Melanie's sons could have. Melanie began to feel some hope that rejection was not the only option for her sons. The MHP collaboratively explored what Melanie considered her strengths in her communication skills with her sons and her typical role in their lives. Melanie shared that she had sought to be an honest, truthful, and hands-on parent. The MHP encouraged her to use these skills as she rehearsed interacting with her sons in role-play situations. Melanie was also encouraged to explore support networks and TGNC-affirming resources she may draw on during the disclosure process. The MHP encouraged Melanie to use TGNC parent-affirming online resources as well as a local TGNC parent support group to further access support and empowerment. For Melanie, watching media depictions of TGNC parents and children dealing with similar concerns validated her experience and feelings.

TGNC Reproductive Considerations

The topic of pursuing reproduction as a means of becoming a primary caregiver is multifaceted. This section focuses on reproductive approaches for TGNC people who have the goal of becoming primary caregivers through pregnancy and/or assisted reproduction techniques, either as solo parents or with partners. Before discussing the different ways in which this may occur, it is important to recognize, historically, and throughout the world, how the requirements imposed on TGNC people seeking gender-affirming medical services have influenced reproduction and family building options, and other components influencing this process.

HISTORICAL AND GLOBAL CONSIDERATIONS

In the university gender clinics of the 1960s and 1970s, strict medical criteria were used to determine whether a TGNC person was an appropriate candidate for medical transition (Benjamin, 1966). One requirement was that existing marriages (i.e., marriages considered heterosexual with respect to sex assigned at birth) be dissolved to access medical interventions such as hormones or surgery (Denny, 2002). Therefore, for some TGNC people, pursuing medical transition to affirm their authentic gender identity was in direct opposition with the option of contributing genetic material to unassisted reproduction with their spouses prior to transition. Though this requirement no longer exists, and TGNC people are increasingly supported in their desires to engage in reproduction, there are other potential barriers that TGNC people may face. In many countries, TGNC people are still required to be sterilized to medically transition or be legally recognized in their affirmed gender (European Commission Directorate-General for Justice, 2012; European Parliament, Directorate General for Internal Policies, 2010; World Health Organization, 2014). Despite the World Professional Association for Transgender Health's (WPATH, 2015) statement urging governments to remove forced sterilization requirements for TGNC people "regardless of reproductive capacity," historical and present barriers such as these may affect the options TGNC people feel are available to them.

GENDER IDENTITY AND/OR EXPRESSION AND REPRODUCTIVE CONCERNS

TGNC people vary widely in terms of desires to build families or engage in reproduction. In a 2012 survey of 50 trans men, over half reported a desire to have children, and over a third reported that they would have considered freezing gametes (i.e., eggs) if the option had been available to them (Wierckx et al., 2012). In another survey of TGNC women, equal numbers reported wanting and not wanting children (De Sutter, Kira, Verschoor, & Hotimsky, 2002). Beliefs and value systems related to gender socialization may play a part in the available options for different individuals. Some TGNC people may feel grief at not being able to contribute genetic material in a way that is in line with their authentic gender.

PRETRANSITION PRESERVATION OF GAMETES

The WPATH "Standards of Care for the Health of Transsexual, Transgender, and Gender Nonconforming People" (Coleman et al., 2012) recommends that health care providers discuss reproductive concerns before initiating gender-affirming medical interventions. MHPs can aid in the exploration of questions regarding having children and making decisions based on informed consent. It is important that TGNC people know the risks and benefits of the medical procedures they may choose with regard to transition and how these choices could impact future reproductive options. Hormone therapy can limit the reproductive options available to TGNC people (Coleman et al., 2012). For TGNC people taking testosterone, ovulation will be suppressed and pregnancy may not be possible. This effect may be reversed if hormone therapy is discontinued and hormones return to a balance considered normal in typical females. However, there are TGNC people who have become pregnant while taking testosterone, and thus it should not be used as a means of birth control (Gorton & Grubb, 2014). For TGNC people taking feminizing hormones (e.g., estrogen), there is evidence of decreased sperm production and decreased erectile function, and this could prevent pregnancy from occurring as well (Hembree et al., 2009; Mueller, Kiesewetter, Binder, Beckmann, & Dittrich, 2007). Some TGNC people consider delaying or stopping hormone therapy to preserve gametes (i.e., cryopreservation of eggs or sperm). The cryopreservation of embryos leads to higher success rates for pregnancy than the cryopreservation of eggs (Noyes, Boldt, & Nagy, 2010), but this may be more costly depending on access to a sperm (e.g., donor, partner) at the time of cryopreservation. Both procedures are invasive, costly, require sedation, and successful results are not guaranteed. On the other hand, if a TGNC person stops feminizing hormones until sperm reaches viable levels, sperm can be frozen indefinitely and pregnancies may occur even after many years (Gorton & Grubb, 2014). The main costs with this procedure are associated with storage. For all of these procedures, the cost of future assisted reproductive techniques (e.g., in vitro fertilization), including the use of a surrogate or gestational carrier if needed, should also be factored in.

TGNC PREGNANCY AND BIRTH

Some transmasculine and gender-nonbinary people (i.e., people with ovaries) may want to get pregnant and give birth a child. Pregnancy is made possible by the cessation of testosterone therapy until former hormone levels are reached, which could take weeks to months for testosterone injections or a matter of days for topical testosterone (Gorton & Grubb, 2014). Some transmasculine people may be interested in chest feeding, and they may be able to find online communities and resources to learn more about this (Baker, n.d.; Milk Junkies, 2012). Transmasculine people who get pregnant may need support in navigating societal reactions and the possible forced disclosure of being TGNC.

INTERACTIONS WITH MEDICAL PROVIDERS

Regardless of the means by which a TGNC person builds a family or prepares to become a primary caregiver, they will want their doctors, nurses, midwives, and other health professionals to display cultural competency and to be sensitive to their identities and concerns. This includes the use of affirming language that respects self-identification and self-determination (Smith, Shin, & Officer, 2012), such as the use of correct pronouns and affirming terms to describe gender identities and body parts. TGNC people are encouraged to talk to their medical providers about limits in electronic medical records systems that may affect their utilization of services.

Adoption and Fostering

Some TGNC people arrive at primary caregiving through adoptive or foster care. Research and data here are limited (Mallon, 2006); for instance, the majority of articles about LGBTQ caregivers offering or being considered for foster or adoptive care refer to LGB caregivers and do not directly discuss TGNC caregivers (Brooks & Goldberg, 2001; Gates, 2013; Hicks, 2013). Therefore, this section draws from the literature with LGB primary caregivers, which is then adapted to apply to TGNC parents. Although some families pursue adoption through private agencies or internationally, this section focuses on domestic foster care and adoption with an emphasis on children coming from the child welfare system. MHPs can help TGNC prospective primary caregivers consider such factors as motivation for adoption, level of need children arrive with (e.g., physical, developmental, or emotional disability, among other things), age of children on entering the child welfare system, cultural concerns (e.g., transracial adoption), and shared parenting (e.g., biological and foster or adoptive efforts to continue to care for children as a team; Mallon, 2006). MHPs can also aid in considerations of attachment, trauma, kinship and biological family connection, and the high needs of children and youth often exposed to negligent and abusive conditions (Berrick, 1998). Studies looking at children's adjustment and prognosis over time within LGBT families are favorable, citing no differences in those children's mental health status or overall happiness (Wainright, Russell, & Patterson, 2004). If adverse outcomes are determined in LGBT homes, it is crucial to consider the preexisting background risks of the child and the tendency for LGBTQ parents to adopt higher needs children rather than assume it is because of family status of having a LGBT caregiver (Lavner, Waterman, & Peplau, 2012). A 2011 report of private adoption agencies cited that 61% of private agencies have not placed children with lesbian or gay families and 40% would not even accept an application from these families (Movement Advancement Project, Family Equality Council, & Center for American Progress, 2011). These findings have implications for TGNC primary caregivers and the bias they may face when seeking to adopt a child. MHPs can help prospective TGNC caregivers address feelings that come up in navigating systemic bias.

The data available regarding TGNC women and more specifically, TGNC women of color, remind us that growing families with caregivers that have traditionally lacked acceptance need that much more support. For many TGNC women, their first experience of being rejected or experiencing violence occurred within their family of origin homes (Koken, Bimbi, & Parsons, 2009). In thinking of caregivers interested in adoption and foster care, rates of attachment disruption and, in turn, posttraumatic stress disorder (PTSD) evidenced in the children are high. Over 20% of foster care alumni report experiencing PTSD (Pecora et al., 2005). A TGNC caregiver may understand deeply what the experience of family disruption or rejection can be like. The capacity to empathize in this way can serve as a protective factor for many children. Additionally, caregivers who have experienced trauma or rejection need adequate support to offer a corrective experience for their children, as children's self-image can be greatly affected by how they view their parents (Portney, 2003). MHPs versed in family systems theory and attachment-based approaches can assist TGNC caregivers in creating a sound and adequate support system.

Chapter Summary

In this chapter, we discussed important considerations for MHPs working with TGNC people engaged in family building and primary caregiving, including cultural backgrounds and values and the everyday experiences TGNC primary caregivers may have as they care for children across the lifespan. Because research in TGNC parenting is still in its early stages, especially with regard to TGNC people with nonbinary identities, MHPs working with TGNC caregivers and families can benefit from ongoing consultation and supervision, as well as professional development in this area.

References

Baker, M. (n.d.). *Pregnancy, birthing & chestfeeding: An illustrated guidebook*. Retrieved from http://issuu.com/miyukibaker/docs/pregnancy

Benjamin, H. (1966). *The transsexual phenomenon*. New York, NY: Warner.

Berrick, J. D. (1998). When children cannot remain home: Foster family care and kinship care. *The Future of Children, 8*, 72–87. http://dx.doi.org/10.2307/1602629

Brooks, D., & Goldberg, S. (2001). Gay and lesbian adoptive and foster care placements: Can they meet the needs of waiting children? *Social Work, 46*, 147–157. http://dx.doi.org/10.1093/sw/46.2.147

Coleman, E., Bockting, W., Botzer, M., Cohen-Kettenis, P., DeCuypere, G., Feldman, J., . . . Zucker, K. (2012). Standards of care for the health of transsexual, transgender, and gender-nonconforming people, 7th version. *International Journal of Transgenderism, 13*, 165–232. http://dx.doi.org/10.1080/15532739.2011.700873

De Sutter, P., Kira, K., Verschoor, A., & Hotimsky, A. (2002). The desire to have children and the preservation of fertility in transsexual women: A survey. *International Journal of Transgenderism, 6*, 215–221.

Denny, D. (2002). The politics of diagnosis and a diagnosis of politics: How the university-affiliated gender clinics failed to meet the needs of transsexual people. *Transgender Tapestry, 98*, 17–27.

European Commission Directorate-General for Justice. (2012). *Trans and intersex people—discrimination on the grounds of sex, gender identity, and gender expression*. Retrieved from http://www.teni.ie/attachments/35bf473d-1459-4baa-8f55-56f80cfe858a.PDF

European Parliament, Directorate General for Internal Policies. (2010). *Transgender persons' rights in the EU member states*. Retrieved from http://www.lgbt-ep.eu/wp-content/uploads/2010/07/NOTE-20100601-PE425.621-Transgender-Persons-Rights-in-the-EU-Member-States.pdf

Fischer, K. W. (1980). A theory of cognitive development: The control and construction of hierarchies of skills. *Psychological Review, 87*, 477–531. http://dx.doi.org/10.1037/0033-295X.87.6.477

Gates, G. J. (2013). *LGBT parenting in the United States*. Retrieved from http://escholarship.org/uc/item/9xs6g8xx

Goldberg, A. (2010). Children of lesbian and gay parents: Adjustment and experiences. In A. Goldberg (Ed.), *Lesbian and gay parents and their children: Research on the family life cycle* (pp. 125–156). Washington, DC: American Psychological Association. http://dx.doi.org/10.1037/12055-005

Gorton, N., & Grubb, H. M. (2014). General, sexual, and reproductive health. In L. Erickson-Schroth (Ed.), *Trans bodies, trans selves* (pp. 390–405). New York, NY: Oxford University Press.

Grant, J. M., Mottet, L. A., Tanis, J., Harrison, J., Herman, J. L., & Keisling, M. (2011). *Injustice at every turn: A report of the national transgender discrimination survey.* Washington, DC: National Center for Transgender Equality and National Gay and Lesbian Task Force.

Haines, B. A., Ajayi, A. A., & Boyd, H. (2014). Making trans parents visible: Intersectionality of trans and parenting identities. *Feminism & Psychology, 24,* 238–247. http://dx.doi.org/10.1177/0959353514526219

Hembree, W. C., Cohen-Kettenis, P., Delemarre-van de Waal, H. A., Gooren, L. J., Meyer, W. J., III, Spack, N. P., . . . Montori, V. M., & the Endocrine Society. (2009). Endocrine treatment of transsexual persons: An Endocrine Society clinical practice guideline. *The Journal of Clinical Endocrinology and Metabolism, 94,* 3132–3154. http://dx.doi.org/10.1210/jc.2009-0345

Hicks, S. (2013). Lesbian, gay, bisexual, and transgender parents and the question of gender. In A. E. Goldberg & K. R. Allen (Eds.), *LGBT-parent families* (pp. 149–162). New York, NY: Springer. http://dx.doi.org/10.1007/978-1-4614-4556-2_10

Hill, J. P., & Lynch, M. E. (1983). The intensification of gender-related role expectations during early adolescence. In J. Brooks-Gunn & A. Petersen (Eds.), *Girls at puberty: Biological and psychosocial perspectives* (pp. 201–228). New York, NY: Plenum. http://dx.doi.org/10.1007/978-1-4899-0354-9_10

Hopkins, J., Gouze, K. R., & Lavigne, J. V. (2013). Direct and indirect effects of contextual factors, caregiver depression, and parenting on attachment security in preschoolers. *Attachment & Human Development, 15,* 155–173. http://dx.doi.org/10.1080/14616734.2013.750702

Koken, J. A., Bimbi, D. S., & Parsons, J. T. (2009). Experiences of familial acceptance–rejection among transwomen of color. *Journal of Family Psychology, 23,* 853–860. http://dx.doi.org/10.1037/a0017198

Landry, S. H., Smith, K. E., & Swank, P. R. (2006). Responsive parenting: Establishing early foundations for social, communication, and independent problem-solving skills. *Developmental Psychology, 42,* 627–642. http://dx.doi.org/10.1037/0012-1649.42.4.627

Lavner, J. A., Waterman, J., & Peplau, L. A. (2012). Can gay and lesbian parents promote healthy development in high-risk children adopted from foster care? *American Journal of Orthopsychiatry, 82,* 465–472. http://dx.doi.org/10.1111/j.1939-0025.2012.01176.x

Lev, A. I. (2004). *Transgender emergence: Therapeutic guidelines for working with gender-variant people and their families.* New York, NY: Haworth Clinical Practice.

Lofquist, D. (2011). *Same-sex couple households: American Community Survey briefs.* Retrieved from http://www.census.gov/prod/2011pubs/acsbr10-03.pdf

Main, M. (2000). The organized categories of infant, child, and adult attachment: Flexible vs. inflexible attention under attachment-related stress. *Journal of the American Psychoanalytic Association, 48,* 1055–1096. http://dx.doi.org/10.1177/00030651000480041801

Mallon, G. P. (2006). *Lesbian and gay foster and adoptive parents: Recruiting, assessing, and supporting an untapped resource for children and youth.* Washington, DC: Child Welfare League of America.

Meeus, W., Iedema, J., Maassen, G., & Engels, R. (2005). Separation-individuation revisited: On the interplay of parent-adolescent relations, identity and emotional adjustment in adolescence. *Journal of Adolescence, 28,* 89–106. http://dx.doi.org/10.1016/j.adolescence.2004.07.003

Milk Junkies. (2012). *Tips for transgender breastfeeders and their lactation educators.* Retrieved from http://www.milkjunkies.net/2012/03/tips-for-transgender-breastfeeders-and.html

Movement Advancement Project, Family Equality Council, & Center for American Progress. (2011). *All children matter. How legal and social inequalities hurt LGBT families.* Retrieved from http://www.lgbtmap.org/file/all-children-matter-full-report.pdf

Mueller, A., Kiesewetter, F., Binder, H., Beckmann, M. W., & Dittrich, R. (2007). Long-term administration of testosterone undecanoate every 3 months for testosterone supplementation in female-to-male transsexuals. *The Journal of Clinical Endocrinology and Metabolism, 92,* 3470–3475. http://dx.doi.org/10.1210/jc.2007-0746

Noyes, N., Boldt, J., & Nagy, Z. P. (2010). Oocyte cryopreservation: Is it time to remove its experimental label? *Journal of Assisted Reproduction and Genetics, 27,* 69–74. http://dx.doi.org/10.1007/s10815-009-9382-y

Pecora, P. J., Kessler, R. C., Williams, J., O'Brien, K., Downs, A. C., & English, D., . . . Holmes, K. (2005). *Improving family foster care: Findings from the Northwest Foster Care Alumni Study.* Retrieved from http://www.casey.org/resources/publications/pdf/improvingfamilyfostercare_fr.pdf

Polly, K., & Polly, R. G. (2014). Parenting. In L. Erickson-Schroth (Ed.), *Trans bodies, trans selves* (pp. 390–405). New York, NY: Oxford University Press.

Portney, C. (2003). Intergenerational transmission of trauma: An introduction for the clinician. *Psychiatric Times, 20,* 1–3.

Prout, H. T., & Fedewa, A. L. (2015). Counseling and psychotherapy with children and adolescents: Historical, developmental, integrative, and effectiveness perspectives. In H. T. Prout & A. L. Fedewa (Eds.), *Counseling and psychotherapy with children and adolescents: Theory and practice for school and clinical settings* (5th ed., pp. 1–24). Hoboken, NJ: John Wiley & Sons.

Pyne, J., Bauer, G., & Bradley, K. (2015). Transphobia and other stressors impacting trans parents. *Journal of GLBT Family Studies, 11,* 107–126. http://dx.doi.org/10.1080/1550428X.2014.941127

Smith, L. C., Shin, R. Q., & Officer, L. M. (2012). Moving counseling forward on LGB and transgender issues: Speaking queerly on discourses and microaggressions. *The Counseling Psychologist, 40,* 385–408. http://dx.doi.org/10.1177/0011000011403165

Tando, D. (2015, September 8). *Private vs. secret* [Blog post]. Retrieved from http://darlenetandogenderblog.com/2015/09/08/private-vs-secret/

Valentine, D. (1998). *Gender identity project: Report on intake statistics, 1989–April, 1997.* New York, NY: Lesbian and Gay Community Services Center.

Veldorale-Griffin, A. (2014). Transgender parents and their adult children's experiences of disclosure and transition. *Journal of GLBT Family Studies, 10,* 475–501. http://dx.doi.org/10.1080/1550428X.2013.866063

Wainright, J. L., Russell, S. T., & Patterson, C. J. (2004). Psychosocial adjustment, school outcomes, and romantic relationships of adolescents with same-sex parents. *Child Development, 75,* 1886–1898. http://dx.doi.org/10.1111/j.1467-8624.2004.00823.x

Waters, E., & Cummings, E. M. (2000). A secure base from which to explore close relationships. *Child Development, 71,* 164–172. http://dx.doi.org/10.1111/1467-8624.00130

White, T., & Ettner, R. (2004). Disclosure, risks and protective factors for children whose parents are undergoing a gender transition. *Journal of Gay & Lesbian Psychotherapy, 8,* 129–147.

White, T., & Ettner, R. (2007). Adaptation and adjustment in children of transsexual parents. *European Child & Adolescent Psychiatry, 16,* 215–221. http://dx.doi.org/10.1007/s00787-006-0591-y

Wierckx, K., Van Caenegem, E., Pennings, G., Elaut, E., Dedecker, D., Van de Peer, F., . . . T'Sjoen, G. (2012). Reproductive wish in transsexual men. *Human Reproduction, 27,* 483–487. http://dx.doi.org/10.1093/humrep/der406

World Health Organization. (2014). *Eliminating forced, coercive and otherwise involuntary sterilization: An interagency statement.* Retrieved from http://www.unaids.org/sites/default/files/media_asset/201405_sterilization_en.pdf

World Professional Association for Transgender Health. (2015). *WPATH statement on legal recognition of gender identity.* Retrieved from http://tgeu.org/wp-content/uploads/2015/01/WPATH-2015-Statement-on-Gender-Identity-Recognition.pdf

lore m. dickey and Kyle L. Bower

Aging and TGNC Identities
Working With Older Adults

7

I n some ways, transgender and gender nonconforming (TGNC) older adults are no different than their younger counterparts. The age at which a person comes to realize their TGNC identity varies from one person to the next (American Psychological Association [APA], 2015). As a TGNC adult, coming out or disclosing one's gender identity can have significant challenges. However, these challenges do not mean that a person is any less TGNC than a person who came out in adolescence or childhood. Anecdotally, some older TGNC people have faced difficulties in making social or medical transitions because providers have believed that by waiting so long to come out, they were not truly TGNC.

This chapter reviews the typical concerns when counseling TGNC older adults. Issues unique to disclosing a TGNC identity later in life are discussed. Strategies for working with families and geriatric care are described. This chapter not only addresses concerns, but also discusses what should be done to create a more inclusive aging environment for TGNC

http://dx.doi.org/10.1037/14957-008

Affirmative Counseling and Psychological Practice With Transgender and Gender Nonconforming Clients, A. A. Singh and l. m. dickey (Editors)

individuals. As is true with all TGNC people, mental health providers (MHPs) should affirm a person's identity. Older adults may use the terms *elder, older adult, senior citizen,* or something else to describe their identity relative to their age. Providers are encouraged to be respectful of the ways in which a person self-identifies, and we use those self-identified terms.

Navigating TGNC Identities

Each TGNC individual has a personal journey they must navigate, and for older adults who transition later in life, their journey is of unique importance to the TGNC community. These older individuals have lived in a social climate that was much less accepting than it is today and may have experienced injustices that today's TGNC youth are protected against (Ippolito & Witten, 2014). For instance, many TGNC adults, when making a medical transition prior to the 1990s, were treated for mental illness and were encouraged to remove themselves from their social environment, which included divorce if they were married and moving to a different town, city, or even state (Kimmel, Rose, & David, 2006). Although these types of social requirements (e.g., leaving jobs and abandoning relationships) are still practiced in some places, they are much less common today.

Even though TGNC individuals are becoming more visible to the mainstream society, there remains a discrepancy between the needs of this aging population and the services to which they are entitled. A study conducted by Services and Advocacy for Gay, Lesbian, Bisexual, and Transgender Elders (SAGE; 2014) emphasized the impact of the residual fear toward discriminatory medical practices that remains evident among TGNC older adults. The study found that 65% of TGNC respondents reported feeling fearful because they believed access to health care will be limited at some point during later adulthood, and 55% expected to be denied medical coverage completely. Compounding the issue of care, nearly half of the TGNC individuals expressed concern about being a burden to their loved ones in old age (only 33% of cisgender individuals expressed feeling burdensome). If older adults experience fear of being denied care and are concerned about being a burden to their loved ones, this makes care planning more difficult (Ippolito & Witten, 2014). To begin, MHPs must take the time to learn about the older adult's life trajectory, their individual pathways, and transitions. There is a need for MHPs to take a lead role in ensuring that clinical practice with TGNC adults and older adults is respectful and compassionate. The history of gatekeeping and pathologization of TGNC people cannot be changed, but MHPs can help to ensure that the future does not repeat the past.

TGNC people of color, including older adults, may use terminology that does not fit within the gender binary and is more consistent with their cultural background (Battle & Bennett, 2005; FORGE, 2012). Providers who work with these individuals are encouraged to use terminology that is self-determined. For a more complete listing of culturally competent terms, readers are referred to Chapter 2 of this volume. For TGNC older adults, one challenge relates to end-of-life care. The combination of the barriers that TGNC people have faced over their lifetime may further complicate the decisions they need to make about care at the end of life (Kishore, 2013). It is important to assist TGNC older adults in culturally appropriate end-of-life activities. MHPs are encouraged to explore this with their clients in a way that is respectful.

Gender Role Expectations

TGNC adults have been subject to gender socialization with rigid expectations of what it means to be male or female (Burdge, 2007; Stockard, 2006). These gender role expectations influence the choices a person makes across all aspects of their life. To the extent a person is able to push the edges of what it means to be a gendered person, this may not create any internal conflict (Burdge, 2007; Stockard, 2006). However, if the expectations are especially rigid, it stands to reason that a person will experience internal conflict, if not dysphoria (Wester, McDonough, Taylor, Vogel, & White, 2010). TGNC older adults who are successful in working through the challenges with gender role expectations are more likely to thrive. Individual resilience is evident in the ways in which TGNC people manage the day-to-day challenges and microaggressions they face (Nadal, 2013; Nadal, Davidoff, Davis, & Wong, 2014; Singh & McKleroy, 2011). Community resilience is evident in the ways in which the TGNC community has built support systems and networks (Singh, Hays, & Watson, 2011). According to SAGE (2014), 40% of the lesbian, gay, bisexual, and transgender (LGBT) community relies on the Internet for information about aging. Examples of resources that are available online include the Transgender Aging Network (TAN) which is a program of FORGE (http://www.forge-forward.org). TAN offers an e-mail server for TGNC older adults and also provides technical assistance and consultation. Older adults with intersecting or marginalized identities may have additional challenges. TGNC older adults who socially and medically transitioned 25 or more years ago may have been living in stealth (i.e., not out to others as having a TGNC history). When these people are faced with decisions about health care and other end-of-life decisions, they may struggle to find TGNC-affirmative resources (Applebaum & Maddux, 2011).

TGNC older adults are less likely to report a sense of belonging and have fewer supports than other members of the LGBT community; this may be especially true for elder TGNC people of color (Auldridge, Tamar-Mattis, Kennedy, Ames, & Tobin, 2012). In addition, TGNC older adults are at greater risk for health disparities (Cook-Daniels, 2016; Makadon & Cahill, 2012). According to Fredriksen-Goldsen and colleagues (2011), older adults who identify as TGNC are more likely to experience victimization, internalized stigma, and verbal and physical abuse. This in turn puts this group at higher risk for health complications. For example, TGNC older adults have poorer physical health than their cisgender peers, and their general mental health is also compromised, as this group has the highest percentage of reported depression (48%) and anxiety (39%).

However, literature suggests that when faced with adversity, some individuals have shown extraordinary resilience (Singh & McKleroy, 2011; Witten, 2014). Resilience, "the ability to handle adversity and challenges successfully, is an important key to maintaining good physical and mental health" (Fredriksen-Goldsen et al., 2011, p. 15), can take a number of forms. Although the percentages were not as high as their cisgender peers, the majority (82%) of TGNC respondents in this study reported a positive sense of belonging to the LGBT community, adequate levels of perceived social support, and involvement in religious and/or spiritual practices, all of which reinforce feelings of resilience among those who identify as LGBT (Fredriksen-Goldsen et al., 2011). TGNC older adults are at greater risk and do not have the same level of support; however, it is important to keep in mind that this population is making strides to overcome adversity and is in the process of creating a more inclusive environment for themselves and educating others in order to benefit future older adult cohorts. MHPs are encouraged to be aware of the ways that TGNC people of color are adversely affected by discrimination and abuse. TGNC women of color are especially at risk of violence (Witten, 2009).

Coming Out Concerns With Family and Peer Groups

Coming out as a TGNC person is a lifelong process for some (APA, 2015). TGNC people need to decide when and with whom to share their TGNC history. In families and peer groups, it is important to have social support, and it is unlikely that a TGNC person will not be able to share their history. Unlike sexual orientation, most TGNC people experience a number of social or medical changes that make it difficult to remain closeted.

FAMILY

Many TGNC people face challenges in their family of origin. These range from mild tension to outright shunning. One survey reported that 43% of participants had enduring family bonds, whereas 57% had experienced significant rejection from family members (Grant et al., 2011). Rejection from one's family members can have devastating effects from homelessness, to incarceration, and even attempted or completed suicide. For older adults, family acceptance is an important factor in determining access to and utilization of health care by the TGNC individual. According to the National Center for Transgender Equality (NCTE) report,

> In the face of extensive institutional discrimination, family acceptance had a protective affect against many threats to well-being including health risks such as HIV infection and suicide. Families were more likely to remain together and provide support for TGNC family members than stereotypes suggest. (Grant et al., 2011, p. 5)

RELATIONSHIPS AND MARRIAGE

There have been mixed findings on the nature of relationship satisfaction among TGNC people (Brown, 2009; dickey, Burnes, & Singh, 2012). Relationship issues include negotiating sexual identity and can be challenging. Because TGNC people decide to present themselves as male, female, or gender nonconforming, the issue of sexual identity can become particularly complicated to the general public and for the couple themselves. Some marriages dissolve over this issue and family members pull away (Malpas, 2012). A TGNC woman may identify as a lesbian, or be perceived as a lesbian, as she is attracted to women. For people of color, these labels may not fit with their lived experience, as the terms *lesbian, gay,* and *bisexual* are often attributed to White people (Battle & Bennett, 2005).

The meaning of gender identity, as a nonbinary concept, should be negotiated between the couple, and these answers depend solely on the individuals involved. Older adults who transition later in life may have a more difficult time navigating intimate relationships because they have lived a large portion of their life assuming a certain gender identity. It can be assumed that for many older adults embarking on a later-life romantic relationship may include the negotiation of financial assets, health benefits, and relationships outside the partnership. Adding to the complexity are the evolving changes to laws and policy. For example, up until the summer of 2015, same-sex marriages were only recognized by individual states. If individuals married as a different-sex couple, their marriage was legally upheld regardless of where they lived or were married. However, if one partner transitioned, creating a same-sex union, the couple risked losing their shared benefits, as well as legal recognition of their union (Monnin-Browder, 2012). However, it is expected that these challenges to marital unions will decrease with the recent U.S. Supreme Court decision on marriage equality (*Obergefell v. Hodges*, 2015).

Currently there is no research to confirm whether or not older adults have a more difficult time than younger cohorts. As our older population increases, MHPs can expect to see more diversity, and there is a need to create a space for answers. As previously mentioned, having a social support network is necessary for the maintenance of resiliency. For older TGNC individuals who transition later in life the complications with relationships can be challenging because partners may feel betrayed on learning of the TGNC person's history of identifying as TGNC.

CHILDREN AND CUSTODY CONCERNS

One of the challenges faced by adults and older adults relates to changes in their relationship with their children. At worst, TGNC people may be at risk of losing custody of their children in an acrimonious divorce proceeding (Minter & Wald, 2012). At best, children are supportive of their parent's transition process. Research has indicated that there are no adverse consequences to children as a result of their parent's transition process (White & Ettner, 2004, 2007). Readers are encouraged to read Chapter 6, this volume, which discusses parenting.

Peer Groups

Finding peers to build a support community can be an important part of developing a support system. Depending on where a person lives, this can be challenging and limited to online connections. Depending on when a person transitioned, they may or may not be out as TGNC (known by some as being *stealth*). If a person is living as stealth, it is unlikely that they will have any connection to the TGNC community. Reasons for living as stealth vary from workplace concerns to family considerations. Before the 1990s it was common for people to live as stealth in part because the old transsexual narrative assumed that a TGNC person would make a medical transition and leave behind the life they had prior to transition (Lev, 2004). For many people, finding in-person or online support groups can be critical to understanding the kinds of resources that are available for social and medical transition (Ippolito & Witten, 2014).

In response to nonacceptance by family members, many TGNC individuals turn to their peers and develop what has become known as a *family of choice* (Giammattei & Green, 2012; Hughes & Kentlyn, 2011).

Families of choice can help to provide basic care for TGNC older adults as they face health concerns and end-of-life issues.

Intergenerational Connections

Presently there is a dearth of literature on the intergenerational inter-actions between TGNC people. However, TGNC individuals rely on close friendships when family members do not accept their transition, and it is reasonable to assume that these friendships may form between age cohorts. It could also be hypothesized that the formation of an inter-generational relationship may have unique effects on older TGNC people. Young adults are coming of age during a time of more cultural awareness and acceptance and may have acquired language that helps them express their identities most truthfully. However, their ability to live openly and embrace their self-awareness was paved by an earlier generation that was highly stigmatized and made to feel as if they were mentally ill. Although advocacy should continue to make the general population aware of the inadequacy of the gender binary, advancement around TGNC issues has occurred because older people made space for change and younger gen-erations are now utilizing the space that was created.

These unique relationships are not one-sided, but instead may be reciprocal. Older adults have valuable experiences they can share with younger cohorts as well as an acquired wisdom that may help younger adults rationalize their intense feelings and understand the long-term impact of their decisions. Younger TGNC adults may be able to help their older contemporaries become more integrated into the community after having been stealth for so many years. Older individuals may have a dif-ficult time finding a place to feel comfortable as their new selves. These are only a couple examples of how people from different age cohorts might impact each other in a positive way. More research in this area will assist in developing an understanding of the reciprocity that mem-bers of varying generations use to support one another.

Addressing Career Issues

In later life, many TGNC older adults are not faced with beginning a career, but with ending one. For some, retirement allows older adults to feel more comfortable making the transition they sought for so many years. Auldridge et al. (2012) found that 70% of TGNC older adults reported delaying their transition because of fear of being discriminated against in the work force. According to the NCTE (2015), their fear is not unfounded, as less than half of the U.S. states have nondiscrimination laws that protect gender identity and sexual orientation.

Retirement brings certain entitlements, such as Social Security and Medicare. Medicare recently expanded coverage to include more procedures that help older adults transition in later life. According to the NCTE (2014), "Medicare beneficiaries have a right to access services that are appropriate to their individual medical needs and necessary care should be provided regardless of the gender marker in one's Social Security or other records." This includes medically necessary hormone therapy under Medicare Part D, and as of 2014 medically necessary gender affirmation surgery (NCTE, 2014). Although progress is being made in recognizing the health needs and concerns regarding TGNC older adults, more can and should be done. For example, the NCTE (2014) has suggested that the gender marker should be removed from Medicare cards. This would make services more universally available and individuals would not be denied services in the case that their gender markers do not match their expressed gender. A person's gender marker can be changed through the Social Security office (NCTE, 2015), but the process can be long and may rely on outsiders to approve the change. For example, to change a person's gender on his or her Social Security card, that person must present either a signed letter from a doctor confirming the individual has undergone the necessary clinical treatment or a government-issued document reflecting the gender change, such as a passport, birth certificate, or court order.

As previously discussed, it is not always easy for TGNC individuals to find practitioners who accept their desire to transition, and when they do, they are dependent on the practitioner to approve of their gender identity. Finding providers who accept Medicare coverage is challenging for TGNC people. Exacerbating this issue is that although there are policies in effect, personnel are not always accommodating and, at times, people working for theses social services discriminate against TGNC people. To combat these prejudices, the NCTE consistently monitors federal policies and provides information to educate people on how to contest perceived maltreatment. Although advocates are working to provide more inclusive care to all people, not all health practitioners hold the same thought. Continued advocacy is needed for TGNC people to receive proper care later in life (Witten, 2009). TGNC individuals who have served their country in a branch of the military may be a need to rely on the resources that are available through the U.S. Department of Veterans Affairs (VA). The climate at VA facilities has improved greatly in recent years with the implementation of regulations that allow access to affirmative care in many VA facilities. But this access to care may not be consistent across the country, a reality that may lead some TGNC veterans to not seek care or to rely on access to hormones from Internet or other sources that are not subject to medical management. An additional concern for TGNC veterans is their risk for suicide. In the general population, the risk for suicide is higher for TGNC people (less than 3% for the general population and as high as 65% for TGNC people). However, the risk for TGNC veterans is even higher, and it has been estimated that 4,000 to 5,000 per 100,000 veterans are at risk (Blosnich et al., 2013). The following case vignette explores counseling with a TGNC older adult.

Case Vignette

Oscar is a 68-year-old American Indian. He transitioned at the age of 25 and identifies as male. At the time of his transition he was strongly encouraged to walk away from his work and family, as this would be most respectful. Oscar relocated to another part of the country and was able to find meaningful work. Until recently, he continued to live without coming out to friends and coworkers. But as he began to experience health concerns that may eventually lead to his death, he began reflecting on the nature of life and the spiritual beliefs that were a part of his upbringing in his tribal community. Having been cut off from his American Indian heritage, he was unsure about how to "make peace with his maker" in the face of his failing health. Oscar was questioning his faith and feeling a great deal of grief and loss because he did not have a community of friends from which he could draw support.

In working with Oscar, it was important to explore his spiritual belief system and help him to reconnect, as he desired, to a faith community. Equally important was the need to explore Oscar's feeling of grief and loss. Too often TGNC people assume that grief and loss may be an indication that a decision to make a transition was ill-formed. This is not necessarily the case, however. There are few reports of regret from TGNC people. Oscar should be encouraged to explore the source of his grief and loss as it was more likely to have been related to being cut off from family and friends.

Affirmative Counseling With Older Adults

TGNC older adults may present to counseling for a variety of reasons (Ippolito & Witten, 2014). Clinical concerns may or may not be related to the client's gender identity (APA, 2015). Common clinical concerns for older adults may relate to cognitive decline, which is a normal part of the aging process for most people (APA, 2014).

Another common clinical concern is grief. This may be due to the loss of friends and family members because of aging and death. It may also be related to changes that are made as a part of transition. It is a normal reaction to experience grief as a person moves through a social or medical transition. To date, there is only anecdotal information about this phenomenon. MHPs are encouraged to explore this idea with their clients in a way that allows space to discuss this important clinical concern.

MENTAL HEALTH PROVIDERS AND ADVOCACY RELATED TO GERIATRIC INSTITUTIONS

Returning to the closet is a phenomenon among older TGNC older adults who find themselves doing so out of fear of being discriminated against by formal care institutions, health aides, and even physicians (Applebaum & Maddux, 2011; Ippolito & Witten, 2014). It is difficult for TGNC individuals because their expressed gender identity is not consistent with their sex as assigned at birth. TGNC individuals are more likely to put their health at risk because of perceived fear of being discriminated against (Fredriksen-Goldsen et al., 2014; Ippolito & Witten, 2014). Because it is more difficult to cover up or hide, many TGNC older adults are fearful of not only formal care but also the health care system. In one study, 40% of participants feared accessing health services due to discrimination and their "internalized stigma" (Fredriksen-Goldsen et al., 2014). Furthermore, people who identify as a racial and/or ethnic minority access health care services even less frequently (SAGE & National Center for Transgender Equality, 2012) and are thus at higher risk for health complications. A seemingly simple, yet impactful, response would be to educate care providers on appropriate use of pronouns. Using the proper pronoun seems small, but it conveys a message of respect and acceptance. In addition, care providers should also become more aware of the perceived and experienced fear TGNC individuals possess regarding institutionalized care and work toward creating more inclusive care environments.

NEED FOR AFFIRMATIVE PROVIDERS

Although the health care industry is becoming more inclusive, much work still needs to be done to make TGNC people feel safe and supported. Discrimination and prejudice still exist, and educational resources should be made available to formal care facilities about the diverse older adult population they are serving. Without informal caregiving support from family and friends, some TGNC people are forced to rely on institutional care and are finding that they need to return to the closet to do so (Applebaum & Maddux, 2011). When working with those who identify as TGNC, MHPs are urged to adopt a life course perspective by taking into consideration the client's entire life of experiences, not just who they are in the present moment. The cumulative advantage/disadvantage concept helps to explain the rewards or challenges individuals face in old age (Crystal & Shea, 1990). This concept is helpful when trying to understand how older adults came to be the person they are today. When applied to the TGNC population, practitioners could better understand the weight of certain implications early in life and how they will affect the individual later in life. Also, there is much to learn from older adults by listening to their life course narratives. It should be conveyed to providers that for many TGNC individuals, gender is not binary. Instead, gender should be considered as a continuum (APA, 2015). This progressive thinking is a way to begin discussions with anyone about gender identity, not just those who identify as TGNC.

Chapter Summary

Clinical work with TGNC older adults can be a very enriching experience for the MHP and for the client. TGNC people have needs across the lifespan and into older adulthood. This chapter described some of the concerns including workplace issues, relationship concerns, and common clinical concerns. MHPs are encouraged to work with adult TGNC clients in an affirmative manner. Clients who are from marginalized communities (e.g., genderqueer, poverty, ethnic minorities) are more likely to experience discrimination and, as a result, have higher rates of mental health concerns. MHPs are encouraged to work with these clients to ensure their needs are met and their experiences are normalized within the context of their life.

References

American Psychological Association. (2014). Guidelines for psychological practice with older adults. *American Psychologist, 69,* 34–65. http://dx.doi.org/10.1037/a0035063

American Psychological Association. (2015). Guidelines for psychological practice with transgender and gender nonconforming people. *American Psychologist, 70,* 832–864. http://dx.doi.org/10.1037/a0039906

Applebaum, J. (Producer), & Maddux, S. (Producer & Director). (2011). *Gen silent* [Motion Picture]. United States: Interrobang! Productions, LLC.

Auldridge, A., Tamar-Mattis, A., Kennedy, S., Ames, E., & Tobin, H. J. (2012). *Improving the lives of transgender older adults: Recommendations for policy and practice.* Retrieved from http://www.lgbtagingcenter.org/resources/resource.cfm?r=520

Battle, J. J., & Bennett, N. D. A. (2005). Striving for place: Lesbian, gay, bisexual, and transgender (LGBT) people. In A. Hornsby, Jr. (Ed.), *A companion to African American history* (pp. 412–445). Malden, MA: Blackwell. http://dx.doi.org/10.1002/9780470996720.ch26

Blosnich, J. R., Brown, G. R., Shipherd, J. C., Kauth, M., Piegari, R. I., & Bossarte, R. M. (2013). Prevalence of gender identity disorder and suicide risk among transgender veterans utilizing Veterans Health Administration care. *American Journal of Public Health, 103,* e27–e32. http://dx.doi.org/10.2105/AJPH.2013.301507

Brown, N. R. (2009). "I'm in transition too": Sexual identity renegotiation in sexual-minority women's relationships with transsexual men. *International Journal of Sexual Health, 21,* 61–77. http://dx.doi.org/10.1080/19317610902720766

Burdge, B. J. (2007). Bending gender, ending gender: Theoretical foundations for social work practice with the transgender community. *Social Work, 52,* 243–250. http://dx.doi.org/10.1093/sw/52.3.243

Cook-Daniels, L. (2016). Understanding transgender elders. In D. A. Hurley & P. B. Teaster (Eds.), *Handbook of LGBT elders: An interdisciplinary approach to principles, practices, and policies* (pp. 285–308). New York, NY: Springer. http://dx.doi.org/10.1007/978-3-319-03623-6_14

Crystal, S., & Shea, D. (1990). Cumulative advantage, cumulative disadvantage, and inequality among elderly people. *The Gerontologist, 30,* 437–443. http://dx.doi.org/10.1093/geront/30.4.437

dickey, L. M., Burnes, T. R., & Singh, A. A. (2012). Sexual identity development of female-to-male transgender individuals: A Grounded Theory inquiry. *Journal of LGBT Issues in Counseling, 6,* 118–138. http://dx.doi.org/10.1080/15538605.2012.678184

FORGE. (2012). *Terms paradox.* Retrieved from http://forge-forward.org/wp-content/docs/FAQ-06-2012-terms-paradox.pdf

Fredriksen-Goldsen, K. I., Cook-Daniels, L., Kim, H. J., Erosheva, E. A., Emlet, C. A., Hoy-Ellis, C. P., . . . Muraco, A. (2014). Physical and mental health of transgender older adults: An at-risk and underserved population. *The Gerontologist, 54,* 488–500. http://dx.doi.org/10.1093/geront/gnt021

Fredriksen-Goldsen, K. I., Kim, H., Emlet, C. A., Muraco, A., Erosheva, E. A., Hoy-Ellis, C. P., & Petry, H. (2011). *The aging and health report: Disparities and resilience among lesbian, gay, bisexual, and transgender older adults.* Retrieved from http://caringandaging.org/wordpress/wp-content/uploads/2011/05/Full-Report-FINAL-11-16-11.pdf

Giammattei, S., & Green, R.-J. (2012). LGBTQ couple and family therapy. In J. J. Bigner & J. L. Wetchler (Eds.), *Handbook of LGBT-affirmative couple and family therapy* (pp. 1–22). New York, NY: Routledge.

Grant, J. M., Mottet, L., Tanis, J. E., Harrison, J., Herman, J., & Keisling, M. (2011). *Injustice at every turn: A report of the National Transgender Discrimination Survey.* Retrieved from http://transequality.org/issues/resources/national-transgender-discrimination-survey-full-report

Hughes, M., & Kentlyn, S. (2011). Older LGBT people's care networks and communities of practice: A brief note. *International Social Work, 54,* 436–444. http://dx.doi.org/10.1177/0020872810396254

Ippolito, J., & Witten, T. M. (2014). Aging. In L. Erickson-Schroth (Ed.), *Trans bodies, trans selves: A resource for the transgender community* (pp. 476–500). New York, NY: Oxford University Press.

Kimmel, D. C., Rose, T., & David, S. (2006). *Lesbian, gay, bisexual, and transgender aging: Research and clinical perspectives.* New York, NY: Columbia University Press.

Kishore, S. A. (2013). *Dying with dignity: Considerations for treating elder transgender people of color.* Retrieved from http://www.asaging.org/blog/dying-dignity-considerations-treating-elder-transgender-people-color

Lev, A. I. (2004). *Transgender emergence: Therapeutic guidelines for working with gender-variant people and their families.* New York, NY: Haworth Clinical Practice.

Makadon, H. J., & Cahill, S. (2012). *Aging in the LGBT community: Improving services and eliminating barriers to care.* Retrieved from http://www.healthandtheaging.org/wp-content/uploads/2012/05/Aging-Conference-FINAL-JW-3-13.pdf

Malpas, J. (2012). Can couples change gender? Couple therapy with transgender people and their partners. In J. J. Bigner & J. L. Wetchler (Eds.), *Handbook of LGBT-affirmative couple and family therapy* (pp. 69–85). New York, NY: Routledge.

Minter, S. P., & Wald, D. H. (2012). Protecting parental rights. In J. L. Levi & E. E. Monnin-Browder (Eds.), *Transgender family law: A guide to effective advocacy* (pp. 63–85). Bloomington, IN: AuthorHouse.

Monnin-Browder, E. E. (2012). Relationship recognition and protections. In J. L. Levi & E. E. Monnin-Browder (Eds.), *Transgender family law: A guide to effective advocacy* (pp. 36–62). Bloomington, IN: AuthorHouse.

Nadal, K. L. (2013). *That's so gay! Microaggressions and the lesbian, gay, bisexual, and transgender community.* Washington, DC: American Psychological Association. http://dx.doi.org/10.1037/14093-000

Nadal, K. L., Davidoff, K. C., Davis, L. S., & Wong, Y. (2014). Emotional, behavioral, and cognitive reactions to microaggressions: Transgender perspectives. *Psychology of Sexual Orientation and Gender Diversity*, *1*, 72–81. http://dx.doi.org/10.1037/sgd0000011

National Center for Transgender Equality. (2014). *Medicare and transgender people: Updated 2014*. Retrieved from http://transequality.org/sites/default/files/docs/kyr/MedicareAndTransPeople.pdf

National Center for Transgender Equality. (2015). *Map: State nondiscrimination laws*. Retrieved from http://transequality.org/issues/resources/map-state-nondiscrimination-laws

Obergefell v. Hodges, 135 S. Ct. 2584 (2015).

Services and Advocacy for Gay, Lesbian, Bisexual, and Transgender Elders. (2014). *Out and visible: The experiences and attitudes of LGBT older adults, ages 45–75*. Retrieved from http://www.sageusa.org/files/LGBT_OAMarketResearch_Rpt.pdf

Services and Advocacy for Gay, Lesbian, Bisexual, and Transgender Elders, and National Center for Transgender Equality. (2012). *Improving the lives of transgender older adults: Recommendations for policy and practice*. Retrieved from http://transequality.org/sites/default/files/docs/resources/TransAgingPolicyReportFull.pdf

Singh, A. A., Hays, D. G., & Watson, L. (2011). Strategies in the face of adversity: Resilience strategies of transgender individuals. *Journal of Counseling & Development*, *89*, 20–27. http://dx.doi.org/10.1002/j.1556-6678.2011.tb00057.x

Singh, A. A., & McKleroy, V. S. (2011). "Just getting out of bed is a revolutionary act": The resilience of transgender people of color who have survived traumatic life events. *Traumatology*, *20*(10), 1–11.

Stockard, J. (2006). Gender socialization. In J. S. Chafetz (Ed.), *Handbook of the sociology of gender* (pp. 215–227). New York, NY: Springer. http://dx.doi.org/10.1007/0-387-36218-5_11

Wester, S. R., McDonough, T. A., Taylor, L., Vogel, D. L., & White, M. (2010). Using gender role conflict theory in counseling male-to-female transgender individuals. *Journal of Counseling & Development*, *88*, 214–219. http://dx.doi.org/10.1002/j.1556-6678.2010.tb00012.x

White, T., & Ettner, R. (2004). Disclosure, risks and protective factors for children whose parents are undergoing a gender transition. *Journal of Gay & Lesbian Psychotherapy*, *8*, 129–147.

White, T., & Ettner, R. (2007). Adaptation and adjustment in children of transsexual parents. *European Child & Adolescent Psychiatry*, *16*, 215–221. http://dx.doi.org/10.1007/s00787-006-0591-y

Witten, T. M. (2009). Graceful exits: Intersection of aging, transgender identities, and the family/community. *Journal of GLBT Family Studies*, *5*, 35–62. http://dx.doi.org/10.1080/15504280802595378

Witten, T. M. (2014). It's not all darkness: Robustness, resilience, and successful transgender aging. *LGBT Health*, *1*, 24–33. http://dx.doi.org/10.1089/lgbt.2013.0017

Theodore R. Burnes, Stacie Fishell Rowan, and Parrish L. Paul

Clinical Supervision With TGNC Clients in Health Service Psychology

8

T he necessity for transgender and gender nonconforming (TGNC)-affirmative supervision is built on the foundation that broad multicultural competence within supervision and practice is integral to the welfare of clients and to one's competence as a psychologist (Falender & Shafranske, 2014; Falender, Shafranske, & Falicov, 2014). Subsequently, supervision that celebrates gender-diverse people and communities creates space for exploration and understanding of personal and professional worldviews that may differ from one's own, and the opportunities to increase awareness, insight, and ability to provide multiculturally competent mental health services (Burnes, Wood, Inman, & Welikson, 2013). However, a stance affirming gender diversity may also be challenging for some supervisors or for those striving to enter the profession. Concurrent with the use of supervision to train the next generation of professionals and maintain ethical care for clients of health service psychology, the need for clinical supervision to specifically address the concerns of TGNC clients and their communities remains an

http://dx.doi.org/10.1037/14957-009
Affirmative Counseling and Psychological Practice With Transgender and Gender Nonconforming Clients, A. A. Singh and l. m. dickey (Editors)

area in critical need of attention within the discipline of professional psychology as a whole. Such ethical care mandates that mental health professionals work within the boundaries of their competence and with populations for whom the professional has received appropriate education and training (American Counseling Association [ACA], 2014; American Psychological Association [APA], 2003, 2010). Scholars have noted the absence of literature that addresses clinical training for MHPs who work with TGNC clients (Falender et al., 2014; Richmond, Burnes, & Carroll, 2012).

The need for TGNC-affirmative supervision comes in large part from the increasing documentation that clinical supervision is a significant part of MHPs' professional practice. The provision of supervision has been ranked as one of the top five activities in which professional MHPs spend their time (Norcross, Hedges, & Castle, 2002) and the supervisory relationship is one of the most pivotal ones in the profession (Riggs & Bretz, 2006). Supervision is also cited as the most frequently used training method for teaching clinical skills and has increasingly become a focal point for the training and education of counselors and psychologists (Milne & James, 2002). Specifically, supervision provides a foundational place for clinical growth, reflection, challenge, and movement toward a professional identity as a competent MHP (Burnes et al., 2013). On a more personal level, a positive and connected supervision relationship allows space for the exploration of cultural attitudes and awareness (Falender, Burnes, & Ellis, 2013), such as TGNC gender experiences, narratives, and bias.

Although supervision continues to be recognized as a distinct professional practice with its own respective literature and competencies, literature specific to working with TGNC clients is noticeably absent. Scholars have consistently documented that training in working with TGNC clients is lacking in many training programs (APA, 2015; Carroll, Gilroy, & Ryan, 2002). Specifically, there is a lack of graduate training in curricula related to knowledge, attitudes, and skills for working with TGNC clients (Burnes & Stanley, in press). Unfortunately, this lack of TGNC-focused curricula creates a framework for lack of competence. Not only are psychologists who are competent addressing the needs of TGNC clients better able to provide mental health interventions, but they are also better equipped to serve as allies and advocates for social justice (Levitt & Ippolito, 2014).

There has long been an undercurrent of tension within the "LGBT"[1] community that not all groups are treated with equal importance. A

---

[1]The quotations are meant to denote the often-used language regarding sexual and gender minority individuals, and it is essential to note the limitation of the term *LGBT* (lesbian, gay, bisexual, and transgender) in reflecting the much more complex identities within, such as those of intersex, queer, questioning, and transgender individuals.

significant amount of the previous literature regarding therapy with LGBT-identified individuals has focused on sexual orientation and sexual minority status, whereas TGNC identities have been relatively invisible outside of the context of intersectionality with sexual identity (Bieschke, Blasko, & Woodhouse, 2014). Spade (2008) referred to the movement as the "LGBfakeT" movement, which reflects the history of invisibility of TGNC individuals, even within the larger LGB and queer community. This contributes to the ways in which TGNC individuals have been marginalized (Marine & Nicolazzo, 2014). Even within the larger multicultural competency movement within the field, supervision regarding work with TGNC individuals has not consistently had a place at the table.

In answer to these calls and in response to the multitude of absences in the counseling and psychology literature, this chapter provides information related to current theory and practice in clinical supervision and the application of these practices to working with TGNC clients. As authors who are supervisors, our overall definition of *TGNC-affirmative supervision* in individual or group modalities is supervision that consistently explores gender identity and the ways in which gender identity intersect with other salient identities, for the supervisee(s), supervisor, and clients. From our framework, TGNC-affirmative supervision is supportive, challenging, and a space to unpack privilege and oppression of gender identity within a multicultural framework.

We, the chapter authors, believe that identifying one's explicit approach to supervision and gender narrative is important when supervising therapists who are working with TGNC clients, so we have identified our most salient identities here. The first author, Theodore R. Burnes, identifies as a cisgender, queer, White man and uses male pronouns (i.e., he/him/his). His approach to supervision synthesizes competency-based approaches and theories of feminism, social justice, and clinical development to becoming a mental health scientist-practitioner. The second author, Stacie Fishell Rowan, identifies as a cisgender, queer, White woman who uses female pronouns (i.e., she/her/hers). Her approach to counseling and supervision is oriented in feminist, multicultural, and social justice values paired with individual and developmental needs (e.g., Falender & Shafranske, 2004; Porter & Vasquez, 1997; Stoltenberg, Mcneill, & Delworth, 1998). The third author, Parrish L. Paul, identifies as a cisgender, gay, White man. He has been involved primarily in clinical work and supervision and training in his career, in university counseling, academic department, community clinic, and private practice settings. His approach to supervision involves the roles and foci of the discrimination model (Bernard & Goodyear, 2014), along with an ongoing consideration of ways feminist, multicultural, interpersonal, and developmental approaches to supervision (Bernard & Goodyear, 2014) may be relevant in training.

Competency-Based Approaches to TGNC-Affirmative Supervision

Although supervision has long been part of the training model within mental health fields, it has increasingly been recognized as a specific competency requiring training and standards for provision of supervisory services (Falender, 2014). The evolution of competency-based approaches continues to build on a set of standards by which to measure trainee performance, with competencies met through developmental scaffolding and increased trainee responsibility over the course of professional development (Falender et al., 2013). One of the earliest documents on psychology trainee competency, the competency cube (Rodolfa et al., 2005), consists of three domains of professional development (i.e., foundational competency, functional competency, and stages of professional development) that can be synthesized to assess a trainee's learning and development. Fouad et al. (2009) built on this work and subsequently introduced the competency benchmarks, identifying a series of skills that were critical for health service psychologists in their professional activities. We identified a set of skills and corresponding competencies across three levels of professional development (i.e., practicum, internship, and professional practice) for a variety of work functions in health service psychology and MHP work. Although these competency documents do not mention working with TGNC clients specifically, they can be applied to specific domains needed to work with TGNC clients, including the provider's awareness of self, bias with respect to cultural identity and development, and lack of ability to engage in a different worldview.

Since the time these competency documents were published, other publications have increasingly referenced various multicultural identities within the context of diversity education. For instance, the *Guidelines for Clinical Supervision in Health Service Psychology* (APA, 2014) organizes competence in seven domains; five overarching competencies run throughout these domains and connect them. The five domains present clearly defined expectations and best practices and provide research to support assertions of standards within each domain. The specific domain that addresses diversity in these guidelines is overarching for all elements of professional practice of supervision, it states: "Supervisors strive to develop and maintain self-awareness regarding their diversity competence, which includes attitudes, knowledge, and skills" (APA, 2014, p. 10). The five resulting guidelines follow. We elaborate on each with comments on how TGNC-affirmative supervisors may demonstrate competence:

1. *Supervisors planfully strive to enhance their diversity competence to establish a respectful supervisor relationship and to facilitate the diversity competence of their supervisees* (APA, 2014, p. 16). TGNC-affirmative supervisors should forge a strong alliance with trainees to help in the self-examination process with respect to attitudes and awareness about multiple facets of gender diversity, such as gender identity, gender expression, and gender roles.

2. *Supervisors recognize the value of and pursue ongoing training in diversity competence as part of their professional development and lifelong learning* (APA, 2014, p. 17). Supervisors should continue to formally and informally engage in their own professional development as part of the lifelong process of learning about gender.

3. *Supervisors aim to be knowledgeable about the effects of bias, prejudice, and stereotyping. When possible, supervisors model client/patient advocacy and model promoting change in organizations and communities in the best interest of their clients/patients* (APA, 2014, p. 17). From a TGNC-affirmative model, clinical supervisors model the need to move beyond celebration of TGNC identities to the creation of systemic change and the disruption of oppressive paradigms.

4. *Supervisors aspire to be familiar with the scholarly literature concerning diversity competence in supervision and training* (APA, 2014, p. 17). TGNC-affirmative supervisors should strive to integrate scholarly literature into their supervision practices and to facilitate their supervisee's ability to integrate research and practice as gender identities continue to evolve.

5. *Supervisors strive to be familiar with promising practices for navigating conflicts among personal and professional values in the interest of protecting the public* (APA, 2014, p. 17). TGNC-affirmative clinical supervisors should model transparency and openness regarding the intersections of their personal and professional values, with specific focus on decreasing oppression and improving the quality of life for TGNC individuals.

Guidelines and Current Standards of Clinical Supervision With TGNC Clients

In addition to competency-based approaches to supervision, supervisors should also be aware of the mental health services guidelines and standards for work with TGNC clients. The *Guidelines for Psychological Practice With Transgender and Gender Nonconforming* (APA, 2015) is intended to assist MHPs and trainees in developing a "culturally responsive" and competent approach in their work with TGNC clients. These guidelines provide basic knowledge about TGNC persons, along with strengths and challenges that may be related to TGNC experiences. Professionals are asked to be aware of ways their own knowledge and attitudes about gender expression and gender identity could have bearing on the quality of care that is provided to TGNC clients. These guidelines note that competency in this area can be developed by examining personal beliefs about issues of gender, sexuality, identity, stereotypes, and so on. Such a personal exploration would include an examination of one's own experience of gender and privilege and a consideration of the ways that systems, including mental health systems, may have been discriminatory to TGNC persons and their families.

The "Competencies for Counseling With Transgender Clients" (ACA, 2010) provides guideline-informed competencies for practice with transgender clients. These competencies acknowledge that prejudice and discrimination related to TGNC persons are present in society and may be internalized by the counselor, causing a negative influence in counselors' attitudes. Relatedly, the counselor's gender identity, gender expression, and conceptualizations related to gender must be considered in the counseling relationship. Further, counselors are encouraged to consider how the helping professions may have contributed to the discrimination of TGNC persons. The ACA competencies (ACA, 2010) and APA guidelines (APA, 2014, 2015) provide a strong groundwork for MHPs to provide effective TGNC-affirmative supervision that will inform health care for TGNC mental health clients but will also add to the knowledge base of psychological practice with TGNC people and communities. Further, we articulate a series of recommendations that can inform TGNC-affirmative clinical supervision. Specifically, we discuss ways to develop competence for work in supervision with TGNC clients, communities, and concerns using the following clinical vignette.

Applications and Strategies in Competency-Based, TGNC-Affirmative Supervision

A supervisor, Rae, and MHP trainee, Dave, came to supervision and discussed a case on the trainee's caseload. Rae, a 34-year-old, Korean-American, identifies as a queer, cisgender woman of color. Dave, a 26-year-old, White student, identifies as heterosexual and coming from a low-socioeconomic background. They have been working together for 4 months in a community mental health center, and this is Dave's second practicum in his MHP training program. Dave started their 14th supervision session by asking for support with his new client, Jamie. Jamie initiated services with the clinic to address symptoms of anxiety and depression and references strain within family-of-origin relationships. On the day of the appointment, Jamie arrived wearing jeans, a hooded sweatshirt, and jacket. Jamie was provided intake paperwork, which Rae, as supervisor, reviewed prior to starting the session.

Dave noted that Jamie self-identifies as 27 years old, Latino, queer, and partnered. Jamie noted employment at a local university for the past 4 years and endorsed alcohol use one to two per week and marijuana use two to three times per week. Dave noticed that Jamie had not checked any label of gender identity when completing paperwork. During the intake appointment, Jamie shared with Dave feelings of isolation and loneliness and articulated interactions with others that brought up feelings of anxiety, fear of judgment, and generally described feelings of not fitting in. Dave noted that he is becoming increasingly aware that Jamie had not referenced gender identity when sharing information. He was noticing his own feelings related to Jamie's identity, that he probably should have initiated some sort of conversation with Jamie, and began to wonder what other parts of Jamie's multiple identities he should investigate with curiosity. Similarly, Rae also began to wonder what to do in her work with Dave, as she had also reflected that Jamie's gender had not been addressed. Rae wondered what supervision interventions she should implement to help Dave work with these processes.

This vignette brings to life the complexities that arise in TGNC-affirmative supervision. Halpert, Reinhardt, and Toohey (2007) suggested that supervisors and supervisees who are nonaffirmative or unaware of TGNC issues may collude in a way that causes harm to clients, whereas supervisors who take an affirmative stand and demonstrate respect across broad multicultural identities optimize the supervision climate and affirmative interventions. Additionally, for supervisees who also identify as TGNC, a supervisor who takes an affirmative stance and engages in conversations of gender and identity releases the supervisee from the burden of initiating disclosures which may decrease fears and repercussions of coming out in the supervision relationship (and in the field in general). Further consideration of the vignette is integrated into the following sections.

SUPERVISOR AND SUPERVISEE READINESS FOR TGNC-AFFIRMATIVE CARE

The reviewed literature and case vignette illustrate the need for a supervision process that facilitates growth and development of skills when working with TGNC clients, specifically identifying self-awareness within clinical relationships and the willingness and ability to explore gender in various capacities throughout one's professional lifespan as essential (e.g., Bernard & Goodyear, 2014; Knox, Caperton, Phelps, & Pruitt, 2014; Rønnestad & Skovholt, 2003). Research has documented that clinical experience alone cannot provide an environment for optimal growth and emerging competence (Falender et al., 2013). Clear and evaluative feedback through the supervisory process is necessary for clinical progress (Bernard & Goodyear, 2014).

In the vignette, having Rae express her own competence for working with TGNC supervision could enhance Dave's readiness to acknowledge his own gender biases. As practicing MHPs and trainees working with TGNC clients who want to explore their own gender, supervisors should first assess their own readiness with respect to gender-affirmative psychotherapy, diversity, and supervision to assess if they can provide supervision that will result in the most ethical care possible. Falicov (2014) introduced a model that examines a supervisor's readiness through examination of how multiple levels of culture, ecology, and development impact their ways of interaction, understanding hierarchy, and thought processes. She termed these impact factors *maps* that supervisors and trainees have in clinical supervision. Falicov addressed the maps supervisors and their supervisees carry related to these multiple levels, and noted the importance of examining one's own maps to assess whether or not an individual is ready to supervise certain cases and has the appropriate set of knowledge, attitudes, and skills to supervise certain cases. For TGNC-affirmative supervisors, such maps might include cultural values related to gender, messages that the supervisor has received about gender fluidity and transcending of gender norms, and messages they have received about advocacy for individuals of oppressed identities. Further, the supervisor may need to assess whether their values related to transgender-affirmative mental health care match the values of the training program. Singh and Burnes (2010) noted how clinicians may integrate social justice into training models and be met with resistance from an agency or practice's senior administration.

The following scales can help clinicians—supervisors and supervisees—assess their own readiness to work TGNC clients. Such measures include the Psychotherapy Supervisor Development Scale (PSDS; Barnes & Moon, 2006) and the Supervisory Styles Inventory (SSI; Friedlander & Ward, 1984). Supervisors using the PSDS rate themselves using 18 items that measure four factors: effectiveness–competence, identity commitment, self-awareness, and sincerity in supervisory role. The SSI asks supervisors to indicate the perceptions of themselves as a supervisor by rating themselves on 35 traits. The supervisors and trainees can review these assessments together in a supervision session, or the supervisor can assign a trainee to complete one of these assessments outside of the session prior to meeting. The supervisor can also complete a separate copy of the same assessment, and then the supervisor and trainee can compare answers to assess the multiple perspectives of a trainee's readiness to work with issues of gender and multiculturalism within a clinical context.

EXPLORING GENDER AS A CLINICIAN

In the vignette, Dave noted that he wanted to initiate a conversation with Jamie, and that he may have had feelings related to Jamie's gender process thus far in their work. Such a process reflects the needs of supervisees and supervisors to deeply explore their own identities and intersectionalities with respect to gender, gender identity, and gender roles. Further, some trainees may experience work with TGNC clients as challenging; particularly if the trainee's worldview or belief system makes it difficult to fully support TGNC clients or if the trainee has had little experience with this population in the past. Bieschke and Mintz (2012) suggested that training may need to include more than what they have referred to as demographic competence, or learning to work competently with clients who are similar or dissimilar to the counselor in terms of demographics. These authors argued that trainees must also be competent to work with and value a client whose worldview or beliefs are a challenge to their own, which they have termed *demographic worldview inclusivity*. Trainees are not required to abandon their personal values or beliefs in this inclusive stance, but competence includes the ability to work meaningfully with clients (including but not limited to TGNC clients) whose worldviews trainees may experience as challenging.

When working in any new or particularly challenging area of professional practice, supervision, consultation, and collaboration are necessary for supervisors, trainers, and trainees alike (Singh & Burnes, 2010). Mitchell (2009) suggested that it will be important for trainees to explore gender roles, gender identity, gender expression, transphobia, and other TGNC-related concerns. However, we suggest that a scholarly and personal examination of gender-related concerns is necessary for clinical competence. For example, O'Hara, Dispenza, Brack, and Blood (2013) completed a mixed-method research study focused on counselors-in-training and TGNC counselor competence. Eighty-seven counselors in training completed a TGNC counselor competence questionnaire, with seven participants taking part in two focus group interviews. The authors found five major themes that described preparation for counselors to work with TGNC clients: terminology, sources of information and knowledge, emic versus etic worldview in counseling approaches, characteristics of the clinician, and recommendations for training. With such empirical data, Rae could guide Dave in a series of exercises within and outside of supervision to explore gender in terms of language and her own personal characteristics and specific reflections about any challenges of taking clients' perspectives and/or entering their worldviews. Outside of supervision, Dave could journal his thoughts using guided prompts created by Rae and supplement his journaling with readings. Within supervision, Rae could model self-reflection and awareness by appropriately disclosing her own intersecting identities, her journey of gender exploration, and/or her own triumphs with the work.

ENGAGING WITH TGNC-FOCUSED TRAINING AND EDUCATION

The supervision vignette points out the need for clinical supervisors like Rae to engage in their own learning so they feel increased comfort and ability to engage in TGNC-focused supervision process. Workshops, continuing education, and in-service and other training opportunities will be important for competent practice (ACA, 2010; APA, 2015). Learning provided in such settings is invaluable, along with personal review of competencies and guidelines (ACA, 2010; APA, 2015). However, many current training programs and multicultural learning opportunities may focus awareness of the learner on ways the "other" is different or problematic in society in some way (Chao, Okazaki, & Hong, 2011). A focus on difference without enough emphasis on the learner's self-awareness may imply cultural competence, but it is possible that underneath the surface of that implied competence resides assumptions, bias, or prejudice. Chao et al. (2011) suggested that training must also focus on a deep understanding of the learner's own worldview and privilege, to limit the ways in which status, bias, and assumptions may inform interactions and clinical interventions. Therefore, Rae might engage in a consultation group that will allow her to process her own unique combination of privileged and oppressed identities so that she may begin a process of working with Dave. Further, Rae may need to attend continuing education workshops or conference presentations to learn updated information related to gender.

Chavez-Korell and Johnson (2010) argued that awareness of one's own gender identity and gender privilege is essential, along with knowledge of issues that are important to TGNC persons and communities. These authors suggested that integrating personal narratives from the TGNC community may be useful in establishing a conceptual framework for working with TGNC clients. They suggested that understanding may be deepened by exposure to written works (e.g., autobiographies, fiction), videos, websites, and media, along with attending professional conferences. Further, MHPs are encouraged to speak directly to TGNC community members in an effort to deepen their knowledge, awareness, and skills.

For trainees such as Dave, who might struggle initially with discussing personal reactions, case studies (e.g., Budge, 2013) and discussion of possible treatment modalities or interventions could be useful. Budge (2013) argued that such an approach may be useful with TGNC clients, who may have experienced much discrimination and interpersonal struggle, particularly when transition, whether medical or social, is involved. However, after this occurs, it is likely that a return to deeper exploration and dynamic worldview inclusivity will be useful in training (APA, 2015; Bieschke & Mintz, 2012; Singh & Burnes, 2010).

THE NEEDS OF TGNC-IDENTIFIED PROVIDERS

In addition to making sure that MHPs receive appropriate and competent supervision when working with TGNC clients, there is an additional layer of context and consideration for psychology trainees who themselves identify as TGNC. Specifically, provider-allies to the TGNC community have a set of needs that are fundamentally different from those of providers who are questioning their gender identity or who self-identify with one of the many communities of TGNC people (Vance, Halpern-Felsher, & Rosenthal, 2015).

It is important to acknowledge the perspectives of TGNC-identified student-supervisees who may have different reactions to working with TGNC clients than their cisgender peers. Specifically, levels of identity development, experiences of discrimination and oppression, and lack of support in their graduate education can impact their ability to work with TGNC clients effectively (Bieschke et al., 2014). Further, it is important to not assume that TGNC-identified trainees are the best therapists to work with a TGNC-identified client, as trainees may lack competence and skills in basic conceptualization and intervention techniques on the basis of their level of training and professional development. Further, TGNC trainees may experience difficulty in moving through graduate training, experience a lack of support in their academic program, and/or experience a lack of trainee support on-site in clinical supervision. It is important that clinical supervisors do a supportive yet comprehensive assessment of the needs and experiences of TGNC supervisees that is appropriate, ethical, and contextual for their relationship and for the work that the trainee will engage in with clients.

An additional consideration in providing supervision for trainees working with clients who identify as TGNC is the gender identity and expression of the supervisee. Supervisees who identify as TGNC may have various experiences in the development of their TGNC identity that may mirror (or not mirror) the experiences of clients. These similarities and differences in experiences should be monitored carefully. Further, TGNC trainees may have experienced oppression, harassment, and/or invalidation, personally and professionally (Cashore & Tuason, 2009; Levitt & Hiestand, 2004; Levitt & Ippolito, 2014). These experiences may be exacerbated within the power dynamic of the supervisory relationship if supervisors are perceived to struggle to understand and affirm the identity of the supervisee. Such processes may lead to feelings of powerlessness and self-doubt within the supervisor–supervisee relationship (Falender et al., 2013; Singh & Chun, 2010), whereas research has suggested that supervisees who are able to express and claim their TGNC identity experience increased self-confidence and congruence with self and others (Levitt & Ippolito, 2014; Riggle, Rostosky, McCants, & Pascale-Hague, 2011).

Chapter Summary

This chapter highlighted a variety of critical issues for clinical supervisors and MHP trainees who are working with TGNC clients and communities. Supervisors should engage with the APA guidelines (APA, 2014, 2015) and other models of clinical supervision that describe competencies for supervisors and practitioners working with TGNC individuals. Psychologists need to understand the importance of training within the contexts of gender, advocacy, and clinical development. The strategies and interventions we have offered for use in clinical supervision should be considered in the larger contexts of service delivery, development of trainee and supervisor, and needs of the client.

References

American Counseling Association. (2010). Competencies for counseling with transgender clients. *Journal of LGBT Issues in Counseling, 4,* 135–159.

American Counseling Association. (2014). *ACA Code of Ethics.* Alexandria, VA: Author.

American Psychological Association. (2003). Guidelines on multicultural education, training, research, practice, and organizational change for psychologists. *American Psychologist, 58,* 377–402.

American Psychological Association. (2010). *Ethical principles of psychologists and code of conduct* (2002, Amended June 1, 2010). Retrieved from http://www.apa.org/ethics/code/index.aspx

American Psychological Association. (2014). *Guidelines for clinical supervision in health service psychology.* Retrieved from http://www.apa.org/about/policy/guidelines-supervision.pdf

American Psychological Association. (2015). Guidelines for psychological practice with transgender and gender nonconforming people. *American Psychologist, 70,* 832–864. http://dx.doi.org/10.1037/a0039906

Barnes, K. L., & Moon, S. M. (2006). Factor structure of the Psychotherapy Supervisor Development Scale. *Measurement and Evaluation in Counseling and Development, 39,* 130–140.

Bernard, J. M., & Goodyear, R. K. (2014). *Fundamentals of clinical supervision* (5th ed.). Boston, MA: Pearson.

Bieschke, K. J., Blasko, K. A., & Woodhouse, S. S. (2014). A comprehensive approach to competently addressing sexual minority issues in clinical supervision. In C. A. Falender, E. P. Shafranske, & C. Falicov (Eds.), *Multiculturalism and diversity in clinical supervision: A competency-based approach* (pp. 209–230). Washington, DC: American Psychological Association. http://dx.doi.org/10.1037/14370-009

Bieschke, K. J., & Mintz, L. B. (2012). Counseling psychology, model training values statement addressing diversity: History, current use, and future directions. *Training and Education in Professional Psychology, 6,* 196–203. http://dx.doi.org/10.1037/a0030810

Budge, S. L. (2013). Interpersonal psychotherapy with transgender clients. *Psychotherapy, 50,* 356–359. http://dx.doi.org/10.1037/a0032194

Burnes, T. R., & Stanley, J. S. (Eds.). (in press). *Teaching LGBT psychology: Queering psychology pedagogy and instructional practice.* Washington, DC: American Psychological Association.

Burnes, T. R., Wood, J., Inman, J., & Welikson, G. (2013). An investigation of process variables in feminist group clinical supervision. *The Counseling Psychologist, 41,* 86–109. http://dx.doi.org/10.1177/0011000012442653

Carroll, L., Gilroy, P. J., & Ryan, J. (2002). Counseling transgendered, transsexual, and gender-variant clients. *Journal of Counseling and Development, 80,* 131–139. http://dx.doi.org/10.1002/j.1556-6678.2002.tb00175.x

Cashore, C., & Tuason, T. G. (2009). Negotiating the binary: Identity and social justice for bisexual and transgender individuals. *Journal of Gay & Lesbian Social Services, 21,* 374–401. http://dx.doi.org/10.1080/10538720802498405

Chao, M. M., Okazaki, S., & Hong, Y. Y. (2011). The quest for multicultural competence: Challenges and lessons learned from clinical and organizational research. *Social and Personality Psychology Compass, 5,* 263–274. http://dx.doi.org/10.1111/j.1751-9004.2011.00350.x

Chavez-Korell, S., & Johnson, L. T. (2010). Informing counselor training and competent counseling services through transgender narratives and the transgender community. *Journal of LGBT Issues in Counseling, 4*, 202–213. http://dx.doi.org/10.1080/15538605.2010.524845

Falender, C. A. (2014). Clinical supervision in a competency-based era. *South African Journal of Psychology, 44*(1), 6–17. http://dx.doi.org/10.1177/0081246313516260

Falender, C. A., Burnes, T. R., & Ellis, M. V. (2013). Multicultural clinical supervision and benchmarks: Empirical support informing practice and supervisor training. *The Counseling Psychologist, 41*, 8–27. http://dx.doi.org/10.1177/0011000012438417

Falender, C. A., & Shafranske, E. P. (2004). *Clinical supervision: A competency-based approach.* Washington, DC: American Psychological Association. http://dx.doi.org/10.1037/10806-000

Falender, C. A., & Shafranske, E. P. (2014). Clinical supervision: The state of the art. *Journal of Clinical Psychology, 70*, 1030–1041. http://dx.doi.org/10.1002/jclp.22124

Falender, C. A., Shafranske, E. P., & Falicov, C. (Eds.). (2014). *Multiculturalism and diversity in clinical supervision: A competency-based approach.* Washington, DC: American Psychological Association. http://dx.doi.org/10.1037/14370-000

Falicov, C. (2014). Psychotherapy and supervision as cultural encounters: The MECA framework. In C. A. Falender, E. P. Shafransky, & C. J. Falicov (Eds.), *Multiculturalism and diversity in clinical supervision: A competency-based approach.* Washington, DC: American Psychological Association.

Fouad, N. A., Grus, C. L., Hatcher, R. L., Kaslow, N. J., Hutchings, P., Madson, M. B., . . . Crossman, R. E. (2009). Competency benchmarks: A model for understanding and measuring competence in professional psychology across training levels. *Training and Education in Professional Psychology, 3*(4, Suppl.), S5–S26. http://dx.doi.org/10.1037/a0015832

Friedlander, M. L., & Ward, L. G. (1984). Development and validation of the Supervisory Styles Inventory. *Journal of Counseling Psychology, 31*, 541–557. http://dx.doi.org/10.1037/0022-0167.31.4.541

Halpert, S. C., Reinhardt, B., & Toohey, M. J. (2007). Affirmative clinical supervision. In K. J. Bieschke, R. M. Perez, & K. A. DeBord (Eds.), *Handbook of counseling and psychotherapy with lesbian, gay, bisexual, and transgender clients* (2nd ed., pp. 241–258). Washington, DC: American Psychological Association. http://dx.doi.org/10.1037/11482-014

Knox, S., Caperton, W., Phelps, D., & Pruitt, N. (2014). A qualitative study of supervisees' internal representations of supervisors. *Counselling Psychology Quarterly, 27*, 334–352. http://dx.doi.org/10.1080/09515070.2014.886999

Levitt, H., & Hiestand, K. (2004). A quest for authenticity: Contemporary butch gender. *Sex Roles, 50,* 605–621. http://dx.doi.org/10.1023/B:SERS.0000027565.59109.80

Levitt, H. M., & Ippolito, M. R. (2014). Being transgender: The experience of transgender identity development. *Journal of Homosexuality, 61,* 1727–1758. http://dx.doi.org/10.1080/00918369.2014.951262

Marine, S. B., & Nicolazzo, Z. (2014, November 3). Names that matter: Exploring the tensions of campus LGBT centers and trans* inclusion. *Journal of Diversity in Higher Education, 7,* 265–281. http://dx.doi.org/10.1037/a0037990

Milne, D. L., & James, I. A. (2002). The observed impact of training on competence in clinical supervision. *British Journal of Clinical Psychology, 41,* 55–72. http://dx.doi.org/10.1348/014466502163796

Mitchell, V. (2009). Developing the therapeutic self: Supervising therapists with lesbian, gay, bisexual, and transgender clients in the 21st century. *Women & Therapy, 33,* 7–21. http://dx.doi.org/10.1080/02703140903404671

Norcross, J. C., Hedges, M., & Castle, P. H. (2002). Psychologists conducting psychotherapy in 2001: A study of the Division 29 membership. *Psychotherapy: Theory, Research, Practice, Training, 39,* 97–102. http://dx.doi.org/10.1037/0033-3204.39.1.97

O'Hara, C., Dispenza, F., Brack, G., & Blood, R. A. C. (2013). The preparedness of counselors-in-training to work with transgender clients: A mixed methods investigation. *Journal of LGBT Issues in Counseling, 7,* 236–256. http://dx.doi.org/10.1080/15538605.2013.812929

Porter, N., & Vasquez, M. (1997). Covision: Feminist supervision, process, and collaboration. In J. Worell & N. Johnson (Eds.), *Shaping the future of feminist psychology: Education, research, and practice* (pp. 155–171). Washington, DC: American Psychological Association. http://dx.doi.org/10.1037/10245-007

Richmond, K., Burnes, T. R., & Carroll, K. (2012). Lost in trans-lation: Interpreting systems of trauma for transgender clients. *Traumatology, 18*(1), 45–57. http://dx.doi.org/10.1177/1534765610396726

Riggle, E. D. B., Rostosky, S. S., McCants, L. E., & Pascale-Hague, D. (2011). Positive aspects of a transgender self-identification. *Psychology and Sexuality, 2,* 147–158. http://dx.doi.org/10.1080/19419899.2010.534490

Riggs, S. A., & Bretz, K. M. (2006). Attachment processes in the supervisory relationship: An exploratory investigation. *Professional Psychology: Research and Practice, 37,* 558–566. http://dx.doi.org/10.1037/0735-7028.37.5.558

Rodolfa, E., Eisman, E., Rehm, L., Bent, R., Nelson, P., & Ritchie, P. (2005). A cube model for competency development: Implications for psychology educators and regulators. *Professional Psychology: Research and Practice, 36,* 347–354.

Rønnestad, M. H., & Skovholt, T. M. (2003). The journey of the counselor and therapist: Research findings and perspectives on professional development. *Journal of Career Development, 30,* 5–44. http://dx.doi.org/10.1177/089484530303000102

Singh, A., & Chun, K. Y. S. (2010). "From the margins to the center": Moving towards a resilience-based model of supervision for queer people of color supervisors. *Training and Education in Professional Psychology, 4,* 36–46. http://dx.doi.org/10.1037/a0017373

Singh, A. A., & Burnes, T. R. (2010). Shifting the counselor role from gatekeeping to advocacy: Ten strategies for using the competencies for counseling with transgender clients for individual and social change. *Journal of LGBT Issues in Counseling, 4,* 241–255. http://dx.doi.org/10.1080/15538605.2010.525455

Spade, D. (2008). Fighting to win. In M. B. Sycamore (Ed.), *That's revolting! Queer strategies for resisting assimilation* (pp. 47–53). New York, NY: Soft Skull Press.

Stoltenberg, C. D., Mcneill, B., & Delworth, U. (1998). *IDM supervision: An integrated developmental model for supervising counselors and therapists.* San Francisco, CA: Jossey-Bass.

Vance, S. R., Jr., Halpern-Felsher, B. L., & Rosenthal, S. M. (2015). Health care providers' comfort with and barriers to care of transgender youth. *Journal of Adolescent Health, 56,* 251–253. http://dx.doi.org/10.1016/j.jadohealth.2014.11.002

Katherine Richmond, Theodore R. Burnes,
Anneliese A. Singh, and Mel Ferrara

Assessment and Treatment of Trauma With TGNC Clients

A Feminist Approach

9

R esearch has documented high rates of traumatic life experiences for transgender and gender nonconforming (TGNC)
people (Richmond, Burnes, & Carroll, 2012; Singh & McKleroy,
2011). From family and social rejection (Koken, Bimbi, &
Parsons, 2009) to anti-TGNC prejudice experienced when
accessing education, employment, and health care (Bowen,
Bradford, & Powers, 2007; Lombardi, 2001; Lombardi, Wilchins,
Priesing, & Malouf, 2002; Xavier, 2000), TGNC people experience microaggressions (e.g., daily hassles and microinsults;
Nadal, 2013) and macroaggressions (e.g., verbal and physical harassment, overt workplace discrimination) that may
lead to negative health outcomes such as depression, anxiety, suicide attempts, substance abuse, and other mental and
physical health challenges (Institute of Medicine, 2011). In
addition to these traumatic stressors, TGNC people may face
additional obstacles and discrimination related to housing
and TGNC-negative legal policies (Lind, 2004). With regard
to interpersonal violence, literature also indicates that TGNC

http://dx.doi.org/10.1037/14957-010
*Affirmative Counseling and Psychological Practice With Transgender and Gender
Nonconforming Clients*, A. A. Singh and l. m. dickey (Editors)

people are subject to high rates of child sexual abuse and other types of physical abuse (Kersting et al., 2003), such as sexual assault (Kenagy, 2005; Lombardi et al., 2002). Although these high rates of trauma are concerning, these traumatic experiences may become multiplied when seeking counseling for trauma-related experiences with counselors and mental health practitioners (MHPs) who may not have the training necessary in TGNC concerns (Pickering & Leinbaugh, 2006), hold anti-TGNC prejudice, or engage in microaggressions during the counseling process (Nadal, Skolnik, & Wong, 2012). The following case vignette, which we return to throughout the chapter, illustrates the types of traumatic experiences a TGNC client may need to address in counseling.

Zeke is a 23-year-old, White, male-identified individual who entered therapy as a result of urging from his girlfriend. He had been having problems trusting her in their relationship, and had also been displaying difficulty with sleep, waking up two to three times a night due to nightmares. Zeke was assigned female at birth, but came out as TGNC when he was 15 years old; he had engaged in aspects of medical and social transition throughout his later adolescence and early young adulthood. Zeke had been on hormones for 3 years, and desired to one day have surgical procedures to remove his breasts. In his initial therapy session, Zeke noted the difficulty in communicating with his primary care provider about hormones ("My doctor keeps telling me that he thinks I might be a lesbian") and that he had been "feeling really disconnected" from his girlfriend (of 4 years).

In Zeke's initial clinical interview, he noted that he experienced a variety of "difficult" experiences growing up, including parents who were divorced and "neither one believed I was a boy. My dad kept saying that I was trans because my mom hated men and was turning me into a boy to get back at him." Zeke recounted numerous experiences of bullying that began in sixth grade and persisted throughout high school, including being physically beaten by peers, publicly ridiculed by teachers in classrooms, and being called "he-she" by an older brother in the school yard. Zeke noted, "I got through it one day at a time," and mentioned that for almost 3 years he would often cut himself on his arm above his elbow when he came from school.

In this chapter, we hope to advance a feminist, strengths-based, and social justice approach to working with TGNC clients like Zeke who are survivors of traumatic stress. It is important to note that intersex individuals may or may not identify as TGNC (Burnes & Richmond, 2012), and thus the contents of this chapter may not be applicable to intersex clients depending on the identity formation of particular cases. Such an approach acknowledges that many of the daily stressors TGNC individuals face result from living in a hegemonic environment (Maine, 2004). Feminist approaches to trauma counseling acknowledge that trauma may result not just from innate, behavioral symptoms but also from the inability to cope with environments that negate one's traumatic experiences, resulting in further experiences of oppression and marginalization (Brown, 2008). Thus, the goal of feminist therapeutic assessments and interventions is to help clients also develop a *feminist consciousness* through evaluating how social context influences mental health and through a collaborative relationship between the MHP and the client that strives to be as egalitarian as possible (Worell & Remer, 2003). With a developed feminist consciousness, clients and clinicians are able to collaboratively create strategies to combat toxic norms and interactions (Brown, 2004). This consciousness can also result in clinicians' advocacy efforts outside of the therapy office for TGNC clients and communities.

Theoretical Perspectives on Traumatic Experiences of TGNC Individuals

Compared with the general population, TGNC individuals are more likely to experience reoccurring traumatic experiences (Mizock & Lewis, 2008), which increases their vulnerability to developing posttraumatic stress disorder (PTSD)—the most widely acknowledged trauma-related disorder (American Psychiatric Association, 2013). According to the fifth edition of the *Diagnostic and Statistical Manual of Mental Disorders* (*DSM–5*; American Psychiatric Association, 2013), a diagnosis of PTSD can be given when a person is "exposed to death, threatened death, actual or threatened serious injury, or actual or threatened sexual violence" (p. 271) either through direct or indirect exposure (Criterion A). Additionally, there must also be symptoms from each of the following four symptom clusters: intrusive symptoms (Criterion B), avoidance symptoms (Criterion C), negative alterations in cognition and mood (Criterion D), and alterations in arousal and reactivity (Criterion E). If a person experiences at least one symptom from Criteria B and C and at least two symptoms from Criteria D and E, in a way that interferes with daily functioning, for over 1 month following a trauma event, then a diagnosis of PTSD is warranted.

MHPs working with TGNC survivors, however, often describe that the diagnosis of PTSD does not accurately capture these individuals' posttrauma symptoms (Richmond et al., 2012). As in the case of Zeke, complex PTSD may better account for many of the reactions reported by TGNC individuals and observed by clinicians. Herman (1992) introduced complex PTSD as a way to conceptualize trauma reactions following prolonged and repetitive trauma stressors. A distinctive component of complex PTSD is that injury is regularly caused by a trusting person (e.g., family member, caregiver), resulting in betrayal trauma (Courtois & Ford, 2012; Freyd, DePrince, & Gleaves, 2007). Often TGNC individuals' first experience of trauma occurs in their family of origin. According to a proposed change in the upcoming 11th edition of the *International Statistical Classification of Diseases*, an individual will meet criteria for complex PTSD if that person reports the core symptoms of PTSD and also demonstrates persistent impairments in affective functioning, self-functioning, and relational functioning (American Psychiatric Association, 2013). Although the *DSM–5* does not include a distinct diagnosis of complex PTSD, scholars indicated that the two new PTSD subtypes introduced in *DSM–5* (Dissociative and Preschool) are the most similar to complex PTSD (Courtois & Ford, 2012). Because the literature suggests that TGNC clients are likely to encounter multiple types of stress related to their TGNC identity, it is likely that they may present with symptoms associated with PTSD, complex PTSD, or both (Brown, 2008; Lev, 2004).

DIFFICULTIES WITH DIAGNOSES

Feminist scholars, however, have criticized diagnostic categories because the medicalization of mental health often minimizes the sociopolitical and historical explanations for psychological distress and also reaffirms the power of the medical industrial complex (Lafrance & McKenzie-Mohr, 2013). In the case of TGNC individuals, the diagnosis of gender dysphoria (formerly gender identity disorder) ignited significant debate regarding the potential stigmatization posed by psychiatric diagnoses, which understandably created mistrust among some TGNC individuals toward health care providers (Winters, 2007). Yet, feminist scholars generally regard PTSD and complex PTSD more favorably than other diagnostic categories because, to a limited degree, these diagnoses acknowledge that external stressors are at the origin of posttraumatic reactions (Brown, 2008). Because PTSD and complex PTSD are often useful frameworks for researchers and clinicians and have practical benefits (e.g., legal and insurance purposes), many feminist clinicians and researchers still use them (Berg, 2002). Other feminist scholars, however, warn that PTSD and/or complex PTSD should never be used because of the potential to further stigmatize marginalized groups (Lafrance & McKenzie-Mohr, 2013). Because of this concern, it is useful to use strengths-based assessments alongside diagnostic assessments when working with TGNC individuals. For instance, the 25-item Connor–Davidson Resilience Scale (Connor & Davidson, 2003) can help practitioners identify areas of stress-coping that exist or may be expanded in clients. Although this scale has been used primarily with late adolescents and adults, MHPs may also use strengths-based assessments that are specific to earlier developmental stages in childhood and adolescence, such as the Assessing Developmental Strengths Questionnaire (Donnon & Hammond, 2007).

Additionally, a critique of the current criteria for PTSD is that they overlook many important types of traumas that remain invisible to clinicians and trauma survivors (Brown, 2008; Richmond et al., 2012). For example, current PTSD diagnosis does not acknowledge *insidious traumas* (also referred to as *microaggressions*) as traumatic stressors. An example of insidious trauma is recurring exposure to transphobia and other forms of oppression (Espin & Gawelek, 1992). For TGNC clients, an insidious traumatic experience may include having a stranger excessively stare or having a health care provider ask inappropriate and/or invasive questions. Because these events tend to be more subtle than overt experiences of trauma, clinicians and TGNC individuals may not identify them as traumatic (Richmond et al., 2012). Over time, however, the cumulative effects of insidious traumas can increase the likelihood of developing PTSD and/or complex PTSD (Brown, 2008; Root, 1992). Furthermore, such subtle transnegative messages have self-fulfilling tendencies. When internalized, these messages can trigger self-critical thoughts that provoke powerful emotions, such as shame and guilt (Heath, Lynch, Fritch, McArthur, & Smith, 2011). Additionally, these messages can influence the way in which a TGNC individual constructs identity (Lev, 2004). By giving careful attention to how a client discusses identity as well as how a client refers to other TGNC people, a therapist can assess the degree to which insidious traumas have become a part of a client's narrative.

FOCUS ON INTERSECTIONALITY

Gender bias, however, is not the only motive for violence directed at TGNC clients. TGNC survivors of violence are disproportionally young, Black, unemployed, and of lower socioeconomic status, demonstrating that traumatic incidents often involve multiple systemic oppressions (Lombardi et al., 2002; Stotzer, 2008). Older and employed TGNC individuals have a lower probability of experiencing violence (Lombardi et al., 2002). Insidious traumas, in particular, may be motivated by multiple biases, and, for this reason, the consideration of sociocultural variables is critical to understanding the experience and aftermath of any incident of violence or discrimination (Briere & Scott, 2014; Brown, 2008). The power often denied or ascribed to a TGNC individual's social identities (e.g., race, class, disability status, sexual orientation) will influence the type of trauma they experience and their posttrauma reactions

(Briere & Scott, 2014). By taking an intersectional approach, clinicians can more readily conceptualize how to support clients in dealing with multiple oppressions and developing strategies for creating safety (Root, 1992; van der Kolk, McFarlane, & Weisaeth, 1996).

DEVELOPMENTAL PERSPECTIVES ON TRAUMATIC EXPERIENCES OF TGNC INDIVIDUALS

Additionally, traumatic events occur during, and are contextualized by, critical periods of development, particularly in childhood and adolescence (Courtois & Ford, 2012). Baltes (1987) noted the multidirectionality of humans' development, articulating a systemic perspective of development. Because there is no way to divorce an individual's development from environment and context, human development consists of a series of gains and losses (Baltes, 1987). Thus, context continuously shapes what humans developmentally lose and gain. Traumatic stress, in its various forms, presents uniquely in TGNC individuals' psychological functioning at different points across the lifespan. As such, it is important to understand the unique ways in which trauma theory and practice interface with these various developmental levels to provide a comprehensive understanding of trauma assessment and treatment for TGNC clients.

Prenatal/Infancy

With the advancement of obstetric technology, prenatal diagnoses of disorders of sexual development have become more common, albeit controversial. The term *disorders of sexual development* or DSD has become popularized to describe intersex conditions, particularly within the medical context (Accord Alliance, 2008; Hughes, Houk, Ahmed, Lee, & LWPES/ ESPE Consensus Group, 2006). Although not all individuals who have been diagnosed with DSDs identify as TGNC, there are overlaps between the TGNC and intersex communities. Intersex individuals who are TGNC have a unique experience given their interactions with the medical community early in life, which are sometimes characterized as coercive (Ehrenreich & Barr, 2005). When families first learn of their child's diagnosis, there is often a tremendous amount of fear, confusion, and grief (Leidolf, Curran, & Scout, 2008). Decisions about surgery and hormones are frequently made under the expectation that an infant needs medical intervention, even without the consent of the child. This is in spite of the facts that in most cases these procedures are not medical emergencies, with the exception of those allowing for proper waste excretion. Unfortunately, such early surgical interventions have later been associated with feelings of anxiety, betrayal, and helplessness—largely due to the inability to consent to irreversible and invasive surgical and hormonal treatments (Chittenden, 2011; Creighton & Liao, 2004).

Often such interventions occur before a child is even born. One of the most popular forms of treatment is the use of the steroid dexamethasone, which is prescribed to a pregnant person whose fetus may be at risk for congenital adrenal hyperplasia (CAH) to prevent the masculinization of female genitalia (Dreger, Feder, & Tamar-Mattis, 2012; Fausto-Sterling, 2000). The prenatal use of dexamethasone has been associated with many health risks for the pregnant person and the child, including failure to thrive, delayed psychomotor development, and impaired verbal working memory in the child (Fausto-Sterling, 2000; Lajic, Nordenström, & Hirvikoski, 2011). Proponents of this treatment state that the psychological distress caused to parent and child by the presence of genitalia that does not fit societal expectations merits the use of this experimental, prenatal treatment in spite of its potential negative side effects (Dreger et al., 2012; Fausto-Sterling, 2000; Vos & Bruinse, 2010). Opponents of this treatment question how a physically deleterious treatment plan can be justified for treating a non–life threatening and cosmetic condition (Dreger et al., 2012; Fausto-Sterling, 2000).

Only a small number of DSDs result in individuals presenting with genitalia that do not fit into a binary sex assignment, the most notable being CAH and partial androgen insensitivity syndrome (PAIS; APA, 2006; Beers, Porter, Jones, Kaplan, & Berkwits, 2006). Historically, these individuals have undergone sexual reconstruction surgeries within the first 3 to 12 months of life (Kessler, 1998). Sexual reconstructive surgeries for DSD during infancy and childhood, especially feminizing procedures, have been associated with severe physiological and psychological difficulties (Chittenden, 2011; Creighton & Liao, 2004). With regard to the latter, many patients report experiences of trauma, including feelings of shame, confusion, identity issues, and sexual and social anxiety (Creighton & Liao, 2004). This has been attributed largely to the invasiveness of the procedures (focused on genitalia), the lack of disclosure to the patient about their condition, and the lack of informed consent to these procedures by the patient (Chittenden, 2011). With these procedures, one sees how invasive medical interventions could be traumatic for a young individual and could likely trigger developmental losses at a young age, exemplifying Baltes's (1987) theory of multidirectional human development.

Childhood

Scholars have also noted the particular ways in which trauma influences the psychological well-being of children postinfancy (Cohen, Mannarino, & Deblinger, 2012) as a series of obstructions or possible losses. In particular, trauma can negatively influence neurobiological growth and development in children. Specifically, various scholars have suggested the relationship between trauma and the amygdala, as well as trauma and various parts of the frontal lobe and prefrontal cortex (De Bellis & Zisk, 2014). Further, childhood trauma has been associated with difficulty in building and sustaining healthy relationships, which can continue into adulthood (Brown, 2008).

For children who are TGNC, trauma can be incident based (e.g., hate crimes, one-time incidents of assault, physical harassment) or ongoing (e.g., teasing, rejection, bullying). As many children begin to understand notions of gender as early as 5 years old (Broderick & Blewitt, 2010), gender-focused trauma may severely complicate their budding self-concept and cause them to doubt themselves, their abilities, and/or their relationships. Incident-based hate crimes and bullying have been continuously documented as problematic to TGNC children's well-being (Brill & Pepper, 2008; Kosciw, Greytak, Palmer, & Boesen, 2013). Further, as there is growing documentation to suggest that families may be the instigators of some insidious trauma for children (Burnes, Dexter, Richmond, Singh, & Cherrington, 2016), children may begin to internalize caregivers' traumatic responses of hate, rejection, and abuse and begin to engage in negative health-related behaviors to cope with traumatic responses. Unfortunately, these developmental experiences provide a context for TGNC children to experience higher rates of trauma in comparison with their peers (Mallon & DeCrescenzo, 2006). Scholars suggested that TGNC clients report a higher prevalence of emotional maltreatment in childhood compared with a group of psychiatric inpatients (Mallon & DeCrescenzo, 2006). These emotional traumas were in turn associated with higher levels of dissociative symptoms in adulthood (Kersting et al., 2003). Additionally, more than half of TGNC adults in an empirical study reported an unwanted sexual event before the age of 18, which Gehring and Knudson (2005) attributed to the peer-perpetrators' curiosity about the sex of a TGNC person.

Adolescence

Researchers continue to document the increased risk of victimization that TGNC adolescents face in school settings (Gonzalez & McNulty, 2010; Kosciw et al., 2013). Further, scholars have suggested that adolescents are questioning, forming, and experimenting with their various, intersecting identities as a major developmental task to achieve a cohesive sense of self. Thus, some TGNC adolescents will need to cope with incident-based and insidious levels of trauma while concurrently developing an identity (Singh, Meng, & Hansen, 2014).

For adolescents who are TGNC, coping with trauma, particularly in the forms of harassment and victimization, may result in the manifestation of a variety of mental health symptoms, including internalized and externalized behaviors that may be interpreted as mood disturbances, anxiety, dissociation, characterological traits, substance abuse, or conduct and oppositional defiant disorders (Cohen et al., 2012). Like the case of Zeke, some adolescents will cope with trauma through self-injury, accelerated sexual behavior, and/or avoiding professionals (e.g., doctors, school administrators) who may further cause them suffering through aggressive acts. Such behaviors have been documented in TGNC adults who are traumatized (Richmond et al., 2012) and have slowly begun to be generalized to adolescent populations. As their peers begin to engage in the developmental task of peer relationships and the development of social competencies, it may be difficult for the TGNC adolescent to form such relationships, and they may isolate themselves for fear of further ridicule, bullying, or traumatic incidents. A growing literature has focused on the resilience of these youth (e.g., Singh et al., 2014) in finding social support networks through online communities, communities that support them in identifying their own gender, and in reframing mental health challenges as they navigate relationships with family and friends (Burnes et al., 2016).

Adulthood and Aging

Although TGNC adults and older adults may be independent from caregivers, depending on their financial or physical health status, they still experience traumatic incidents at disproportionate rates. Richmond et al. (2012) outlined three specific types of traumatic encounters that TGNC adults are likely to experience on the basis of nomenclature from the World Health Organization: *intrapersonal, interpersonal,* and *collective.* From this ecological framework, TGNC adults are likely to experience trauma from many different types of environmental engagement, including (but not limited to) self-violating behaviors (intrapersonal trauma), verbal harassment (interpersonal trauma), and lack of health care benefits (collective trauma).

For older adults who are TGNC, coping with institutional trauma, particularly in the forms of harassment and victimization from assisted living staff or from marginalizing members of the medical community, can result in trauma-focused symptoms. Although the literature on the experiences of older adults who are TGNC has only begun to accumulate, there is some documentation to suggest that TGNC individuals continue their trauma narrative into older adulthood (Fredriksen-Goldsen et al., 2014). As older adults are beginning to make meaningful contributions and reflect on their lives, TGNC older adults may continue to cope with harassment and victimization while also utilizing their resilience to live the last portions of their lives with meaning (Applebaum & Maddux, 2010). For some TGNC older adults, it may be difficult to engage with a life of insidious trauma, resulting in exacerbated illness and health risks.

Effects

The effects of traumatic stressors on TGNC individuals at these various points throughout the developmental lifespan are well documented in the literature (Richmond et al., 2012; Singh & McKleroy, 2011). TGNC individuals have a high rate of suicide ideation and suicide attempts, with scholars estimating that one third of TGNC people have attempted suicide (Kenagy, 2005; Xavier, 2000). Additionally, in a large online sample of TGNC adults, 42% reported a lifetime history of nonsuicidal self-injurious behavior (dickey, Reisner, & Juntunen, 2015). Further, substance abuse is prevalent among TGNC populations, and financial stress and sex work, in particular, have been associated with substance abuse (Nemoto, Operario, Keatley, & Villegas, 2004; Mizock & Lewis, 2008). HIV rates are also quite high among TGNC women, ranging from 14% (Rodriquez-Madera & Toro-Alfonso, 2000) to 47% (Nemoto et al., 2004), and TGNC adolescents, in particular, are highly vulnerable to contracting HIV (Sausa, 2005). Many of the effects of trauma heighten an individual's vulnerability to experiencing additional traumatic stressors, which creates a vicious cycle of psychological distress (Shipherd, Maguen, Skidmore, & Abramovitz, 2011).

TREATMENT CONSIDERATIONS WITH TGNC SURVIVORS OF TRAUMATIC EXPERIENCES

Assessment

To begin MHP work with a TGNC survivor of traumatic stress, a comprehensive assessment of trauma history is essential (Brown, 2008). A developmental review helps to assess for the presence of traumatic experiences throughout the lifespan, and it is useful to inquire about particular symptoms associated with PTSD and complex PTSD. Using the feminist consciousness, MHPs should collaborate with clients, be transparent about the purposes of the assessment, and empower the client to answer questions in a way that the client feels comfortable. In addition to a semi-structured interview, MHPs should consider utilizing the Trauma Symptom Inventory (TSI; Briere & Scott, 2014). The TSI is sensitive to cultural and gender variations in clients' symptom presentation (Brown, 2008). Additionally, direct questions about identity can be useful in assessing for the experience of microaggressions. For example, a MHP could ask, "Has there ever been a time when you felt you were being treated differently because of your gender/race/class?" During the initial assessment, MHPs should be particularly attentive to process symptoms, including avoidant and/or activation responses, somatization, affect dysregulation, and/or relational disruptions (Briere & Scott, 2014). These symptoms are common among individuals who have experienced traumatic stress, and their assessment will also help in distinguishing between PTSD and complex PTSD. Finally, it is critical that assessments explore contextual stressors (e.g., access to health care, stable employment, safe housing), access to social networks (e.g., supportive friends, family members, support groups), and co-occurring concerns (e.g., substance abuse, eating disorders, medical concerns).

MHPs taking an affirming stance toward working with TGNC clients can use strengths-based assessments to explore sources of resiliency and posttraumatic growth in their assessment and treatment of trauma-related experiences. These assessments may be TGNC focused, such as the gender Minority Stress and Resilience Measure (GMSR; Testa, Habarth, Peta, Balsalm, & Bockting, 2015) or the Transgender Identity Survey (Bockting, Miner, Swinburne Romine, Robinson, Rosser, & Coleman, 2014). Although these are assessments intended for use during mental health research, there are numerous items that trauma practitioners may incorporate into their assessment and treatment planning of trauma and resilience. For instance, items from the GMSR include "I am proud to be a person whose gender identity is different from my sex assigned at birth" and "I feel part of a community of people who share my gender identity."

Treatment Formulation

The development of safety is an essential start to effective trauma counseling (Briere & Scott, 2014). In the case of TGNC individuals, there are unique variables that will influence the degree to which safety is achieved. First, therapists should take a clear TGNC-affirmative stance. This requires that, prior to meeting with clients, MHPs engage in self-reflection about their own gender journey. *My New Gender Workbook: A Step-By-Step Guide to Achieving World Peace Through Gender Anarchy and Sex Positivity* by Kate Bornstein (2013) is an excellent resource for reflecting on gender identity. Additionally, MHPs should have had training in therapeutic work with TGNC individuals. More specifically, MHPs should not rely on a client for education about TGNC identity (Richmond et al., 2012). During the first meeting, MHPs should ask about the pronouns and name(s) a client uses and assure the client that these can change when and if needed (Richmond et al., 2012). Additionally, intake paperwork and other assessment materials should include multiple options for pronouns. For example, paperwork could include open-ended options or allow for multiple selections. Particularly when working with survivors of trauma, using the incorrect pronoun could trigger strong emotions, including anger and helplessness. To create a safe therapeutic environment, the waiting room and surrounding areas should also be TGNC affirming, with materials reflecting that TGNC individuals are welcome. Gender-neutral bathrooms should be available, and where this is not possible, the MHP should discuss this with the client (American Psychological Association, 2015).

Self-Advocacy

Another component of safety (and a critical element of the feminist perspective) is helping clients learn how to advocate for themselves, particularly with other health care providers, from a place of empowerment (Worell & Remer, 2003). It is not uncommon for TGNC individuals to avoid medical assistance because of a fear of mistreatment (Lombardi, 2001). MHPs can remind clients about their rights and also prepare them for interactions by engaging in role-playing activities (Richmond et al., 2012). Further, assertiveness training can help clients address discriminatory and/or invasive questions. For example, a TGNC individual can practice how to address a health care provider who uses an incorrect pronoun or learn how to negotiate with health insurance companies regarding authorization for coverage of medical care.

Safety also includes attention to high-risk behavior and self-care (Richmond et al., 2012). Self-injurious behaviors, substance abuse, and chaotic interpersonal relationships can be disruptive to the process of creating safety. MHPs can help to reduce these concerns by providing psychoeducation about the reasons such behaviors developed and their likely connection to traumatic stress. Prior to reducing high-risk behaviors, however, alternative coping strategies should be collaboratively developed (Briere & Scott, 2014). Such strategies, for example, include relaxation training, mindfulness, stress management techniques, trauma-sensitive yoga, support groups, and psychotropic medications (Briere & Scott, 2014). MHPs can also assist clients like Zeke in learning how to self-sooth and self-nurture, which are critical skills used to contain trauma symptoms (e.g., flashbacks, dissociative experiences) and to help with processing of traumatic memories during therapy (Briere & Scott, 2014).

Although not every TGNC individual will be able to achieve safety and stabilization, for those who do, it is appropriate to revisit trauma experiences and carefully rework and integrate trauma material. Evidence-based treatments, including exposure therapy (Foa, Hembree, & Rothbaum, 2007), eye movement desensitization and reprocessing (Shapiro & Solomon, 1995), cognitive processing therapy, and dialectical behavior therapy (Linehan, 1993), are useful during this process. The goal of revisiting trauma material is to assist in reprocessing and integrating difficult memories and emotions. This process can be destabilizing, so it is critical that the TGNC individual have developed sufficient stabilization skills to manage the affect associated with reprocessing (Courtois & Ford, 2012). It is especially critical that a TGNC individual have a strong social support network during this phase of counseling. Often it is helpful for a TGNC person to connect with other survivors who can normalize and validate their experiences (Schrock, Holden, & Reid, 2004). If a TGNC person joins a support group, the therapist should assist the client in learning how to evaluate the safety of such groups.

Once trauma memories are processed, it is not uncommon for survivors to construct a survivor identity (Brown, 2008). Self-reflective exercises assist the client in understanding their evolving thoughts and feelings about their identity, and they can also help the client begin to trust their own insights (Bockting, Knudson, & Goldberg, 2006). Such exercises can include journal writing, artistic expressions, or thought-based records (Richmond et al., 2012). An additional goal of these exercises is to promote resiliency through the process of meaning making, particularly as it relates to the larger challenges associated with living in a hegemonic context. Research on the resilience of TGNC people in response to anti-TGNC stigma indicates that having a sense of pride in one's gender identity, cultivating a sense of hope, and access to health care are important sources of resilience (Singh, Hays, & Watson, 2011). Some of these sources of resilience may be influenced by a TGNC person's multiple social identities (e.g., race/ethnicity, age) and multiple experiences of oppression (e.g., racism, ableism). For instance, research on resilience of TGNC adults of color who have survived traumatic life experiences has suggested that pride in both their gender and racial/ethnic identity may be a source of resilience to trauma (Singh & McKleroy, 2011). Research has also suggested that the resilience strategies of TGNC youth of color may be connected to how they self-identify their racial/ethnic and gender identities; advocate for themselves in educational systems; experience predominantly White, queer, and TGNC youth centers; and use social media to connect with TGNC people of color (Singh, 2013).

WORKING TO CHANGE THE SYSTEM

In addition to the very important clinical work conducted within a therapeutic context, it is also critical for MHPs to engage with the social context outside of the therapeutic relationship. Ultimately, systemic social change is necessary to eliminate many of the daily traumatic stressors that individuals face (Nelson & Prilleltensky, 2010). A feminist approach considers engagement with the social context a critical component of therapy (Brown, 2004). A variety of macrolevel policy reports (e.g., Grant et al., 2011) have noted that verbal and physical harassment of TGNC individuals occur at disproportionate rates and therefore create a wide range of traumatic symptoms. Such reports note the importance of individuals having support on a variety of ecological levels to ensure safety and TGNC-affirmative care. Specifically, the need for policy that ensures safety for TGNC people is of primary importance. MHPs can lobby their elected officials for legislation ensure nondiscrimination at the local, state, and national levels. Peck and DeLeon (2011) noted that although MHPs are often not trained to advocate for the rights of their clients and of the profession and the need for advocacy from MHPs is increasing drastically. To answer this call to action, MHPs must advocate for the needs of TGNC people, including nondiscrimination policies in private and public sectors. Further, policies must be created to ensure that TGNC people can receive appropriate insurance coverage for all aspects of their medical transition (National Center for Transgender Equality, 2014). Finally, educating policymakers about the unique psychosocial stressors that TGNC people encounter is also of importance.

Singh and Burnes (2011) noted the importance of street activism for feminist MHPs, articulating innovative strategies for enhancing well-being through activism at microecological levels, such as acknowledging White privilege, breaking through silence, and communicating openly about resistance in the counseling room. We believe that such a feminist framework is a crucial component of engaging processes and outcomes of social justice on behalf of TGNC individuals. MHPs advocating for and with TGNC communities must acknowledge the multiple complexities of engaging in activism for individuals who hold multiple identities other than being TGNC, many of which might also be systematically oppressed (Burnes & Chen, 2012). Such activism can occur through critical self-examination as individuals or in small groups or facilitated large groups to understand the multiple layers of privilege and oppression that may exist. Further, scholars have noted the importance of recognizing resilience through activism (Singh, Richmond, & Burnes, 2013) and the historical precedent that TGNC people have had in local and street-based resistance initiatives (e.g., the Stonewall riots; The TransAdvocate, 2013).

MHPs who engage with such activist initiatives on behalf of TGNC clients can seek to collaborate with TGNC community-based organizations, working on micro-, meso-, and macrolevels of systemic change (Singh & Burnes, 2010). Advocating for TGNC communities without asking TGNC individuals what they need can replicate trauma-based hierarchies in the lives of these individuals. Therefore, engaging gender-diverse individuals in critical conversations about experiences of privilege and marginalization are extremely crucial to not replicate the systems of neglect that TGNC people have experienced (Singh et al., 2013).

MENTAL HEALTH PROVIDER SELF-CARE

MHPs working with gender-diverse survivors of trauma will also need to attend to their own self-care, particularly because such work can influence a MHP's emotional and professional well-being, including vicarious trauma (VT) and secondary traumatic stress (STS). VT is a condition that results directly from working with traumatized clients and is characterized by interference with the MHP's feelings, cognitive schemas, memories, self-esteem, and/or sense of safety (Hernández, Engstrom, & Gangsei, 2010). STS is a term for a condition resulting from the "natural consequences of caring" for an individual who has been affected by a traumatic experience, and it is characterized by symptoms almost identical to PTSD (Devilly, Wright, & Varker, 2009, p. 374). There are few studies directly analyzing the experience of these conditions in mental health care providers working with gender-diverse clients (Devilly et al., 2009). Research on these conditions indicates that the following factors could influence the manifestation of VT specifically: amount of exposure to traumatized clients, frequency of working with traumatized clients, capacity for empathetic response, and a personal history of trauma (Devilly et al., 2009).

Although working with traumatized clients can have deleterious effects on the well-being of MHPs, research suggests that these therapeutic processes can also benefit professionals. *Vicarious resilience*, for example, can work to counteract VT and STS. Vicarious resilience is characterized by a renewed sense of motivation and meaning spurred by the resilience and posttraumatic growth of a client as this individual is "positively transformed" in spite of or because of her/his/their experience of trauma (Hernández et al., 2010). Such meaning can be derived from connecting with other health care providers and organizations that support MHPs who work with TGNC individuals (e.g., World Professional Association for Transgender Health).

Chapter Summary

As researchers and clinicians who work with TGNC individuals, we have found our work to be tremendously rewarding, yet complicated. So often, TGNC individuals deal with multiple systemic and interpersonal barriers that stem from TGNC-bias and discrimination. This creates additional challenges for the therapeutic process, particularly when working with TGNC survivors of trauma. We believe that a feminist, strengths-based, and social justice approach that addresses immediate therapeutic individual concerns and attends to transforming hegemonic social norms and policies is ultimately the best treatment option.

References

Accord Alliance. (2008). *Clinical guidelines for the management of disorders of sex development in childhood.* Retrieved from http://www. accordalliance.org/dsdguidelines/htdocs/clinical/index.html

American Psychiatric Association. (2013). *Diagnostic and statistical manual of mental disorders* (5th ed.). Washington, DC: Author.

American Psychological Association. (2006). *Answers to your questions about individuals with intersex conditions.* Retrieved from http://www.apa.org/topics/lgbt/intersex.pdf

American Psychological Association. (2015). Guidelines for psychological practice with transgender and gender nonconforming people. *American Psychologist, 70,* 832–864. http://dx.doi.org/10.1037/a0039906

Applebaum, J. (Producer), & Maddux, S. (Producer & Director). (2010). *Gen Silent* [Motion picture]. United States: Interrobang! Productions, LLC.

Baltes, P. B. (1987). Theoretical propositions of life-span developmental psychology: On the dynamics between growth and decline. *Developmental Psychology, 23,* 611–626. http://dx.doi.org/10.1037/0012-1649.23.5.611

Beers, M. H., Porter, R. S., Jones, T. V., Kaplan, J. T., & Berkwits, M. (2006). *The Merck Manual of Diagnosis and Treatment* (18th ed.). Sacramento, CA: Merck.

Berg, S. H. (2002). The PTSD diagnosis: Is it good for women? *Affilia, 17,* 55–68. http://dx.doi.org/10.1177/0886109902017001004

Bockting, W. O., Knudson, G., & Goldberg, J. M. (2006). Counseling and mental health care for transgender adults and loved ones. *International Journal of Transgenderism, 9,* 35–82. http://dx.doi.org/10.1300/J485v09n03_03

Bockting, W. O., Miner, M. H., Swinburne Romine, R. E., Robinson, B. E., Rosser, B. R. S., & Coleman, E. (2014). *The Transgender Identity Survey: A measure of internalized transphobia.* Manuscript submitted for publication.

Bornstein, K. (2013). *My new gender workbook: A step-by-step guide to achieving world piece through gender anarchy and sex positivity.* New York, NY: Routledge.

Bowen, D. J., Bradford, J., & Powers, D. (2007). Comparing sexual minority status across sampling methods and populations. *Women & Health, 44,* 121–134. http://dx.doi.org/10.1300/J013v44n02_07

Briere, J., & Scott, C. (2014). *Principles of trauma therapy: A guide to symptoms, evaluation and treatment* (2nd ed.). Thousand Oaks, CA: Sage.

Brill, S. A., & Pepper, R. (2008). *The transgender child: A handbook for families and professionals*. San Francisco, CA: Cleis Press.

Broderick, P. C., & Blewitt, P. (2010). *The life span: Human development for helping professionals* (3rd ed.). New York, NY: Pearson/Prentice Hall.

Brown, L. S. (2004). Feminist paradigms of trauma treatment. *Psychotherapy: Theory, Research, Practice, Training, 41*, 464–471. http://dx.doi.org/10.1037/0033-3204.41.4.464

Brown, L. S. (2008). *Cultural competence in trauma therapy: Beyond the flashback*. Washington, DC: American Psychological Association. http://dx.doi.org/10.1037/11752-000

Burnes, T. R., & Chen, M. (2012). Multiple identities of transgender individuals: Incorporating a framework of intersectionality to gender crossing. In R. Josselson & M. Harway (Eds.), *Navigating multiple identities: Race, gender, culture, nationality and roles* (pp. 113–128). New York, NY: Oxford University Press. http://dx.doi.org/10.1093/acprof:oso/9780199732074.003.0007

Burnes, T. R., Dexter, M. D., Richmond, K., Singh, A. A., & Cherrington, A. (2016). The experiences of transgender survivors of trauma who undergo social and medical Transition. *Traumatology, 22*, 75–84. http://dx.doi.org/10.1037/trm0000064

Burnes, T. R., & Richmond, K. (2012). Counseling strategies with intersex clients: A process-based approach. In S. H. Dworkin & M. Pope (Eds.), *Casebook for counseling lesbian, gay, bisexual, and transgender persons and their families* (pp. 35–44). Alexandria, VA: American Counseling Association.

Chittenden, K. S. (2011). *The cost of normal: The subjective experience of intersexed individuals who have undergone corrective genital surgery* (Doctoral dissertation). Retrieved from RUcore (10001800001).

Cohen, J. A., Mannarino, A. P., & Deblinger, E. (2012). *Trauma-focused CBT for children and adolescents: Treatment implications*. New York, NY: Guilford Press.

Connor, K. M., & Davidson, J. R. T. (2003). Development of a new resilience scale: The Connor-Davidson Resilience Scale (CD-RISC). *Depression and Anxiety, 18*, 76–82. http://dx.doi.org/10.1002/da.10113

Courtois, C. A., & Ford, J. D. (2012). *Treatment of complex trauma: A sequenced, relationship-based approach*. New York, NY: Guilford Press.

Creighton, S. M., & Liao, L.-M. (2004). Changing attitudes to sex assignment in intersex. *BJU International, 93*, 659–664. http://dx.doi.org/10.1111/j.1464-410X.2003.04694.x

De Bellis, M. D., & Zisk, A. (2014). The biological effects of childhood trauma. *Child and Adolescent Psychiatric Clinics of North America, 23*, 185–222. http://dx.doi.org/10.1016/j.chc.2014.01.002

Devilly, G. J., Wright, R., & Varker, T. (2009). Vicarious trauma, secondary traumatic stress or simply burnout? Effect of trauma therapy on mental health professionals. *Australian and New Zealand Journal of Psychiatry,* *43,* 373–382. http://dx.doi.org/10.1080/00048670902721079

dickey, l. m., Reisner, S. L., & Juntunen, C. L. (2015). Non-suicidal self-injury in a large online sample of transgender adults. *Professional Psychology: Research and Practice, 46,* 3–11. http://dx.doi.org/10.1037/a0038803

Donnon, T., & Hammond, W. (2007). A psychometric assessment of the self-reported youth resiliency: Assessing Developmental Strengths questionnaire. *Psychological Reports, 100,* 963–978. http://dx.doi.org/10.2466/pr0.100.3.963-978

Dreger, A., Feder, E. K., & Tamar-Mattis, A. (2012). Prenatal dexamethasone for congenital adrenal hyperplasia: An ethics canary in the modern medical mine. *Journal of Bioethical Inquiry, 9,* 277–294. http://dx.doi.org/10.1007/s11673-012-9384-9

Ehrenreich, N., & Barr, M. (2005). Intersex surgery, female genital cutting, and the selective condemnation of 'cultural practices'. *Harvard Civil Rights-Civil Liberties Law Review, 40,* 71–140.

Espin, O. M., & Gawelek, M. A. (1992). Women's diversity: Ethnicity, race, class, and gender in theories of feminist psychology. In L. S. Brown & M. Ballou (Eds.), *Personality and psychopathology: Feminist reappraisals* (pp. 88–109). New York, NY: Guilford Press.

Fausto-Sterling, A. (2000). *Sexing the body: Gender politics and the construction of sexuality.* New York, NY: Basic Books.

Foa, E. B., Hembree, E. A., & Rothbaum, B. O. (2007). *Prolonged exposure therapy for PTSD.* New York, NY: Oxford University Press.

Fredriksen-Goldsen, K. I., Cook-Daniels, L., Kim, H. J., Erosheva, E. A., Emlet, C. A., Hoy-Ellis, C. P., . . . Muraco, A. (2014). Physical and mental health of transgender older adults: An at-risk and underserved population. *The Gerontologist, 54,* 488–500.

Freyd, J. J., DePrince, A., & Gleaves, D. (2007). The state of betrayal trauma theory: Reply to McNally—Conceptual issues and future directions. *Memory, 15,* 295–311. http://dx.doi.org/10.1080/09658210701256514

Gehring, D., & Knudson, G. (2005). Prevalence of childhood trauma in a clinical population of transsexual people. *International Journal of Transgenderism, 8,* 23–30.

Gonzalez, M., & McNulty, J. (2010). Achieving competency with transgender youth: School counselors as collaborative advocates. *Journal of LGBT Issues in Counseling, 4,* 176–186. http://dx.doi.org/10.1080/15538605.2010.524841

Grant, J. M., Mottet, L. A., Tanis, J., Harrison, J., Herman, J. L., & Keisling, M. (2011). *Injustice at every turn: A report of the national transgender discrimination survey.* Washington, DC: National Center for Transgender Equality and National Gay and Lesbian Task Force.

Heath, N. M., Lynch, S. M., Fritch, A. M., McArthur, L. N., & Smith, S. L. (2011). Silent survivors: Rape myth acceptance in incarcerated women's narratives of disclosure and reporting of rape. *Psychology of Women Quarterly, 35,* 596–610. http://dx.doi.org/10.1177/0361684311407870

Herman, J. (1992). Complex PTSD: A syndrome in survivors of prolonged and repeated trauma. *Journal of Traumatic Stress, 5,* 377–391. http://dx.doi.org/10.1002/jts.2490050305

Hernández, P., Engstrom, D., & Gangsei, D. (2010). Exploring the impact of trauma on therapists: Vicarious resilience and related concepts in training. *Journal of Systemic Therapies, 29,* 67–83.

Hughes, I. A., Houk, C., Ahmed, S. F., Lee, P. A., & the Lawson Wilkins Pediatric Endocrine Society/European Society for Paediatric Endocrinology Consensus Group. (2006). Consensus statement on management of intersex disorders. *Journal of Pediatric Urology, 2,* 148–162. http://dx.doi.org/10.1016/j.jpurol.2006.03.004

Institute of Medicine. (2011). *The health of lesbian, gay, bisexual, and transgender people: Building a foundation for better understanding.* Washington, DC: National Academy of Sciences.

Kenagy, G. P. (2005). Transgender health: Findings from two needs assessment studies in Philadelphia. *Health & Social Work, 30,* 19–26.

Kersting, A., Reutemann, M., Gast, U., Ohrmann, P., Suslow, T., Michael, N., & Arolt, V. (2003). Dissociative disorders and traumatic childhood experiences in transsexuals. *Journal of Nervous and Mental Disease, 191,* 182–189. http://dx.doi.org/10.1097/01.NMD.0000054932.22929.5D

Kessler, S. J. (1998). *Lessons from the intersexed.* New Brunswick, NJ: Rutgers University Press.

Koken, J. A., Bimbi, D. S., & Parsons, J. T. (2009). Experiences of familial acceptance–rejection among transwomen of color. *Journal of Family Psychology, 23,* 853–860. http://dx.doi.org/10.1037/a0017198

Kosciw, J., Greytak, E., Palmer, N., & Boesen, M. (2013). *The 2013 National School Climate Survey.* Retrieved from http://www.glsen.org/article/2013-national-school-climate-survey

Lafrance, M. N., & McKenzie-Mohr, S. (2013). The DSM and its lure of legitimacy. *Feminism & Psychology, 23,* 119–140. http://dx.doi.org/10.1177/0959353512467974

Lajic, S., Nordenström, A., & Hirvikoski, T. (2011). Long-term outcome of prenatal dexamethasone treatment of 21-hydroxylase deficiency. *Endocrine Development, 20,* 96–105.

Leidolf, E. M., Curran, M., & Scout, B. J. (2008). Intersex mental health and social support options in pediatric endocrinology training programs. *Journal of Homosexuality, 54,* 233–242. http://dx.doi.org/10.1080/00918360801982074

Lev, A. I. (2004). *Transgender emergence.* Binghamton, NY: Haworth.

Lind, A. (2004). Legislating the family: Heterosexist bias in social welfare policy frameworks. *Journal of Sociology and Social Welfare, 31,* 21–35.

Linehan, M. (1993). *Cognitive-behavioral treatment of borderline personality disorder.* New York, NY: Guilford Press.

Lombardi, E. (2001). Enhancing transgender health care. *American Journal of Public Health, 91,* 869–872. http://dx.doi.org/10.2105/AJPH.91.6.869

Lombardi, E. L., Wilchins, R. A., Priesing, D., & Malouf, D. (2002). Gender violence: Transgender experiences with violence and discrimination. *Journal of Homosexuality, 42,* 89–101. http://dx.doi.org/10.1300/J082v42n01_05

Maine, C. (2004). *Feminist-narrative therapy: Treating PTSD and substance abuse in women* (Doctoral dissertation). Alliant International University, San Francisco, CA.

Mallon, G. P., & DeCrescenzo, T. (2006). Transgender children and youth: A child welfare practice perspective. *Child Welfare, 85,* 215–241.

Mizock, L., & Lewis, T. K. (2008). Trauma in transgender populations: Risk, resilience, and clinical care. *Journal of Emotional Abuse, 8,* 335–354. http://dx.doi.org/10.1080/10926790802262523

Nadal, K. L. (2013). *That's so gay! Microaggressions and the lesbian, gay, bisexual, and transgender community.* Washington, DC: American Psychological Association. http://dx.doi.org/10.1037/14093-000

Nadal, K. L., Skolnik, A., & Wong, Y. (2012). Interpersonal and systemic microaggressions toward transgender people: Implications for counseling. *Journal of LGBT Issues in Counseling, 6,* 55–82. http://dx.doi.org/10.1080/15538605.2012.648583

National Center for Transgender Equality. (2014, March). *Health care rights for transgender people.* Washington, DC: Author.

Nelson, G., & Prilleltensky, I. (2010). *Community psychology: In pursuit of liberation and well-being* (2nd ed.). Basingstoke, England: Palgrave Macmillan.

Nemoto, T., Operario, D., Keatley, J., & Villegas, D. (2004). Social context of HIV risk behaviours among male-to-female transgenders of colour. *AIDS Care, 16,* 724–735.

Peck, J. A., & DeLeon, P. H. (2011). Representing psychology in California at the state and federal levels: The big picture. *The California Psychologist, 44*(2), 6–9.

Pickering, D., & Leinbaugh, T. (2006). *Counselor self-efficacy with transgender clients* (Unpublished doctoral dissertation). Ohio University, Athens.

Richmond, K., Burnes, T. R., & Carroll, K. (2012). Lost in trans-lation: Interpreting systems of trauma for transgender clients. *Traumatology, 18*(1), 45–57. http://dx.doi.org/10.1177/1534765610396726

Rodriquez-Madera, S., & Toro-Alfonso, J. (2000, August). *An exploratory study regarding social vulnerability, high-risk sex conduct, and HIV/AIDS in Puerto Rico's transgender community.* Paper presented at the United States Conference on AIDS, Atlanta, GA.

Root, M. P. (1992). Reconstructing the impact of trauma on personality. In L. S. Brown & M. Ballou (Eds.), *Personality and psychopathology: Feminist reappraisals* (pp. 229–265). New York, NY: Guilford Press.

Sausa, L. A. (2005). Translating research into practice: Trans youth recommendations for improving school systems. *Journal of Gay & Lesbian Issues in Education, 3,* 15–28.

Schrock, D., Holden, D., & Reid, L. (2004). Creating emotional resonance: Interpersonal emotion work and motivational framing in a transgender community. *Social Problems, 51,* 61.

Shapiro, F., & Solomon, R. M. (1995). *Eye movement desensitization and reprocessing.* Hoboken, NJ: John Wiley & Sons.

Shipherd, J. C., Maguen, S., Skidmore, W. C., & Abramovitz, S. M. (2011). Potentially traumatic events in a transgender sample: Frequency and associated symptoms. *Traumatology.* http://dx.doi.org/10.1177/1534765610395614

Singh, A. A. (2013). Transgender youth of color and resilience: Negotiating oppression, finding support. *Sex Roles, 68,* 690–702. http://dx.doi.org/10.1007/s11199-012-0149-z

Singh, A. A., & Burnes, T. R. (2010). Shifting the counselor role from gatekeeping to advocacy: Ten strategies for using the ACA Competencies for Counseling Transgender Clients for individual and social change. *Journal for Lesbian, Gay, Bisexual, and Transgender Issues in Counseling, 4,* 241–255.

Singh, A. A., & Burnes, T. R. (2011). Feminist therapy and street-level activism: Revisiting our roots and "acting up" in the next decade. *Special Issue on 21st Century Feminism. Women & Therapy, 34,* 129–142. http://dx.doi.org/10.1080/02703149.2011.532457

Singh, A. A., Hays, D. G., & Watson, L. (2011). Strategies in the face of adversity: Resilience strategies of transgender individuals. *Journal of Counseling & Development, 89,* 20–27. http://dx.doi.org/10.1002/j.1556-6678.2011.tb00057.x

Singh, A. A., & McKleroy, V. S. (2011). "Just Getting Out of Bed Is a Revolutionary Act": The resilience of transgender people of color who have survived traumatic life events. *Traumatology, 20*(10), 1–11.

Singh, A. A., Meng, S., & Hansen, A. (2014). "I am my own gender:" Resilience strategies of trans youth. *Journal of Counseling & Development, 92,* 208–218. http://dx.doi.org/10.1002/j.1556-6676.2014.00150.x

Singh, A. A., Richmond, K., & Burnes, T. R. (2013). Feminist participatory action research with transgender communities: Fostering the practice of ethical and empowering research designs. *International Journal of Transgenderism, 14,* 93–104. http://dx.doi.org/10.1080/15532739.2013.818516

Stotzer, R. L. (2008). Gender identity and hate crimes: Violence against transgender people in Los Angeles County. *Sexuality Research & Social Policy, 5,* 43–52. http://dx.doi.org/10.1525/srsp.2008.5.1.43

Testa, R. J., Habarth, J., Peta, H., Balsalm, K., & Bockting, W. (2015). Development of the Gender Minority Stress and Resilience measure. *Psychology of Sexual Orientation and Gender Diversity, 2,* 65–77. http://dx.doi.org/10.1037/sgd0000081

The TransAdvocate. (2013, January 25). *So, what was Stonewall?* Retrieved from http://www.transadvocate.com/so-what-was-stonewall_n_8424.htm

van der Kolk, B. A., McFarlane, A. C., & Weisaeth, L. (1996). *Traumatic stress: The effects of the overwhelming experience on mind, body, and society.* New York, NY: Guilford Press.

Vos, A. A., & Bruinse, H. W. (2010). Congenital adrenal hyperplasia: Do the benefits of prenatal treatment defeat the risks? *Obstetrical & Gynecological Survey, 65,* 196–205. http://dx.doi.org/10.1097/OGX.0b013e3181d61046

Winters, K. (2007). *Issues of GID diagnosis for transsexual women and men.* Retrieved from https://gidreform.wordpress.com

Worell, J., & Remer, P. (2003). *Feminist perspectives in therapy: Empowering diverse women* (2nd ed.). Hoboken, NJ: John Wiley & Sons.

Xavier, J. M. (2000). *The Washington, DC Transgender Needs Assessment Survey.* Washington, DC: Us Helping Us, People Into Living. Retrieved from http://www.glaa.org/archive/2000/tgneedsassessment1112.shtml

Ruben A. Hopwood and Tarynn M. Witten

Spirituality, Faith, and Religion
The TGNC Experience

10

R eligious, spiritual, and faith beliefs and practice play a central role in the daily lives of many, including transgender and gender nonconforming (TGNC) people (Porter, Ronneberg, & Witten, 2013). Religion, spirituality, and faith have been shown to contribute to mental health (Vahia, Chattillion, Kavirajan, & Depp, 2011), provide a framework around which people order and make sense of their lives (Koenig, 2009), give a means of perceived personal control (Fiori, Hays, & Meador, 2004), and contribute to resilience in the face of ordinary to significant adversity (McFadden, Frankowski, Flick, & Witten, 2013; Singh & McKleroy, 2011). These effects are found across the lifespan, including for TGNC people (Fiori et al., 2004; Porter et al., 2013).

In this chapter, we provide an overview of religion and spirituality, their relationship with TGNC people, and general effects of religious and spiritual beliefs and practices on mental health and well-being. We conclude the chapter with suggestions for clinical practice in working with TGNC

http://dx.doi.org/10.1037/14957-011
Affirmative Counseling and Psychological Practice With Transgender and Gender Nonconforming Clients, A. A. Singh and l. m. dickey (Editors)

people around issues of faith, belief, and religious and spiritual practice. We strive to be inclusive of Western and Eastern systems of spirituality and faith, as well as cultural differences, while acknowledging that exhaustive coverage of the experiences of TGNC people within all possible religious and spiritual systems and cultures is simply not possible in one chapter.

Understanding Religiosity, Spirituality, Faith, and TGNC People

Just as there is no homogeneous experience, identity, or expression across TGNC people, there is no homogeneous understanding of or approach to the myriad religions, faiths, and spiritualties of TGNC people (Levy & Lo, 2013). Religion and spirituality address a search for what is sacred, meaningful, or outside the ordinary, and may involve specific behaviors, beliefs, rituals, objects, symbols, expressions, and thoughts. Historically, *religion*—a word coming from the Latin *religio*—signified a bond between humans and a power greater than humanity—the sacred (Wulff, 1997). Over time, as some societies became less religious and more secular, many people rejected religious institutions as a hindrance to their personal experiences and expressions of the sacred (Zinnbauer et al., 1997), religiosity became differentiated from spirituality. This distinction resulted in a narrowing of the understanding of religion and religiousness as signifying negative aspects of institutional structures, rules, and moral codes of conduct (Zinnbauer et al., 1997), whereas spirituality became the signifier for personal experience, meaningfulness, and personal wholeness (Hill et al., 2000). Both terms, however, overlap significantly and involve a focus on the "Sacred"—a power greater than humanity that may entail a being, an object, a principle, or a concept that transcends the self, whether found within the self or outside it. However, at the core of many religious and spiritual canons addressing assigned birth sex and gender is a rigid and binary understanding of the sexes (Appleton, 2011; Levy & Lo, 2013). These binary conceptualizations of sex and gender typically shape language, laws, customs, privileges, and economies (Fausto-Sterling, 2000) and inevitably leads to beliefs and mandates from which it follows that no individual may change their assigned birth sex. This rigidity leaves no room for those who have a TGNC experience in life; an experience in which their gender self-perceptions/presentations, or even bodies, do not align with their birth sex (Conroy, 2010; Kennedy, 2008).

In spite of this more typically binary conceptualization of sex in many religions and spiritualities, TGNC individuals may still identify with a broad spectrum of religious and spiritual beliefs and practices. Hopwood (2014) examined the literature on transsexual populations and found no statistically significant differences between male-to-female (MTF) people and cisgender people in formal religious affiliation. In one study, MTF people were less affiliated with Christianity than the general U.S. population (Kosmin, Mayer, & Keysar, 2001). Other research shows a variance in religious affiliation and participation between MTF and female-to-male (FTM) people (Rosser, Oakes, Bockting, & Miner, 2007). Reasons for the underlying difference in religious affiliation and participation between FTM and MTF populations, and between TGNC and cisgender populations, are unknown at this time (Hopwood, 2014). Still, there are some important studies that help to illuminate possible religious and spiritual trends and characteristics within the larger TGNC community. For instance, Table 10.1 contains the responses of 1,963 participants of the Trans MetLife Survey on Later-Life Preparedness and Perceptions in Transgender-Identified Individuals (TMLS; Porter et al., 2013) to the question "With which particular religious/spiritual/faith tradition would you currently identify yourself?" There was a wide spectrum of religious, spiritual, and faith structures in this sample, although study limitations included that the sample was primarily White, Western-oriented, and middle to upper-middle class (Porter et al., 2013). Other literature suggests that TGNC people of color, those from non-Western cultures, with non-Western religious and spiritual beliefs and practices, and those with less economic means, may also identify with religious and spiritual beliefs and practices in a way that offers strength and resilience in the face of discrimination and trauma (bautista, Mountain, & Reynolds, 2014).

TGNC people's affiliations with and participation in religious and spiritual practices and communities may reduce stress, enhance coping, increase spiritual support and meaningful integration of significant events in life (bautista et al., 2014; Singh & McKleroy, 2011), contribute to identity formation (Vieten et al., 2013), and inform end-of-life processes (Porter et al., 2013). Although one of the main functions of religion and spirituality may be to enable people to cope with their lives, for marginalized groups religious belief systems may cause more harm than good, such as removing meaning and support (Hopwood, 2014).

For TGNC people, spirituality and religion may contribute to negative outcomes, fear, oppression, rejection, and condemnation arising from religious and spiritual prejudices and bias (McFadden et al., 2013; Porter et al., 2013). It is not surprising, then, given TGNC people's experiences of religious and spiritual biases, that a cyclical pattern emerges

TABLE 10.1

Trans MetLife Survey Religious, Spiritual, Faith Tradition Affiliation

Affiliation	No. (%)
Dominant traditions	
Catholic	154 (7.85)
Mainline Protestant	183 (9.32)
Unitarian	53 (2.7)
Quaker	19 (0.97)
Christian Scientist	14 (0.71)
Pentecostal/Charismatic/Fundamentalist	14 (0.71)
Evangelical	43 (2.19)
Mormon	5 (0.25)
Lutheran	17 (0.87)
Anglican	5 (0.25)
Baptist	7 (0.36)
United Church of Christ	7 (0.36)
Metropolitan Community Churches	10 (0.51)
Christian	29 (1.48)
Episcopal	5 (0.25)
Judaism	140 (7.13)
Islam	10 (0.51)
Nondominant traditions	
Taoist/Buddhist/Confucianist	65 (3.31)
Bahá'í	2 (0.1)
Wiccan	58 (2.95)
Earth Goddess/Sun Worship/Goddess Worship	12 (0.61)
Alternative Healing Circles	7 (0.36)
First Nations Traditional	7 (0.36)
Celtic/Pagan	43 (2.19)
Other or no traditions	
Atheist	260 (13.25)
Agnostic	192 (9.78)
Nonspecific Spirituality	414 (21.09)
Not Sure	53 (2.7)
Other	70 (3.57)
None	10 (0.51)
Mix of Beliefs	55 (2.8)
Total	1,963 (100)

Note. Data from the Trans MetLife Survey (Porter et al., 2013) question, "With which particular religious/spiritual/faith tradition would you currently identify yourself?" Overall, 28.78% affiliate with some form of Christian faith; 11.05% with a non-Christian traditional faith (Judaism, Bahá'í, Islam, and Taoist/Buddhist/Confucianist); and 6.47% fall into the categories of Celtic/Pagan, Alternative Healing Circles, First Nations Traditional, Wiccan and Earth/Sun Goddess worship. Individuals who fell into the Atheist, Agnostic, Not Sure, or None groups constituted a total of 26.24% of the respondents. Individuals who specified that they had a mixed belief set, non-specific spirituality or other form of religious, spiritual or faith represented 27.46% of the respondents.

of sexual and gender minorities rejecting religion and religious communities and those communities in turn rejecting these groups (Clark, Brown, & Hochstein, 1989). These patterns and experiences of rejection from the very systems that often provide the foundations of meaning and purpose in one's life compound the challenges of living life for TGNC people. Rejection from religious and spiritual communities combined with myriad experiences of discrimination and trauma in society leads to high rates of mental health issues, substance abuse, and alarmingly high rates of attempted suicide among TGNC people in general (Clements-Nolle, Marx, & Katz, 2006; Grant et al., 2011), and increased suicidality in TGNC older adults (Witten, 2014).

Other TGNC people fear rejection by their religious and spiritual community from significant life and death rituals, and they may make plans to return to "the closet" to feel safe or to experience those spiritual and religious traditions that are important to them, such as some TGNC Muslim women in Malaysia who chose to forego genital reconstruction and return to living as male at the end of life so that they may be buried according to their religious traditions (Koon Teh, 2001). Some TGNC people are denied funereal ceremony rights and burial rights in a religious graveyard (Koon Teh, 2001); have been returned to a sex assigned at birth for burial (Rothaus, 2014); and are denied marriage ceremonies, last rights, and access to spiritual counseling (Witten, 2014). For TGNC individuals and their families, denial of access to spiritual and religious care and rituals for various stages of life may be a significant loss beyond the normal losses experienced in life—they are potentially losses of one's soul or losses beyond human existence that cannot be recaptured or replaced in this lifetime. These experiences may leave TGNC people with negative self-images and the concept that they are of lesser or no personal worth and value to something or someone Sacred or beyond them. From this basic overview of religion, spirituality, and TGNC people, we review dominant and nondominant religious and spiritual communities, beliefs, faith, and practices within the United States in the lives of TGNC people.

DOMINANT U.S. RELIGIOUS, SPIRITUAL, AND FAITH GROUPS AND TGNC PEOPLE

Within the United States, the dominant religious groups (e.g., Jewish, Christian, Muslim) tend to codify and reify binary concepts of sex and gender, often viewing TGNC people with bias as people going against a divinely determined and immutable binary sex and gender system. This situation may put TGNC people at odds with the predominance of religious systems and dominant cultures given that 77% of Americans identify as Christian, 2% as Mormon,[1] 2% as Jewish, 1% as Muslim, 3% as non-Christian, and the remaining 16% as having atheist, agnostic, or no religious preference (Newport, 2014).

Kidd and Witten's (2008) data included several illustrations of some of the challenges that TGNC individuals face when dealing with various faith-based entities. Respondents made comments about this experience, for example, one respondent indicated she was "insulted by [my] Catholic priests [regarding] my chosen dress being incongruent with my gender." A similarly rejecting albeit somewhat embracing response was reflected in the comment by another transwoman who said, "My church said that they didn't mind [me] being a transsexual woman and that I could attend services as long as I promised to remain celibate for the rest of my life." All these experiences illustrate the difficult challenges faced by TGNC people who work to remain in their more dominant cultural religious and faith systems. Similarly, another respondent reported her disappointment in her religious community by saying, "Religion let me down. The Bible, which meant so much to me, is being used against me." Further, respondents from the TMLS study spoke of being denied funeral ceremony rights, burial rights in the church graveyard, marriage ceremonies, last rights, and even access to spiritual counseling when needed because they were transgender-identified (Porter et al., 2013). Still, a few religious or spiritual groups may not reject atypical people[2] (Kaldera, 2009; Rodriguez & Ouellette, 2000). Some of these less rejecting, or accepting, groups are found within nondominant religious and spiritual categories.

NONDOMINANT U.S. RELIGIOUS, SPIRITUAL, AND FAITH GROUPS AND TGNC PEOPLE

Although making up just 3% of the population, other religious and spiritual groups within the US are nonetheless important in the lives of TGNC people. These groups are most often from Eastern, indigenous, and earth-based traditions. The following is a very brief overview of the impact of these traditions on TGNC lives.

Earth-Based

By comparison, there may be less rejection of, or discrimination against, TGNC people within non-Christian, or non-Abrahamic, religious and

---

[1] The term *Mormon* is listed as it appears as a term of self-identification in the research cited. This is a term that may be used by some people to refer to The Church of Jesus Christ of Latter-day Saints, or LDS. This term may or may not be used by individual members of the LDS Church.

[2] For example, Unitarian Universalism has a policy of welcoming people of all gender identities (http://www.uua.org/lgbtq).

spiritual traditions. Earth-based faiths and spiritualties, including Pagan, Wiccan, and more modern groups such as Radical Faeries may have a broader acceptance and celebration of gender variance in expressions and identities (Appleton, 2011; Kaldera, 2009; Smith & Horne, 2007) and some TGNC people have found acceptance and significant support from such religious communities.

Buddhism

Other traditions, such as some within Buddhism, may offer opportunities for acceptance of TGNC people within their myriad communities. Some Buddhist groups have stories of magical sex changes within their sacred texts (*Mahayana*) or reincarnation in another sex (*Jain*). This may be more complicated than this simplistic and brief comment can address, as many stories of sex change are nonetheless based on an overarching belief that it is a punishment to be reborn a woman and that a third sex (i.e., intersex, asexual, homosexual) person is incapable of understanding *dharma*, or religious and moral law governing human conduct (Appleton, 2011). Despite this apparent negative view of changing sex, at least toward femaleness, there may be more acceptance of TGNC people within the few U.S. Buddhist groups serving lesbian, gay, bisexual, transgender, intersex and queer/questioning (LGBTIQ) communities (*Sanghas*).[3]

Hindu and Native Indian

Within the wide spectrum of beliefs and practices of Hinduism there may be a broader acceptance of TGNC people than in other traditions, though this seems open to interpretation as well, with some Hindu cultures expressing prejudice and violence toward lesbian, gay, bisexual, and TGNC people (Wilhelm, 2010).[4] Some TGNC people, however, find acceptance and personal meaning based in a variety of the Hindu forms of God and sacred narratives that represent a blending of two sexes (intersex; *Shiva, Siva/Durga, Ardhanarisvara*), three genders (male, female, and intersex; *Sri Arjuna, Brihannala*), deities for crossdressing (*Sri Bhagavati-devi*), and other representations of the Hindu concept of a third sex (i.e., LGBTIQ people collectively; Wilhelm, 2010). As of 2014, one TGNC group in India known as *Hijra* (eunuchs, intersex, and TGNC people) has full legal recognition and may participate in some historic

---

[3]See listing at http://www.queersangha.com/links.html

[4]See http://www.galva108.org for a further description of Vaishnava and Hindu views on a third gender from the Gay & Lesbian Vaishnava Association.

cultural spiritual rituals and rites (blessing marriages and births).[5] The concept of third sex, similar to two-spirit in some Native Indian belief traditions, represents a combination of gay and lesbian sexual identities, intersex conditions, and a blending of male and female gender characteristics, expressions, or identities that may or may not represent a more modern interpretation and understanding of TGNC people, yet certainly seems wide enough to include them (Gilley, 2006; Wilhelm, 2010).

RECLAIMING RELIGIOSITY AND SPIRITUALITY

Internalizing these negative self-images and losses from rejecting religious and spiritual experiences within dominant and nondominant groups may lead to hopelessness and increased depression in TGNC populations. However, joining or developing an affirming religious or spiritual community or practice may counter the harmful effects from condemning groups and messages and may lend increased meaning to a TGNC experience (Lease, Horne, & Noffsinger-Frazier, 2005; Levy & Lo, 2013; Sullivan-Blum, 2004). Some TGNC people may equate their changing life course and coming out experiences to a form of spiritual discernment and integration of their bodies and spirits (Bockting & Cesaretti, 2001). Other TGNC people may use the experiences of religious or spiritual prejudice to develop their own individual spiritual and religious beliefs that may help them integrate their gender and faith (Levy & Lo, 2013; see also Table 10.1). Still other TGNC people may encounter spiritual struggles as they affirm and express their identities and may nonetheless use spiritual and religious beliefs and practices to provide them hope for the future and as a way to cope with and recover from negative life events (Singh & McKleroy, 2011). TGNC people search for meaning and belonging throughout their TGNC identity development. Therefore, reframing and redefining religiosity and spirituality may provide a pathway for TGNC individuals to recreate or discover new practices and beliefs, as well as defining how to engage in spiritual and religious practices in new roles (Bockting & Cesaretti, 2001; Levy & Lo, 2013).

CASE VIGNETTES

This section provides two brief vignettes as examples of the ways an MHP might encounter and work with a client's religion or spirituality in treatment. The individuals' names and particular situations are changed to protect their identity.

---

[5]For more information, see http://www.theguardian.com/society/2014/apr/16/india-third-gender-claims-place-in-law and http://www.worldpolicy.org/blog/2014/01/29/hijras-battle-equality

Julia

Julia is a Caribbean American TGNC woman who came to see Jeff, an MHP in a large group practice, for support around her gender affirmation process and to help her manage distress and advocacy having to do specifically with her religious community. Julia was in a very conservative spiritual community that was deeply meaningful to her, yet rejecting of her relationship with a man because community members viewed it as "homosexual" in nature, and they had trouble understanding a TGNC experience. Members were rejecting of her gender identity on the basis that it goes against "God's mandated and immutable" binary of sex and gender, and they rejected her relationship secondary to not accepting her identity as a straight woman. This experience of rejection was painful for Julia and was a primary focus of treatment in understanding her need to stay actively connected to this community and how the connection continued to provide strength and empowerment in ways that were at times difficult to comprehend clinically. A significant portion of Julia's resilience was based in her personal religious beliefs that she was being faithful to the particular religion that was the only "true" religion.

Jeff honored Julia's religious and spiritual beliefs and practices by supporting her continued involvement with her religious community despite the challenges she had faced from their rejecting behaviors, which enabled treatment to be collaborative and ultimately effective in helping Julia manage stressors in her gender affirmation process. Other providers who, contrary to her religious community, supported her gender but not her religious beliefs and practices had been discouraging of Julia's involvement in her faith community. This had been destructive to several therapeutic relationships and had forced her to choose between her beliefs and religious supports and her MHPs. Her beliefs were primary, not secondary, to her well-being. Working in gender-affirming treatment with a spiritually sensitive and open approach that invited her beliefs into the dialogue and included her religious practices in her available coping tools, Julia was able to increase her internal sense of self-worth and empowerment and make changes within her personal and religious life that allowed her to feel accepted and affirmed as a trans woman. These changes in turn led to improvements in all her relationships inside and outside her religious community and to significant improvements in her physical health and self-care.

Raul

Raul is a first-generation immigrant from the Dominican Republic who prefers to use gender-neutral pronouns (i.e., they/them/theirs). They came to see Susan, an MHP in an integrated multidisciplinary practice. Raul's presentation involved many religious and spiritual references to what they had interpreted as a Divine directive to change or express a "transgender identity." It became evident during the evaluation process that Raul's descriptions of spiritual experiences that were encoded and presented as gender dysphoria—which involved unusual physiological sensations outside Raul's control, loss of consciousness, and ego-dystonic thoughts and behaviors—were better explained as either tactile and auditory hallucinations (e.g., psychosis) or an undiagnosed neurological disorder needing a referral for further evaluation. This did not mean that gender dysphoria was not present or that Raul's core spirituality was illusory and detrimental. However, it required further exploration of the experiences of spirituality and gender from a place of spiritual sensitivity and valuing the place of belief in Raul's life. During the extended evaluation, it remained important to be respectful of Raul's strong religious and spiritual beliefs because a large portion of their future-oriented hopefulness was based in the spiritual meaning and interpretation of these events. Maintaining a balance between assessment of possible risks and attention to religious and spiritual beliefs was vital to continue to work with Raul, who was reluctant to continue the assessment when full support of their desire to begin medical gender affirmation needed to be suspended while gaining an accurate clinical picture of the processes and needs present. Through intentional sensitivity to and respect for Raul's religious, spiritual, and cultural beliefs first, and how a TGNC identity made sense within their religious and spiritual framework, the therapeutic work moved forward toward more in-depth assessments of the underlying concerns and to support appropriate care.

Exploring Religious and Spiritual Coping in Counseling Practice With TGNC People

There is evidence that the majority of people seeking counseling for serious concerns prefer an MHP who has spiritual values and who integrates the client's religious and spiritual concerns into counseling. However, there is little to no training for MHPs in how to integrate religion and spirituality into their practice (Plante, 2007; Vieten et al., 2013). The foundational mission and purpose of the American Psychological Association (APA) is "to advance the creation, communication and application of psychological knowledge to benefit society and improve people's lives [and champion] the application of psychology to promote human rights, health, well-being and dignity" (APA, n.d.). MHPs are encouraged to fulfill this mission as it concerns TGNC people. Promoting well-being and dignity includes supporting people as they sort out and integrate their religious and spiritual beliefs and practices. Skilled and affirmative care includes competency in spiritual and religious diversity and issues as well as in sexual and gender identity diversity and issues.

Nevertheless, being familiar with LGB communities does not equate to a familiarity with TGNC people. Therefore, MHPs need to engage in intentional work to become familiar with the unique needs of TGNC individuals to provide competent clinical care (American Counseling Association, 2010; APA, 2015; Israel & Tarver, 1997; Lev, 2004). In a similar way, being familiar with one's own religious and spiritual beliefs and practices does not equate to competence in or awareness of a diversity of beliefs and practices. It is important for MHPs to seek training in religious and spiritual diversity issues in addition to training in gender issues and to recognize their limitations in knowledge and refer or seek supervision when appropriate (American Counseling Association, 2010; Vieten et al., 2013).

Counseling with TGNC people, at its basic level, should include the MHP's use of gender-affirmative language (e.g., names, pronouns, body, sexuality, partner references) and demonstrate awareness and knowledge of fundamental concerns of TGNC communities that includes religious and spiritual issues, beliefs, and practices (APA, 2015). Providing a means for TGNC people to express their identities, beliefs, and values in their terms, with the confidence that these will be respected and reflected, is important. Procedures to ask for details, such as names, pronouns, sexuality, and religious and spiritual experiences, beliefs, and practices, will aid in starting treatment in a manner that empowers clients, invites their whole selves into the process, and sets the stage for safety for their complete selves to be present. Safety in the clinical space will allow for exploration of the role of spirituality and religiosity in the person's life. Part of this safety is a clear sense of the distinction between religiously and spiritually sensitive counseling services and religious and spiritual services (Gonsiorek, Richards, Pargament, & McMinn, 2009). Working with clients to understand mental health and TGNC issues with sensitivity to their religious and spiritual beliefs and practices is different from offering religious and spiritual direction. Providing care within an accepted standard of counseling practice remains imperative, while also allowing room to include aspects of the client's spirituality, such as using particularly meaningful language, metaphors, prayers, or imagery as appropriate. Determining the role of religion and spirituality in a client's life, and its potential role in treatment planning, begins with the initial evaluation for services. In providing a comprehensive evaluation, it is critical to inquire about the religious and spiritual beliefs and practices of TGNC individuals who seek care (APA, 2015; Plante, 2007; Rizzuto, 2005). MHPs can strive to understand where a person derives meaning, purpose, and hope, especially TGNC people who may have a damaged sense of hope and self-image due to the effects of discrimination and prejudice (Hendricks & Testa, 2012). In treatment, it can be ineffective, even detrimental, to ignore a client's religious and spiritual beliefs and practices as normal and expected parts of what the MHP and client need to explore and understand (Rizzuto, 2005).

This exploration needs to include a balanced assessment and informed understanding of whether the beliefs and practices are contributing to well-being or are, perhaps, detrimental or indicators of obsessive-compulsive characteristics or psychotic disorders (Vieten et al., 2013; Zinnbauer, 2013). MHPs may be able to support TGNC clients in exploring the gender expectations of their religious and spiritual communities in addition to those of their families and society, to assess areas they would like to change (Levy & Lo, 2013). For TGNC people who have had experiences of religious or spiritual mistreatment, it may be helpful to explore the possible effects these experiences have had on the individual's image of themselves as people of worth and value (Hendricks & Testa, 2012). For other TGNC people, it may be important to explore how positive experiences of religion and spirituality have strengthened their internal sense of self and added protective factors against trauma and suicide attempts. Understanding the impact on functioning and mental health from messages of empowerment and belonging, as well as rejection and condemnation, is important to assess risk, probable resilience, and coping skills as the TGNC person wrestles with daily small, and occasionally devastating, traumas (Hendricks & Testa, 2012). Religious and spiritual practices can be effective when used in counseling (Plante, 2008). It is a fairly common and effective practice in many mental health settings to use spiritually based practices, such as mindfulness and centering techniques, to assist people in managing stress, anger, depression, anxiety, and trauma and to use volunteering, charity, nonjudgment, tolerance, and empathy to improve connections and meaningful relationships (Plante, 2008). It is less common for MHPs to be aware of the spiritual origins of practices (Frankl, 1963; Vieten et al., 2013). In his research, Thomas Plante (2008) offers a list of 13 common spiritual and religious tools used effectively in counseling, including meditation; prayer; vocation, meaning, purpose, calling in life; acceptance of self and others (even with faults); ethical values and behaviors; being part of something larger and greater than oneself; forgiveness, gratitude, love, kindness, compassion; volunteerism and charity; ritual and community support; social justice; spiritual models; bibliotherapy; and sacredness of life.

Having knowledge of the origins of practices, and how to incorporate them into treatment planning in a way that is sensitive to the spirituality of the client, may increase the effectiveness of the MHP in determining how and whether to include these skills in treatment and may provide insights into responses of acceptance or rejection of these practices by clients on the basis of their cultural and personal religious and spiritual beliefs (Plante, 2008; Vieten et al., 2013). Likewise, having some knowledge of meditative or centering practices from various traditions, and exploring what these practices mean to one's client, may enhance the MHP's ability to individualize treatment to strengthen and use the client's existing supports and deepen the client's sense of agency and meaning (Gonsiorek et al., 2009; Zinnbauer, 2013).

An integral part of exploring the spiritual and religious beliefs, practices, and value systems of clients includes the necessity that the therapist explore but not necessarily ascribe to their own particular beliefs, practices, values, and judgments about religion and spirituality (Gonsiorek et al., 2009). Self-awareness on the part of the MHP is important to engaging the client in an effort to understand how and what they hold sacred and where they derive purpose and interpret meaning in their lives without judgment of their religious and spiritual beliefs and practices (Vieten et al., 2013). This means that negative or positive attitudes and biases from MHPs toward religion and spirituality may become negative assessments and conclusions about clients, such as considering the person for whom religion and spirituality are meaningful to be misguided, gullible, or rigid, or considering the person who does not hold religion and spirituality as important to be immoral and unethical (Gonsiorek et al., 2009; Vieten et al., 2013). Not all methods of inquiry and exploration of a client's beliefs and practices are equivalent or even helpful. "Psychological evaluation has the potential to clarify the paths, destinations, and integrity of the sacred, but it also has the potential to insult, pathologize, and oppress" (Zinnbauer, 2013, p. 86). It is important, therefore, for MHPs to be engaged in their own internal exploration to increase self-awareness, but also to be engaged in supervision and training in ways to appropriately address and incorporate religious and spiritual issues in clinical practice (Gonsiorek et al., 2009; Vieten et al., 2013). The following recommendations should guide TGNC-affirmative counseling in this regard:

- MHPs are able to provide respectful, empathetic, and competent treatment to people with a diversity of spiritual and religious backgrounds, beliefs, and practices, taking into consideration and respecting the individual's systems of value, belief, and practice (Vieten et al., 2013). This skill and expectation do not obfuscate the legal and ethical responsibility of the MHP to report instances of abuse or neglect that may be couched within the belief structure or practices of a particular religious group (e.g., refusal to access medical care for a child who is critically ill; the use of corporal punishment or significant physical/emotional harm, as legally defined, against another person; Plante, 2007).

■ MHPs are able to conduct an assessment of religious and spiritual history and current beliefs and practices and understand the role, whether negative or positive, these play in a person's formation and current life and situations, in addition to routine assessments of other psychosocial factors (Plante, 2007; Vieten et al., 2013).

■ MHPs are able to assist a client in exploring ways their beliefs and practices support or hinder their stated goals and support the person in choosing how to use or implement changes to practices and beliefs to improve functioning, mental health, and well-being (Plante, 2008; Vieten et al., 2013).

■ MHPs recognize when their personal beliefs and biases about religion and spirituality are interfering with their ability to provide respectful and unbiased clinical treatment and seek consultation, supervision, or refer the client to another provider for treatment (Plante, 2007).

■ MHPs distinguish between counseling practice and spiritual direction and maintain boundaries in practicing within the scope of their training and expertise, or receive training and supervision in skills that may support more intensive work with religiosity and spirituality in clinical practice (Plante, 2007, 2008; Vieten et al., 2013).

■ MHPs are able to make appropriate referrals when needed for focused work on religious and spiritual issues, or concerns outside their training and knowledge, and are able to adequately assess and identify religious and spiritual problems, or use of religion and spirituality to avoid or justify other psychological problems (Zinnbauer, 2013).

■ MHPs receive regular supervision, consultation, and education on use and exploration of diverse religious and spiritual practices and beliefs in clinical practice (Plante, 2007, 2008; Vieten et al., 2013).

Chapter Summary

This chapter highlighted a variety of the critical issues for members of the TGNC community, their significant others, friends, family, and supporters as well as those in the religious and spiritual communities with which they are affiliated. Although there is a need for additional research into the role and impact of religion and spirituality in the lives of TGNC people, there is an equal need to incorporate TGNC people's religious and spiritual beliefs and practices into the therapeutic work they are engaged in right now to increase relevance and competence in supporting this community. It is important to recognize and explore the role of religiosity and spirituality in the lives of TGNC people, whether positive or negative, and to normalize their involvement in or their desire to be involved in religious and/or spiritual communities. Although there is potential for harm, there remains potential for support and resilience within religious and/or spiritual beliefs, practices, and communities for TGNC people. To increase effective clinical work with TGNC people in a way that is sensitive to their religious and spiritual beliefs and practices, MHPs will need to demonstrate some basic competence skills.

References

American Counseling Association. (2010). Competencies for counseling with transgender clients. *Journal of LGBT Issues in Counseling, 4*, 135–159.

American Psychological Association. (2015). Guidelines for psychological practice with transgender and gender nonconforming people. *American Psychologist, 70*, 832–864. http://dx.doi.org/10.1037/a0039906

American Psychological Association. (n.d.). *Strategic plan*. Retrieved from http://www.apa.org/about/apa/strategic-plan/default.aspx

Appleton, N. (2011). In the footsteps of the Buddha? Women and the bodhisattva path in Theravada Buddhism. *Journal of Feminist Studies in Religion, 27*, 33–51. http://dx.doi.org/10.2979/jfemistudreli.27.1.33

bautista, d., Mountain, Q., & Reynolds, H. M. (2014). Religion and spirituality. In L. Erickson-Schroth (Ed.), *Trans bodies, trans selves: a resource for the transgender community* (pp. 62–79). New York, NY: Oxford University Press.

Bockting, W., & Cesaretti, C. (2001). Spirituality, transgender identity, and coming out. *Journal of Sex Education and Therapy, 26*, 291–300.

Clark, J. M., Brown, J. C., & Hochstein, L. M. (1989). Institutional religion and gay/lesbian oppression. *Marriage & Family Review, 14*, 265–284. http://dx.doi.org/10.1300/J002v14n03_13

Clements-Nolle, K., Marx, R., & Katz, M. (2006). Attempted suicide among transgender persons: The influence of gender-based discrimination and victimization. *Journal of Homosexuality, 51*, 53–69. http://dx.doi.org/10.1300/J082v51n03_04

Conroy, M. (2010). Treating transgendered children: Clinical methods and religious mythology. *Zygon, 45*, 301–316. http://dx.doi.org/10.1111/j.1467-9744.2010.01082.x

Fausto-Sterling, A. (2000). *Sexing the body: Gender politics and the construction of sexuality*. New York, NY: Basic Books.

Fiori, K. L., Hays, J. C., & Meador, K. G. (2004). Spiritual turning points and perceived control over the life course. *The International Journal of*

Aging & Human Development, 59, 391–420. http://dx.doi.org/10.2190/KBXL-18W0-FPJ4-F1GY

Frankl, V. E. (1963). *Man's search for meaning: An introduction to Logotherapy* (I. Lasch, Trans.). New York, NY: Pocket Books.

Gilley, B. (2006). *Becoming two-spirit: Gay identity and social acceptance in Indian country.* Lincoln: University of Nebraska Press.

Gonsiorek, J. C., Richards, P. S., Pargament, K., & McMinn, M. R. (2009). Ethical challenges and opportunities at the edge: Incorporating spirituality and religion into psychotherapy. *Professional Psychology: Research and Practice, 40,* 385–395. http://dx.doi.org/10.1037/a0016488

Grant, J. M., Mottet, L. A., Tanis, J., Harrison, J., Herman, J. L., & Keisling, M. (2011). *Injustice at every turn: A report of the National Transgender Discrimination Survey.* Washington, DC: National Center for Transgender Equality and National Gay and Lesbian Task Force.

Hendricks, M. L., & Testa, R. J. (2012). A conceptual framework for clinical work with transgender and gender nonconforming clients: An adaptation of the Minority Stress Model. *Professional Psychology: Research and Practice, 43,* 460–467. http://dx.doi.org/10.1037/a0029597

Hill, P. C., Pargament, K., Hood, R. W., McCullough, M. E., Swyers, J. P., Larson, D. B., & Zinnbauer, B. J. (2000). Conceptualizing religion and spirituality: Points of commonality, points of departure. *Journal for the Theory of Social Behaviour, 30,* 51–77. http://dx.doi.org/10.1111/1468-5914.00119

Hopwood, R. A. (2014). *Conceptualizations of religion in a sample of female-to-male transsexuals: An interpretative phenomenological analysis* (Doctoral dissertation). Available from ProQuest Dissertations and Theses database. (UMI No. 3645824).

Israel, G. E., & Tarver, D. E., II. (1997). *Transgender care: Recommended guidelines, practical information, and personal accounts.* Philadelphia, PA: Temple University Press.

Kaldera, R. (2009). *Hermaphrodeities: The transgender spirituality workbook.* Hubbardston, MA: Asphodel Press.

Kennedy, J. W. (2008, February 12). The transgender moment. *Christianity Today, 52,* 54–58.

Kidd, J. D., & Witten, T. M. (2008). Understanding spirituality and religiosity in the transgender community: Implications for aging. *Journal of Religion, Spirituality & Aging, 20,* 29–62. http://dx.doi.org/10.1080/15528030801922004

Koenig, H. G. (2009). Research on religion, spirituality, and mental health: A review. *Canadian Journal of Psychiatry, 54,* 283–291.

Koon Teh, Y. (2001). Mak nyahs (male transsexuals) in Malaysia: The influence of culture and religion on their identity. *International Journal of Transgenderism, 5*(3). Retrieved from http://web.archive.org/web/20070429060255/http://www.symposion.com/ijt/ijtvo05no03_04.htm

Kosmin, B. A., Mayer, E., & Keysar, A. (2001). *American religious identification survey 2001*. New York, NY: The City University of New York. Retrieved from http://www.gc.cuny.edu/CUNY_GC/media/CUNY-Graduate-Center/PDF/ARIS/ARIS-PDF-version.pdf

Lease, S. H., Horne, S. G., & Noffsinger-Frazier, N. (2005). Affirming faith experiences and psychological health for Caucasian lesbian, gay, and bisexual individuals. *Journal of Counseling Psychology, 52*, 378–388. http://dx.doi.org/10.1037/0022-0167.52.3.378

Lev, A. (2004). *Transgender emergence: Therapeutic guidelines for working with gender-variant people and their families*. New York, NY: The Haworth Clinical Practice Press.

Levy, D. L., & Lo, J. R. (2013). Transgender, transsexual, and gender queer individuals with a Christian upbringing: The process of resolving conflict between gender identity and faith. *Journal of Religion & Spirituality in Social Work: Social Thought, 32*, 60–83. http://dx.doi.org/10.1080/15426432.2013.749079

McFadden, S. H., Frankowski, S., Flick, H., & Witten, T. M. (2013). Resilience and multiple stigmatized identities: Lessons from transgender persons' reflections on aging. In J. D. Sinnott (Ed.), *Positive psychology* (pp. 247–267). New York, NY: Springer. http://dx.doi.org/10.1007/978-1-4614-7282-7_16

Newport, F. (December 24, 2014). *Three-quarters of Americans identify as Christian*. Princeton, NJ: Gallup News Service. Retrieved from http://www.gallup.com/poll/180347/three-quarters-americans-identify-christian.aspx

Plante, T. G. (2007). Integrating spirituality and psychotherapy: Ethical issues and principles to consider. *Journal of Clinical Psychology, 63*, 891–902. http://dx.doi.org/10.1002/jclp.20383

Plante, T. G. (2008). What do the spiritual and religious traditions offer the practicing psychologist? *Pastoral Psychology, 56*, 429–444. http://dx.doi.org/10.1007/s11089-008-0119-0

Porter, K. E., Ronneberg, C. R., & Witten, T. M. (2013). Religious affiliation and successful aging among transgender older adults: Findings from the Trans MetLife Survey. *Journal of Religion, Spirituality & Aging, 25*, 112–138. http://dx.doi.org/10.1080/15528030.2012.739988

Rizzuto, A.-M. (2005). Psychoanalytic considerations about spiritually oriented psychotherapy. In L. Sperry & E. P. Shafranske (Eds.), *Spiritually oriented psychotherapy* (pp. 31–50). Washington, DC: American Psychological Association. http://dx.doi.org/10.1037/10886-002

Rodriguez, E. M. O., & Ouellette, S. C. (2000). Gay and lesbian Christians: Homosexual and religious identity integration in the members and participants of a gay-positive church. *Journal for the Scientific Study of Religion, 39*, 333–347. http://dx.doi.org/10.1111/0021-8294.00028

Rosser, B. R. S., Oakes, J. M., Bockting, W. O., & Miner, M. (2007). Capturing the social demographics of hidden sexual minorities: An internet study of the transgender population in the United States. *Sexuality Research & Social Policy: A Journal of the NSRC, 4,* 50–64. http://dx.doi.org/10.1525/srsp.2007.4.2.50

Rothaus, S. (2014, November 21). Transgender woman dies suddenly, presented at funeral in open casket as a man. *Miami Herald.* Retrieved from http://www.miamiherald.com/news/local/community/gay-south-florida/article4055600.html

Singh, A. A., & McKleroy, V. S. (2011). "Just getting out of bed is a revolutionary act": The resilience of transgender people of color who have survived traumatic life events. *Traumatology, 17,* 34–44. http://dx.doi.org/10.1177/1534765610369261

Smith, B., & Horne, S. (2007). Gay, lesbian, bisexual and transgendered (GLBT) experiences with Earth-spirited faith. *Journal of Homosexuality, 52,* 235–248. http://dx.doi.org/10.1300/J082v52n03_11

Sullivan-Blum, C. R. (2004). Balancing acts: Drag queens, gender and faith. *Journal of Homosexuality, 46,* 195–209. http://dx.doi.org/10.1300/J082v46n03_12

Vahia, I. V., Chattillion, E., Kavirajan, H., & Depp, C. A. (2011). Psychological protective factors across the lifespan: Implications for psychiatry. *The Psychiatric Clinics of North America, 34*(1), 231–248.

Vieten, C., Scammell, S., Pilato, R., Ammondson, I., Pargament, K. I., & Lukoff, D. (2013). Spiritual and religious competencies for psychologists. *Psychology of Religion and Spirituality, 5,* 129–144. http://dx.doi.org/10.1037/a0032699

Wilhelm, A. D. (2010). *Tritiya-Prakriti: People of the third sex: Understanding homosexuality, transgender identity, and intersex conditions through Hinduism.* Philadelphia, PA: Xlibris.

Witten, T. M. (2014). It's not all darkness: Robustness, resilience, and successful transgender aging. *LGBT Health, 1,* 24–33. http://dx.doi.org/10.1089/lgbt.2013.0017

Wulff, D. M. (1997). *Psychology of religion: Classic and contemporary* (2nd ed.). New York, NY: John Wiley & Sons.

Zinnbauer, B. J. (2013). Models of healthy and unhealthy religion and spirituality. In K. I. Pargament, A. Mahoney, & E. P. Shafranske, K. I. (Eds.), *APA handbook of psychology, religion, and spirituality: Vol. 2. An applied psychology of religion and spirituality* (pp. 71–89). Washington, DC: American Psychological Association.

Zinnbauer, B. J., Pargament, K., Cole, B., Rye, M. S., Butter, E. M., Belavich, T. G., . . . Kadar, J. L. (1997). Religion and spirituality: Unfuzzying the fuzzy. *Journal for the Scientific Study of Religion, 36,* 549–564. http://dx.doi.org/10.2307/1387689

Jae Sevelius, lore m. dickey, and Anneliese A. Singh

Engaging in TGNC-Affirmative Research

11

Over the last 50 years, research with transgender and gender nonconforming (TGNC) people has often been fraught with a pathologizing and sometimes unethical history (Namaste, 2009; Singh, Richmond, & Burnes, 2013). Now, more than ever, there is increasing interest in research with TGNC people from a variety of disciplines and agents (e.g., faculty and student researchers in university settings, government agencies). Because of the history of deficit-focused research, TGNC people and communities are often suspicious of the intent, goals, and end products of research, as the following blog post demonstrates:

> Dear Mr. or Ms. Grad Student, I am sorry to report that I will not participate in your study as a data point. I don't understand what you're trying to accomplish. I don't trust you. I don't like you. I don't care if you succeed. In fact, I kind of think you suck. Here's why. . . . Let me tell you something: trans people have already been studied. We've been interviewed,

http://dx.doi.org/10.1037/14957-012
Affirmative Counseling and Psychological Practice With Transgender and Gender Nonconforming Clients, A. A. Singh and l. m. dickey (Editors)

sampled, tested, cross-referenced, experimented on, medicated, shocked, examined, and dissected post-mortem. You've looked at our chromosomes, our families, our blood levels, our ring fingers, our mothers' medicine cabinets, and our genitalia (over and over again with the genitalia—stop pushing condoms on us, dumbass, we know what they're for). You've watched us play with dolls, raise children, fall in love, look at pornography, get sick, die, and commemorate ourselves. . . . But you've never listened to our voices and you need to do that now. (Anne, 2009, p. 1)

TGNC people, who often experience invisibility and marginalization, are certainly justified in questioning why interest in their lives has intensified. Therefore, it is important that researchers aim to understand how to engage in affirmative TGNC research and initiate research that empowers and involves TGNC individuals and communities. In this chapter, key aspects of conducting affirmative research with TGNC people are described, including research strategies (e.g., TGNC-inclusive data collection), outlets for publishing research, and funding for research. The authors will also address important ethical considerations when working with TGNC research participants. Suggestions are provided to ensure that the conclusions drawn from TGNC studies appropriately reflect the generalizability of results. The chapter concludes with encouragement to investigate a broad range of concerns and address gaps in research with TGNC people from diverse cultural backgrounds.

Developing Research Questions

It is not uncommon for people new to the field of counseling and psychology and with an interest in TGNC people to ask about potential research topics. Sometimes people already have a general idea of what they might be interested in studying. These topics range from understanding the coming out process among TGNC people to longitudinal studies exploring the effects of medical transition. Regardless of the topic, researchers should have a clear research question that is designed to further understand the many areas of life that impact TGNC people. An Institute of Medicine report (2011) discussed many of these research gaps (e.g., demographic research, health care inequities, transgender-specific health care). Experts in culturally competent research methodology advise that members of the community of interest also be involved in generating appropriate and relevant research questions (Lee & Zaharlick, 2013).

In examining the current state of TGNC-focused research, it is clear that TGNC people's voices need to be included. By addressing research gaps, investigators must ensure that TGNC people have the opportunity to discuss their lived experiences. Too often, small numbers of TGNC participants are aggregated with lesbian, gay, bisexual, and queer (LGBQ) people, which effectively renders the unique experiences of TGNC people invisible. Furthermore, if TGNC people are to be included in studies and adequately represented, researchers must develop data collection methods that ensure sufficient sample sizes of TGNC people. Related to this concern is the need to ensure that the diversity of TGNC people is represented in the literature. A number of large, important studies completed in recent years have relied on a variety of data collection techniques (Bockting, Miner, Swinburne Romine, Hamilton, & Coleman, 2013; Conron, Scott, Stowell, & Landers, 2012; Tate, Ledbetter, & Youssef, 2013). However, the participants in these studies have largely been White TGNC people, who are already disproportionately represented in the literature (Rosser, Oakes, Bockting, & Miner, 2007). To address this disparity, researchers need to reach out to diverse TGNC people where they live and work, and not rely solely on word of mouth and snowball samples (i.e., participant referrals) to ensure that people participate. In this way, psychologists may want to follow the example of many sociologists and anthropologists by taking their data collection procedures to the people they are studying rather than relying on participants to come to them (Bernard, 2011; Lee & Zaharlick, 2013).

Similarly, much of the research with TGNC women in particular has been generated within the field of HIV prevention and treatment, where they have historically been subsumed under the behavioral risk group of men who have sex with men (MSM; Baral et al., 2013). Public health researchers introduced behavioral risk groups in an attempt to avoid addressing the complexities of identities by aiming to describe behavior (Young & Meyer, 2005). However, by describing TGNC women as MSM, much of the research has effectively obscured the unique cultural contexts in which TGNC women's experiences of sexuality and sexual health often put them at disparate risk for acquiring HIV (Sevelius, 2013). Furthermore, studies that include TGNC women with MSM often include them in very small numbers and fail to disaggregate them when presenting their findings (Sevelius, Keatley, Calma, & Arnold, 2016). Researchers should examine their research questions to determine if they are able to include TGNC people in a meaningful and affirming way, rather than tacking them on to a larger group in the name of inclusion without addressing and incorporating their unique concerns. If TGNC people are included as part of a larger group in a study design, the sample size should permit disaggregation of the TGNC subsample for separate analyses and the study design (e.g., measures) should consider unique TGNC participant issues.

Understanding and Using TGNC-Affirming Language in Research

Using appropriate language and terminology is essential to planning, conducting, and distributing research that is affirming to TGNC communities. Language used to describe and articulate the diversity of TGNC communities is continuously evolving and varies by age cohort, region, race/ethnicity, sociocultural status, and more. Therefore, it can be challenging to identify language that is inclusive, appeals to various subgroups of TGNC people, and is descriptive enough for TGNC research purposes. Current best practices for TGNC-affirming language emphasize the use of language that privileges the gender of identity, rather than the sex assigned at birth (Gender Identity in U.S. Surveillance Group [GenIUSS], 2014). This emphasis means that current TGNC-affirming literature is moving away from the use of acronyms such as MTF (male-to-female) and FTM (female-to male) to describe TGNC people. Although the term *transgender* may not capture all of the cultural nuances that are present in diverse TGNC communities, many TGNC-affirming researchers (especially in the United States) are using this as an umbrella term to describe people whose gender identity differs from their sex assigned at birth. Some authors shorten the term to *trans* to indicate inclusivity of people with other identities, such as transsexual people.

Placing the emphasis on a person's gender identity also means that the sexual orientation of TGNC people should be described in relation to the person's gender identity, rather than their sex assigned at birth. For example, a TGNC man who is sexually oriented toward men may be most appropriately described as gay, whereas a TGNC man who is sexually oriented toward women may be most appropriately described as straight or heterosexual (dickey, Burnes, & Singh, 2012). These best practices have not always been used in research with TGNC people, so when reviewing the literature it is important to pay close attention to how researchers are using language to describe their populations. When designing and publishing studies, researchers should be specific about how they are defining terminology when describing their samples.

Cultural Humility and TGNC Community-Based Research Strategies

Cultural humility is a process that requires ongoing self-reflection and self-critique, including identifying and examining one's own patterns of enacting racism, classism, and other oppressions, and actively addressing power imbalances in relationships to better equalize the power (Tervalon & Murray-García, 1998). Many community-based researchers and other professionals emphasize the importance of cultural humility over cultural competence. *Cultural competence* implies that one can have mastery over another's culture and this mastery is static once achieved (Tervalon & Murray-García, 1998). In contrast, cultural humility encourages continuous examination of one's assumptions and refraining from imposing the lens of the dominant culture on one's research and in partnerships with communities.

When building community research partnerships, each one will be unique, and the members must decide collectively what their vision, core values, and guiding principles for decision-making will be. Some partnerships may be time-limited, other community partnerships will involve a long-term process and a commitment to sustainability to develop and maintain trust beyond a single research project or funding period. TGNC-affirmative research identifies, acknowledges, and builds on strengths, resources, and relationships that exist within TGNC communities. Strengths may include skills of individuals or group knowledge of community history, resources may include organizations whose mission includes a commitment to fostering the health of TGNC communities, and relationships may include networks of mutual trust. TGNC-affirming research seeks to support and expand social structures and processes that contribute to community health.

TGNC-affirmative research seeks to identify opportunities for mutual education and capacity building of the researchers and the community partners. Acknowledging that all contributors bring diverse skills and knowledge to the research process can result in increased expertise and capacity of the team as a whole (Benoit, Jansson, Millar, & Phillips, 2005). Fostering collaborative and equitable partnerships within TGNC communities requires the recognition that many TGNC people have experienced social, educational, and economic marginalization that has resulted in diminished power to name or define their experience. Intentionally creating empowering decision-making and information sharing processes that center on the experiences and expertise of TGNC community members can help to create more equitable partnerships that focus on issues and concerns identified by community members.

An example of cultural humility in community-based research is *participatory action research* (PAR). In PAR, researchers and community members work collaboratively, from generating research questions to collecting and analyzing data and translating findings to community partners (DiClemente, Salazar, & Crosby, 2015). In a process called *member checking* or *respondent validation*, participants can also review research findings to ensure that what is being disseminated resonates with their own lived experiences to improve the accuracy and validity of results. PAR studies can be grounded in various theories to clarify the role and intent of researchers and community partners. Scholars have asserted that feminist PAR approaches may be helpful to theoretically frame TGNC studies (Singh et al., 2013). By recognizing that socially and economically marginalized communities, such as TGNC communities, have not historically had the power to name and define their own experience, PAR approaches seek to empower communities of interest to participate in shaping research processes from their inception.

Involvement of Community Experts: Peer Staff and Community Advisory Boards

In some TGNC communities, especially among communities of color, individuals may have ample exposure to the experience of being a research participant without opportunities to help shape the research questions, learn about findings, or observe any direct benefit to the community. Hiring TGNC staff is often critical to the success of TGNC-affirming research (Paxton, Guentzel, & Trombacco, 2006). In addition to the value of their lived expertise in shaping the research processes and implementation, TGNC staff can help devise strategies for engaging TGNC communities, help build trust, and assist in translating research goals and findings into accessible language for members of the TGNC community (Paxton et al., 2006). Hiring TGNC staff provides opportunities for economic empowerment and capacity building for people who have often been marginalized by traditional education and employment sectors. Because of this marginalization, researchers must be committed to taking the time to properly train TGNC staff, provide opportunities for professional development, and continuously support their staff by providing adequate supervision (Benoit et al., 2005).

TGNC women living with HIV report disproportionate levels of trauma, including intimate partner violence, sexual abuse (both in childhood and as adults), survival sex work, family dysfunction, poverty, and homelessness (Machtinger, Haberer, Wilson, & Weiss, 2012). TGNC women living with HIV can benefit tremendously from services using peer-based support and health navigation, which have been shown to increase engagement in care and address issues of mistrust of the medical system (Sevelius, Patouhas, Keatley, & Johnson, 2014). However, peer staff may experience vicarious trauma, or secondary traumatic stress, because of exposure to highly traumatic stories and situations experienced by their interactions with participants coupled with high levels of identification with participants on the basis of their peer status (Canfield, 2005). Vicarious trauma is a pervasive experience among peer staff working with transgender women living with HIV due to extremely high levels of trauma experienced by this population. This phenomenon should be considered more explicitly in peer-based interventions to adequately support staff and prevent burnout. Considerations for preventing burnout and supporting staff include providing positive coping skills training, helping staff develop and maintain healthy boundaries with participants, debriefing traumatic content in supervision, and following up with staff to identify ongoing difficulties and early signs of burnout (Bercier & Maynard, 2015).

Engaging a community advisory board (CAB) to help guide research can be a vital source of inspiration, insight, and expertise for engaging in TGNC-affirming studies. The composition of a CAB should reflect the specific communities at the center of the research question. If a research project focuses on TGNC women of color, the CAB should primarily comprise TGNC women of color. It may also be appropriate to include representatives from community-based organizations that serve the community of interest, depending on what type of community expertise is needed to guide the research. Jae Sevelius is currently engaged in intervention development research that aims to support TGNC women who are reentering the community after a period of incarceration. The CAB for this project includes TGNC women who have been affected by incarceration and providers (including TGNC women) who work with incarcerated or recently released TGNC women, such as representatives from probation and community health providers. It is important to support the participation of TGNC people on CABs by providing food, monetary compensation for their time, and/or transportation. It is also important to ensure that all participants feel supported in contributing to decision-making and feedback processes, especially in the context of a CAB where some participants may have more experience in research than others. Such support can be accomplished by developing group agreements designed to support every CAB member sharing early in the formation of the CAB and by incorporating capacity-building activities into the CAB meetings to provide opportunities for less experienced CAB members to learn about the research process (Lee & Zaharlick, 2013).

Working With Institutional Review Boards

Research often requires approval from a human subjects committee or institutional review board (IRB). IRBs were developed in response to repeated use of research techniques that failed to protect or safeguard participants. IRBs in a university setting typically include members from across colleges and disciplines, and may additionally include a member of the general public. Members of the IRB are tasked with reviewing research proposals and determining if sufficient safeguards are in place to ensure the safety of research participants. Some community-based and governmental organizations also maintain IRB committees for the purpose of reviewing research.

Concerns that an IRB is attentive to include informed consent, risks to participants, benefits of participating, and assurance that researchers have been trained in the basic concepts of human subjects protections. Participants should be provided with basic information about the nature of the research in which they are agreeing to partake, such as basic information about the research question, what participants will be asked to do, and how long they can reasonably expect to be engaged in the research study. Research fatigue in studies that require a great deal of time may result in skewed results, so researchers need to carefully determine the amount of time it will take the average person to complete a study. For lengthy Internet studies, researchers may also want to use software that allows a person to take a break and return to the study at a later time. Informed consent also includes the concepts of "capacity, disclosure, understanding, voluntariness, and permission" (Joffe, Cook, Cleary, Clark, & Weeks, 2001, p. 139).

Risks of research can include breach of confidentiality, security of data storage, psychological harm, and injury. For some research, risks are an inherent element of the research process. However, researchers still need to manage those risks in a way that does not cause significant harm to the participants. One of the most common ethical failures of psychologists is a breach of confidentiality (Bodenhorn, 2006). It is vital to anticipate and prevent potential breaches in TGNC research. For some TGNC people, providing basic demographic information is sufficient to identify the participant. For example, the second author has participated in TGNC research as a participant but by the time he had indicated his gender, race, age, and ZIP code, it was relatively easy to figure out his identity. This is one reason why ZIP codes are considered personally identifying information.

Researchers may be reluctant to engage in research with participants under the age of 18 because of the perceived or actual challenges associated with gaining IRB approval for such a study. Family support can be important in obtaining consent for research (Mustanski, 2011); however, some lesbian, gay, bisexual, transgender, and questioning (LGBTQ) youth do not have that support as they may have been banished from their homes (Durso & Gates, 2012). Although the challenges to gaining IRB approval can be significant, there is much to learn from the lives of TGNC adolescents and children. Researchers must work closely with their IRB to ensure that the approval process does not become unnecessarily slowed down.

Recruitment Techniques With TGNC People

In TGNC-affirming research, there may be many factors that inhibit the participation of TGNC people. Economic marginalization that results in homelessness, food insecurity, and health issues may limit TGNC people's time and inclination to engage in research. Recruitment techniques that prioritize building trust and incorporating the priorities of the communities to be reached are more successful with TGNC people. Building community trust that enhances recruitment includes hiring peer staff, engaging the community early on in the research process, and providing money, food, and other types of compensation to acknowledge the time and effort contributed by participants. Depending on the sampling strategies used, peer staff and CABs are often very helpful in identifying appropriate recruitment venues, tapping into social networks, and advising on outreach strategies. In-person outreach conducted at venues where TGNC people gather and outreach locations on the street should always prioritize staff and participant safety. Peer staff should be extensively trained on how to appropriately approach potential participants on the street, with an emphasis on ensuring the safety of everyone.

Until recently, researchers have relied on face-to-face interviews, telephone surveys, or postal mail surveys to collect survey research. This reliance shifted with increased access to the Internet. In some ways this has helped to develop new avenues for finding research participants who were previously thought to be hard to reach (Rosser et al., 2007). Social media has truly revolutionized the ways in which people connect with one another. Online venues, such as Yahoo! Groups, replaced the online discussion boards that were popular in the 1980s. There are millions of Yahoo! Groups on topics ranging from business and finance to health, wellness, and relationships, and it is in this last category that most LGBTQ groups are found. Groups provide a means to connect with people without having to be in person, and TGNC people are able to access resources about the transition process and names of known TGNC-affirming providers. This type of community has quickly become a venue for research. Many of these online groups require a person to "belong" to the group and to declare that they meet any eligibility requirements. For example, there is a Yahoo! Group titled Transgender Women of Color Los Angeles. The description of the group says: "This group is a channel for on-line communication for Transgender women of color in Los Angeles County area and abroad." To join the group, prospective members must provide the moderator with information about why they believe they are eligible to join. A TGNC-affirming researcher could craft a message to the moderator that sufficiently covers the eligibility criteria. Once a person's membership has been approved, they are free to post messages recruiting research participants. If a person joins the group under false pretenses, it is likely their membership will be revoked, yet they still may have been able to recruit people to participate in research studies, which is an ethical concern.

Publication, Distribution, and Translation of Research Findings

From the outset of research, investigators should consider where they publish, distribute, and translate study findings. This consideration should not be isolated to the benefit of the researcher, such as a faculty member publishing in a peer-reviewed journal. Researchers should also account for how to make study findings accessible to TGNC communities to facilitate capacity building. This is important because many of the areas of TGNC research highlight ways that experiences of stigma and discrimination influence mental and physical health outcomes; however, many of these study findings do not make their way back to TGNC communities. This disconnect between individual and community participation in research and the translation of findings to benefit

TGNC people creates distrust, exemplified by the blog post that opened this chapter. Researchers should consider a variety of publication outlets, from academic research journals to TGNC-specific organizations. TGNC studies will vary in terms of quality, scope, and size. However, there can be merit in publishing the studies that do not achieve their aim in outlets such as newsletter bulletins, academic and community blogs, and other venues to share information about what has not been working in TGNC research.

Initiating community forums or joining preexisting forums can also be a helpful way to share research findings (Lee & Zaharlick, 2013). Researchers can identify these forums prior to commencing their study, so that the translation of findings is planned as an integral part of the research process and does not end with publication. Some large TGNC surveys have produced research briefs (e.g., UCLA Williams Institute), extensive reports for policymakers (e.g., National Center for Transgender Equality), brochures (e.g., American Psychological Association), webinars (e.g., UCSF Center of Excellence for Transgender Health), and podcasts (e.g., American Counseling Association).

Support for TGNC Research: Funding and Mentors

Securing grant funding for TGNC-focused research can be challenging. Grant reviewers may not be familiar with the literature on TGNC communities, and researchers often need to educate reviewers about not only the issues the TGNC people face but also why these issues are unique and important to consider and explore. The first author has ample experience with grant reviewers who wonder if the TGNC population is large enough to warrant focused studies. Although we still do not have probability-based national estimates of the size of the TGNC population in the United States, we do have regional studies that allow us to suggest to reviewers that TGNC people likely constitute anywhere from 0.5% to 3.0% of the population (Conron et al., 2012; GenIUSS, 2014).

In recent years, funding for research with TGNC people has been focused predominantly on the HIV-related disparities experienced by TGNC women. Although this is certainly a pressing and critical topic, there are other important TGNC-focused research topics that have received less attention. Leveraging HIV funding to address multiple health issues and supporting community-based partnerships can help build the knowledge base on other important topics such as resilience, mental health, and trauma within TGNC communities (Sevelius, Keatley, & Gutierrez-Mock, 2011). See the following case vignette for a discussion of some of these issues.

Case Vignette

Antonia is a new researcher in TGNC health. She identifies as a cisgender Latina from a middle class background, and she is the third generation in her family to pursue graduate studies. She became interested in TGNC research during a qualitative study she conducted on the sexual orientation disclosure experiences of Latinas in the United States. During this study, a TGNC Latina responded to the call for participants and Antonia was surprised about this, as she had not anticipated a TGNC participant in her study sample. At that time, she began reading about TGNC people, and TGNC Latinas specifically, and she noticed there was very little on sexual orientation disclosure of TGNC Latinas. During this time, Antonia engaged in extensive self-reflection on how her race/ethnicity, education level, and other identities intersected with her cisgender identity—and how these identities may influence her in TGNC research. Antonia contacted a researcher (Jeanine) who had been working in TGNC research for over a decade for consultation. Jeanine encouraged Antonia to continuously self-reflect on her intersectional identities during all aspects of the TGNC research process and the importance of cultural humility, as well as how her own gender liberation might be connected to the liberation of TGNC people. Jeanine also shared how she has worked with CABs, other TGNC community-based organizations, and TGNC leaders to collaboratively design TGNC research studies and questions. Antonia asked Jeanine about the history of TGNC research and learned about TGNC research studies that have not been TGNC-affirming. Antonia asked to contact Jeanine as Antonia prepared her IRB submission and throughout her study activities.

After this consultation, Antonia met with TGNC leaders in her community and scheduled online consultations with TGNC Latina leaders in the United States to learn and reflect on how to build trust with TGNC communities. She read several manuscripts on TGNC-affirmative research and how to engage in ethical research with TGNC people, as well as on the diverse recruitment strategies that have been used with TGNC people. As she designed her study, Antonia ensured that her sampling strategy sought to include a diverse sample of TGNC Latinas in terms of social class, citizenship status, geographic region, and other participant demographics. As Antonia entered the field, she first established a CAB that she worked with during the study. The CAB provided consultation and guidance when Antonia faced challenges. When her recruitment stalled, CAB members were able to help Antonia with recruitment efforts in their communities. At the end of the study, Antonia planned for publication and presentation of her findings in professional venues in her discipline. Simultaneously, Antonia worked with her CAB to schedule a community forum sharing study findings and she wrote a policy brief and newsletter articles on her findings for a local TGNC community-based organization. She welcomed feedback on the experiences TGNC people have while participating in research, and conveyed community feedback in blog and listserv posts in her professional discipline. Finally, Antonia integrated TGNC advocacy into these publications and presentations.

Challenges and Limitations to TGNC-Affirming Research

Throughout this chapter, there has been a focus on involving TGNC people and communities as an important aspect of ethical and TGNC-affirming research. However, a major challenge to collaborative and participatory approaches involves time. TGNC communities, especially diverse ones, may be hidden or difficult to find, making it challenging to identify TGNC experts to consult on studies and involve communities in the process of identifying community needs. Therefore, researchers should take ample time to identify TGNC study partners in advance of a study commencing. Care should be taken to ensure that these community partners do not represent only a limited part of the TGNC community. For example, identifying TGNC partners from culturally diverse backgrounds, gender identities, age, class, and other demographics can be helpful.

Other limitations that researchers may face in TGNC research entail the very real and current stressors influencing TGNC participants. The third author has engaged in qualitative studies of TGNC resilience for the past 15 years, and over that time has repeatedly witnessed these stressors firsthand. TGNC participants may be scheduled for an interview but may not have the money for public transportation because they were fired from their job for being TGNC or were experiencing homelessness and were not able to locate a safe place for their belongings prior to the interview. In these instances, having a TGNC resource list detailing a wide range of TGNC-affirming mental and physical health services, among other resources, has been critical. Researchers should not underestimate the impact of hearing stories of the lives of TGNC people and the common trauma they experience. In particular, researchers who have conducted TGNC research for multiple years should have a strong support system of personal and professional resources to guard against secondary trauma, as well as avenues of TGNC advocacy, activism, and policy change to foster researcher resilience.

Chapter Summary

In this chapter, major considerations of engaging in TGNC-affirmative research were discussed. Researchers must be mindful of the distrust that exists within TGNC communities regarding research endeavors and the potential for TGNC research to have negative impacts. This harm includes the lack of distribution of findings to TGNC communities and the lack of collaboration and consultation with TGNC people in the design of TGNC-focused research studies. Despite the history of TGNC deficit-focused research, there remains ample need for attention to understudied TGNC areas and ethical, TGNC-affirming studies.

References

Anne. (2009). *Fuck you and fuck your fucking thesis: Why I will not participate in trans studies.* Retrieved from http://tagonist.livejournal.com/199563.html

Baral, S. D., Poteat, T., Strömdahl, S., Wirtz, A. L., Guadamuz, T. E., & Beyrer, C. (2013). Worldwide burden of HIV in transgender women: A systematic review and meta-analysis. *The Lancet Infectious Diseases, 13,* 214–222. http://dx.doi.org/10.1016/S1473-3099(12)70315-8

Benoit, C., Jansson, M., Millar, A., & Phillips, R. (2005). Community-academic research on hard-to-reach populations: Benefits and challenges. *Qualitative Health Research, 15,* 263–282. http://dx.doi.org/10.1177/1049732304267752

Bercier, M. L., & Maynard, B. R. (2015). Interventions for secondary traumatic stress with mental health workers: A systemic review. *Research on Social Work Practice, 25,* 81–89. http://dx.doi.org/10.1177/1049731513517142

Bernard, H. R. (2011). *Research methods in anthropology: Qualitative and quantitative approaches* (5th ed.). Lanham, MD: AltaMira.

Bockting, W. O., Miner, M. H., Swinburne Romine, R. E., Hamilton, A., & Coleman, E. (2013). Stigma, mental health, and resilience in an online sample of the U.S. transgender population. *American Journal of Public Health, 103,* 943–951. http://dx.doi.org/10.2105/AJPH.2013.301241

Bodenhorn, N. (2006). Exploratory study of common and challenging ethical dilemmas experienced by professional school counselors. *Professional School Counseling, 10,* 195–202. http://dx.doi.org/10.5330/prsc.10.2.e1734087234675u4

Canfield, J. (2005). Secondary traumatization, burnout, and vicarious traumatization. *Smith College Studies in Social Work, 75,* 81–101. http://dx.doi.org/10.1300/J497v75n02_06

Conron, K. J., Scott, G., Stowell, G. S., & Landers, S. J. (2012). Transgender health in Massachusetts: Results from a household probability sample of adults. *American Journal of Public Health, 102*, 118–122. http://dx.doi.org/10.2105/AJPH.2011.300315

dickey, l. m., Burnes, T. R., & Singh, A. A. (2012). Sexual identity development of female-to-male transgender individuals: A Grounded Theory inquiry. *Journal of LGBT Issues in Counseling, 6*, 118–138. http://dx.doi.org/10.1080/15538605.2012.678184

DiClemente, R. J., Salazar, L., & Crosby, R. A. (2015). Community-based participatory research in the context of health promotion. In L. Salazar, R. A. Crosby, & R. J. DiClemente (Eds.), *Research methods in health promotion* (pp. 313–335). San Francisco, CA: Jossey-Bass.

Durso, L. E., & Gates, G. J. (2012). *Serving our youth: Findings from a national survey of service providers working with lesbian, gay, bisexual, and transgender youth who are homeless or at risk of homelessness.* Retrieved from http://escholarship.org/uc/item/80x75033#page-5

Gender Identity in U.S. Surveillance Group. (2014). *Best practices for asking questions to identify transgender and other gender minority respondents on population-based surveys.* Retrieved from http://williamsinstitute.law.ucla.edu/research/census-lgbt-demographics-studies/geniuss-report-sept-2014/

Institute of Medicine. (2011). *The health of lesbian, gay, bisexual, and transgender people: Building a foundation for better understanding.* Washington, DC: National Academy of Sciences.

Joffe, S., Cook, E. F., Cleary, P. D., Clark, J. W., & Weeks, J. C. (2001). Quality of informed consent: A new measure of understanding among research subjects. *Journal of the National Cancer Institute, 93*, 139–147. http://dx.doi.org/10.1093/jnci/93.2.139

Lee, M. Y., & Zaharlick, A. (2013). *Culturally competent research: Using ethnography as a meta-framework.* New York, NY: Oxford University Press. http://dx.doi.org/10.1093/acprof:oso/9780199846597.001.0001

Machtinger, E. L., Haberer, J. E., Wilson, T. C., & Weiss, D. S. (2012). Recent trauma is associated with antiretroviral failure and HIV transmission risk behavior among HIV-positive women and female-identified transgenders. *AIDS and Behavior, 16*, 2160–2170. http://dx.doi.org/10.1007/s10461-012-0158-5

Mustanski, B. (2011). Ethical and regulatory issues with conducting sexuality research with LGBT adolescents: A call to action for a scientifically informed approach. *Archives of Sexual Behavior, 40*, 673–686. http://dx.doi.org/10.1007/s10508-011-9745-1

Namaste, V. (2009). Undoing theory: The "transgender question" and the epistemic violence of Anglo-American feminist theory. *Hypatia, 24*, 11–32. http://dx.doi.org/10.1111/j.1527-2001.2009.01043.x

Paxton, K. C., Guentzel, H., & Trombacco, K. (2006). Lessons learned in developing a research partnership with the transgender community.

American Journal of Community Psychology, 37, 349–356. http://dx.doi.org/10.1007/s10464-006-9049-0

Rosser, B. S., Oakes, J. M., Bockting, W. O., & Miner, M. (2007). Capturing the social demographics of hidden sexual minorities: An Internet study of the transgender population in the United States. *Sexuality Research & Social Policy, 4*, 50–64. http://dx.doi.org/10.1525/srsp.2007.4.2.50

Sevelius, J. M. (2013). Gender affirmation: A framework for conceptualizing risk behavior among transgender women of color. *Sex Roles, 68*, 675–689. http://dx.doi.org/10.1007/s11199-012-0216-5

Sevelius, J. M., Keatley, J., Calma, N., & Arnold, E. (2016). 'I am not a man': Trans-specific barriers and facilitators to PrEP acceptability among transgender women. *Global Public Health: An International Journal for Research, Policy and Practice*, 1–16. http://dx.doi.org/10.1080/17441692.2016.1154085

Sevelius, J. M., Keatley, J., & Gutierrez-Mock, L. (2011). HIV/AIDS programming in the United States: Considerations affecting transgender women and girls. *Women's Health Issues, 21*(6, Suppl.), S278–S282. http://dx.doi.org/10.1016/j.whi.2011.08.001

Sevelius, J. M., Patouhas, E., Keatley, J. G., & Johnson, M. O. (2014). Barriers and facilitators to engagement and retention in care among transgender women living with human immunodeficiency virus. *Annals of Behavioral Medicine, 47*, 5–16. http://dx.doi.org/10.1007/s12160-013-9565-8

Singh, A. A., Richmond, K., & Burnes, T. (2013). Feminist participatory action research with transgender communities: Fostering the practice of ethical and empowering research designs. *International Journal of Transgenderism, 14*, 93–104. http://dx.doi.org/10.1080/15532739.2013.818516

Tate, C. C., Ledbetter, J. N., & Youssef, C. P. (2013). A two-question method for assessing gender categories in the social and medical sciences. *Journal of Sex Research, 50*, 767–776. http://dx.doi.org/10.1080/00224499.2012.690110

Tervalon, M., & Murray-García, J. (1998). Cultural humility versus cultural competence: A critical distinction in defining physician training outcomes in multicultural education. *Journal of Health Care for the Poor and Underserved, 9*, 117–125. http://dx.doi.org/10.1353/hpu.2010.0233

Young, R. M., & Meyer, I. H. (2005). The trouble with "MSM" and "WSW": Erasure of the sexual-minority person in public health discourse. *American Journal of Public Health, 95*, 1144–1149. http://dx.doi.org/10.2105/AJPH.2004.046714

lore m. dickey, Anneliese A. Singh, Sand C. Chang, and Mick Rehrig

Advocacy and Social Justice

The Next Generation of Counseling and Psychological Practice With Transgender and Gender Nonconforming Clients

12

A s the previous chapters have noted, mental health providers (MHPs) are often called to engage in the role of advocacy when working with transgender and gender nonconforming (TGNC) clients. MHPs are uniquely positioned to serve as advocates for their TGNC clients as MHP disciplines provide training in interpersonal relationship building, conflict management, and multicultural concerns related to counseling. Each of these domains is an important skill base for MHPs engaging in advocacy. However, the training of MHPs in advocacy and social justice issues, especially related to working with TGNC clients, may vary widely in terms of knowledge and skills. This chapter explores the ways that providers can be engaged in advocacy, including the development of public policy, assurance that workplace interventions are supportive for TGNC people, and promotion of TGNC-empowering ally development.

http://dx.doi.org/10.1037/14957-013

Affirmative Counseling and Psychological Practice With Transgender and Gender Nonconforming Clients, A. A. Singh and l. m. dickey (Editors)

The Role of Advocacy and Social Justice in TGNC-Affirmative Psychological Practice

Counselor advocacy has been defined as the necessary role that MHPs engage in when they are addressing systemic barriers of oppression on the mental and physical well-being of their clients (Fouad, Gerstein, & Toporek, 2006). Advocacy can take many forms, as MHPs can work *with* their clients on removing barriers to their well-being, or MHPs can work *on behalf* of their clients to shift these barriers (Lewis, Arnold, House, & Toporek, 2003). For example, in working with TGNC clients of color to address the anti-TGNC bias and racism they may encounter when seeking housing, MHPs can collaboratively use role-plays to explore self-advocacy skills needed to navigate potential and lived experiences of discrimination (Ratts & Hutchins, 2009). MHPs can also work on behalf of TGNC clients to address systemic barriers that may influence their overall well-being. This work may occur within an individual office setting, such as ensuring safe restroom access for TGNC clients, or on larger system levels, such as engaging in lobbying and policy change. Any of the advocacy interventions that MHPs engage in should consider developmental levels of the client (Ratts, DeKruyf, & Chen-Hayes, 2007), as well as TGNC clients' multicultural and multiple social identities (Wynn & West-Olatunji, 2009).

A focus on advocacy in TGNC counseling also entails a close relationship with multicultural counseling, as these approaches are intertwined. Multicultural approaches help MHPs explore how their multiple social identities influence their thoughts, behaviors, and values. An MHP exploring the salient and multiple social identities of a South Asian, nonbinary TGNC person may find that religious and spiritual concerns are their primary coping resource, yet the client may need MHP advocacy in terms of helping them identify community resources related to religion/spirituality. An advocacy focus continuously seeks to connect the individual level to the larger systemic level with a client's presenting issue. Related to the previous example, the MHP is engaging in advocacy on the individual level by providing resources, however, the MHP can also engage in advocacy related to TGNC people and religion/spirituality on a larger systemic level, such as writing op-ed pieces on this topic or working with interfaith communities to increase TGNC inclusivity in their congregations.

BECOMING A TGNC ALLY

A basic foundation of TGNC advocacy is the journey to becoming a strong TGNC ally. Being an ally is a complex and lifelong process that requires commitment and dedication (Ziegler & Rasul, 2014). Strategies for aligning oneself with true allyship include acknowledging privilege, actively listening, empowering and centering the experiences of people of color and other marginalized TGNC subgroups being curious, learning about the work of other allies, supporting TGNC leadership, and moving beyond guilt into actively supporting the movements of marginalized communities (Ziegler & Rasul, 2014). MHPs are encouraged to self-reflect on how these strategies may be applied in the counseling relationship, especially when they are not members of the communities they serve (e.g., White MHPs working with people of color, heterosexual MHPs working with lesbian, gay, and bisexual clients, cisgender MHPs working with TGNC clients). When cultural or identity difference exists within the counseling relationship, it can be helpful to acknowledge differences, including power and privilege, and to create a safe space to freely discuss with clients their feelings about these dynamics. This is an ongoing process rather than a single statement during the initial session.

As TGNC clients are greatly affected by their environments, an integral part of TGNC-affirmative practice for MHPs is to work to engage with systems to make TGNC clients' experiences better in the sociocultural world. Being an ally and an advocate within the TGNC community needs to be one and the same. In other words, being an ally to TGNC clients means that the role continues even outside the counseling room and beyond affirming each individual client's experience. This must extend to engaging in self-reflection and advocating for the needs of the larger TGNC community. Examples of this include seeking continuing education, engaging in consultation with colleagues (where the clinical and interpersonal work requires investigation into the MHP's own struggles and bias), advocating for TGNC-affirming work environments, and participating in ongoing discourse and knowledge sharing with other providers across disciplines regarding TGNC competency.

Clients who feel supported by a TGNC-affirmative MHP also have to leave the counseling office at the end of the appointment and exist in a highly gendered and, at times, violent world. In addition to anti-TGNC bias, they may experience other forms of oppression, such as racism, sexism, and anti-LGBTQ bias. Living at the intersections of these systems can be especially challenging, and sometimes deadly, especially for TGNC women of color (National Coalition of Anti-Violence Programs, 2011). Being an ally for and with a TGNC client means providing information regarding appropriate TGNC-affirmative resources, including legal and local resources. MHPs engaging in education and consultation across disciplines can ensure that TGNC clients are able to get their needs met in a way that honors their humanity. When a TGNC client comes into the office because of gender or other clinical concerns, part of the work is to provide support in affirming the wholeness of the client, including all aspects that encompass their identity, as the following case vignette demonstrates.

CASE VIGNETTE

Nathan, a young, Black trans man (who is now mostly perceived as a butch female) living in the rural South presented in counseling at the start of his transition, which for him included starting hormone therapy and beginning social transition. Being aware of different forms of societal stigma, Nathan's counselor created a space for Nathan to explore his hopes and expectations, including the question of what Nathan imagined it would be like to be recognized as a young, Black man in the rural South. This made him very quiet, and Nathan stated he had not thought about that part. Nathan and his counselor explored what his experience would be like and how he could resource himself against a different form of racist violence, including coming up with a concrete safety plan that enlisted the help of his partner. The MHP acknowledged his own privilege as a White TGNC man and the dynamic created in even bringing this conversation to the room. Nathan and his counselor spoke about building a larger community and the possible benefit of Nathan getting connected, when he felt ready, to other Black TGNC men in the area who could provide some guidance and support with his transition. Additionally, Nathan's MHP was involved in professional associations to raise awareness about the multiplicity of concerns that TGNC people may have and to advocate for educational resources and policies to better serve TGNC people. The next section further describes the ways in which TGNC clients are affected by larger social systems.

Law, Public Policy, and the TGNC Community

Changes to TGNC-affirming laws and public policy can seem to come slowly. Though the majority of states do not protect TGNC people with regard to discrimination in employment, there have been a number of recent victories in this area. The first victory on this front was an employment discrimination case that ruled that Vandy Beth Glenn, a TGNC woman, was unfairly terminated from her job with the Georgia State Legislature after disclosing her plans to make a social and medical transition (Lambda Legal, 2011). The case cited Title IX, as subsequent cases have done, clearly ruling that discrimination against TGNC people is a form of sex discrimination (see Chapter 4 of this volume for additional discussion of this topic).

Though changes in the interpretation of previously passed laws have been helpful for some people, there is no guarantee that TGNC people will prevail. The effort that is required to bring a lawsuit against an employer is significant (e.g., time, money, emotional support). The psychological consequences of this process can be quite onerous. MHPs are encouraged, therefore, to work with clients who are navigating a legal proceeding by ensuring that the client has a strong support system and engages in adaptive coping techniques.

In addition to supporting TGNC people who are actively pursuing legal remedies to their experiences, MHPs are reminded that they also have a role in working to change public policy. Professional associations (state and national) typically have legislative branches that monitor laws and regulations effecting the profession. One simple way to respond to calls for legislative change is to have people put the phone numbers of elected officials in their cell phone directory, which eliminates the need to find a number when there is urgency to respond (e.g., calling a legislator to advocate for TGNC-affirming laws).

INSURANCE POLICY

Whether a TGNC person can access gender-affirming medical care is greatly dependent on access to financial resources, health insurance coverage, or both. Access to health insurance coverage, in turn, varies depending on many factors, including age, geographical location, and existing laws and policies. Compared with cisgender people, TGNC people are more likely to be without health insurance (Agency for Healthcare Research and Quality, 2011). Survey research suggested that TGNC people of color are most affected by insurance discrimination. One out of every five TGNC people and one out of every three Black TGNC people reported being uninsured in a national survey (Grant et al., 2011).

Recent improved access to health care coverage has resulted from a tremendous amount of lobbying and advocacy by organizations such as the Transgender Law Center, the National Center for Transgender Equality, and the Sylvia Rivera Law Project. Though there have been significant wins for the health care rights of TGNC people, there remain many challenges in access and implementation.

ADVANCEMENTS IN AND BARRIERS TO HEALTH INSURANCE COVERAGE IN THE UNITED STATES

Many TGNC people encounter systemic barriers when attempting to secure health insurance for gender-affirming medical care. Even having access to health insurance coverage does not mean that medical services are affordable, as insurance premiums and copays can be costly. For consumers and patients, the share of costs for medical procedures can be prohibitive, leading TGNC people to avoid or delay seeking necessary treatment (Grant et al., 2011). Therefore, even with health insurance coverage, TGNC people who have the fewest financial resources may still be the least likely to obtain necessary services. Exclusions specific to gender- or transition-related care have negatively impacted TGNC people for decades. Though many of these exclusions have been lifted, there are still barriers in accessing appropriate care. For example, Medicare, which is the main health coverage plan for people over the age of 65 and people with disabilities, had a ban on gender-affirming surgeries for over 30 years (National Center for Transgender Equality, 2016). Although this ban was lifted in May 2014, people with Medicare must nonetheless deal with a great deal of bureaucracy to get the services they need. Requests for surgery are only reviewed on a case-by-case basis, and policy guidelines vary by region and are determined by local Medicare contractors. In addition, as of 2015, there are still few surgeons in the United States who are contracted as Medicare providers and trained in performing these surgeries (Gender Justice League, 2016). This may be the case with other health insurance providers who technically provide coverage but are not contracted with providers who are trained or competent in providing affirmative care to TGNC people.

Another major shift that happened is that, as of January 2016, health insurance companies that insure federal employees and retirees were required to remove blanket exclusions related to TGNC health care (National Center for Transgender Equality, 2016). This was yet another step in removing the barrier of specific health care exclusions. Although the removal of these exclusions is a significant step in reducing the barrier to appropriate care, it does not mean that access is automatically available to all TGNC federal employees.

Though the Affordable Care Act now prohibits insurance carriers from excluding people from coverage on the basis of having preexisting health conditions, some private insurance and self-funded plans may still deny coverage (National Center for Transgender Equality, 2016). Some TGNC people who have been diagnosed with mental health disorders may be denied coverage. This creates a problem in which TGNC people are barred from insurance due to having the very same diagnoses that would allow them to meet medical necessity for the treatment related to these diagnoses. Section 1557, the civil rights provision of the Affordable Care Act, is the first federal civil rights law that explicitly prohibits sex discrimination (including discrimination based on gender identity or expression) in health care (U.S. Department of Health and Human Services, n.d.). Health care settings that receive any form of funding from the U.S. Department of Health and Human Services are required to abide by this law. Though clear mechanisms to enforce this law are still being developed, more health insurance plans have begun to cover gender-affirming health services and complaints may be filed to the Office of Civil Rights by anyone who experiences health care discrimination based on gender identity or expression. As of 2015, at least 10 U.S. states have policies that prohibit exclusions to gender-affirming health care for TGNC people who are state employees.

Determining Medical Necessity

Another issue arises in the determination of who meets criteria for medical necessity and how these criteria are determined. Most insurers now use criteria for the diagnosis of gender dysphoria in the *Diagnostic and Statistical Manual of Mental Disorders, Fifth Edition* (American Psychiatric Association, 2013), and the "Standards of Care for the Health of Transsexual, Transgender, and Gender-Nonconforming People" (7th Version) created by the World Professional Association for Transgender Health (WPATH; Coleman et al., 2012) as a way to determine who is appropriate for medical interventions. However, some of these coverage plans still rely on outdated language and requirements from previous versions of WPATH standards of care with more stringent criteria and even diagnoses that no longer exist, such as gender identity disorder (American Psychiatric Association, 2000; World Health Organization, 2016). As the experience of being TGNC varies widely and is dependent on many contextual factors, such as cultural background and geographical region, these criteria may be very limiting to those people who fit these criteria. This may have a negative impact on those who do not fit a more traditional medicalized narrative (Vipond, 2015), such as people of color and people with nonbinary identities (Harrison, Grant, & Herman, 2012).

What constitutes medically necessary transition-related care (e.g., the specific services or procedures that are included) also varies greatly based on the insurance plan, but current coverage exclusions most negatively impact TGNC women and others on the trans feminine spectrum. For example, chest reconstruction surgeries for trans men or others on the TGNC masculine spectrum are covered far more often than breast augmentation for trans women or those on the trans feminine spectrum. Many insurance companies categorize these procedures as elective or cosmetic, despite the existence of significant gender dysphoria and the fact that the American Medical Association has rejected classifying transition-related care as cosmetic (Cray & Baker, 2012). There has been a recent push in some states to stop covering chest reconstruction for trans masculine people because doing so would require them to also cover breast augmentation for trans feminine people with new nondiscrimination protections (A. Mangubat, personal communication, December 29, 2015).

Aside from gender- or transition-related care, TGNC people need preventative and routine medical care as others do. There is a need for routine health screening based on the organ systems or body parts that are present (regardless of one's gender identity). TGNC men may be denied obstetric or gynecological services that are assumed to be only necessary for women. Many of these procedures are designated for people of a certain gender, therefore making it inaccessible for TGNC people who need them. Some of these concerns are related to electronic medical records systems not accurately reflecting the needs of TGNC people when solely based on gender marker designations (Deutsch & Buchholz, 2015).

Gaining Access to Care

Competent health care is a basic human right. In the past 10 years there have been a number of changes that make health care more accessible. As of the writing of this book, the U.S. Department of Health and Human Services is reviewing a proposed rule that would make it illegal to discriminate in health care. It is too soon to tell if the rule will be enacted. If it is, much of the discrimination that TGNC people experience, including insurance denials, will be addressed. Until that happens, TGNC people are encouraged to appeal any adverse health care decision made by their insurance company. According to the Gender Justice League, a denial must be appealed as many as three times before a favorable decision will be reached (D. Askini, personal communication, August 19, 2015). This favorable decision comes after the third appeal because an outside review of the denial is made after the first two internal decisions.

Environmental Access Issues: Restrooms and Other Sex-Segregated Facilities

Many TGNC people encounter barriers on a day-to-day basis when faced with sex-segregated facilities in their environments. The difficulties that TGNC people face because of these barriers may vary from an everyday hassle or annoyance to severe harm, violence, or threats to safety. Barriers to inclusive environments include sex-segregated restrooms, locker rooms, dormitories, health care facilities, inpatient facilities, prisons, and detention centers. The following is a brief review of some of the ongoing challenges to environmental inclusivity and safety.

RESTROOM ACCESSIBILITY

Using a public restroom or locker room can be very stressful for TGNC people. Most public restrooms are designated for either women or men, creating a forced binary in restroom choice (American Psychological Association, 2015). Although some TGNC people may have passing privilege (Serano, 2013) or have had medical procedures (i.e., surgeries) that allow them to use gendered restrooms with relative ease or comfort, many TGNC people find this experience challenging and even dangerous (Herman, 2013; Transgender Law Center, 2005). Though there are now laws in some states and local jurisdiction that protect the rights of TGNC individuals in using restrooms of their choice (i.e., the restroom that corresponds to one's own sense of gender identity, not necessarily to sex assigned at birth), this does not mean that all restrooms are automatically a safe and inclusive space. Recently, a number of local jurisdictions have passed laws requiring businesses and city buildings to provide "all gender" restrooms (Transgender Law Center, 2016).

MHPs can advocate for all-gender or gender-neutral restrooms in their workplaces or at event spaces. One example of this is that the American Psychological Association implemented all-gender restrooms at its annual convention for the first time in 2014. In counseling centers, psychologists may advocate for all-gender restrooms so that it may be more accessible for TGNC clients to seek mental health services. Advocacy in this form may serve not only to provide a more inclusive, accessible space for TGNC people, but it may also be an intervention to raise awareness about restroom needs and safety for all people. MHPs can also advocate for the need to create gender-neutral restrooms in those situations where the restroom is designed for one person and has a lock on the door.

JAILS, PRISONS, AND DETENTION CENTERS

Criminal justice systems have sex-segregated facilities that create barriers to respectful and appropriate treatment of TGNC individuals (Bassichis, 2007). Jails, prisons, and detention centers are separated into men's and women's units. TGNC people's gender identities are not always respected, and they may be forced to reside in facilities corresponding to their sex assigned at birth. Many TGNC prisoners report physical and sexual assault, sometimes perpetrated by corrections officers, with rates being much higher for Black TGNC prisoners (Grant et al., 2011). The Prison Rape Elimination Act, passed in 2003, allowed for research on the extent of the incidence of rape in prisons at the federal, state, and local levels (National PREA Resource Center, 2015). Another serious obstacle that incarcerated TGNC people often face is lack of access to health care, including transition-related care. Many TGNC people report being denied health care services, including routine and preventative care as well as transition-related care such as hormones (Grant et al., 2011).

Efforts are being made at federal level to address some of these issues in prisons; however, these concerns are not being addressed in many county or local jails. MHPs in prisons, jails, and other facilities within the criminal justice system can educate other staff and personnel about fair, appropriate, and respectful treatment of TGNC people to reduce health disparities for those who are incarcerated (Glezer, McNiel, & Binder, 2013; Merksamer, 2011). The film *Cruel and Unusual* (Baus, Williams, & Hunt, 2006) highlights many of the important issues that need to be addressed within prison systems.

HOMELESS SHELTERS

TGNC people who are homeless or marginally housed face barriers when seeking services. Shelter systems within the United States are sex-segregated, making it difficult for TGNC people to find an appropriate space if they deviate or are perceived as deviating from expectations of sex assigned at birth. This poses huge risks to safety for people in a vulnerable state (Mottet & Ohle, 2003). In many cases, TGNC people are asked to provide identity documentation, and gender markers on this documentation determines placement in a shelter facility. This requirement can be a major barrier for homeless TGNC people in finding safe spaces to sleep and reside. MHPs working within these settings are encouraged to advocate for policies that do not require identity documentation but rather rely on self-identification.

CASE VIGNETTE

Breanna is a 7-year-old, White TGNC girl. She is a second grader at a public elementary school. At the start of the school year Breanna's parents relocated her to this new school. Her parents have long supported Breanna's expressed gender identity and felt it would be best, as Breanna makes a social transition, to start over at a new school.

Breanna and her parents met with school officials prior to the start of the school year and were assured that the school had policies in place that would protect Breanna from bullying and harassment. Unbeknownst to her parents, however, the school principal accepted a job in another district prior to the start of the school year. All of the policies that had been in place were removed, and Breanna is experiencing significant distress and is refusing to go to school.

Breanna confided that she is being required to use the restroom in the nurse's office, her teacher is unwilling to use the correct names and pronouns, and fellow students are bullying her on the playground and in the classroom. Breanna's parents were very upset by this turn of events and would like support in addressing the school administration. The role of the MHP in this case seems quite clear. In addition to working with the emotional distress that Breanna and her parents are facing, the MHP can work directly with school administrators to determine the openness to reestablish the TGNC-affirmative policies. These will include policies addressing the right to use a restroom that is consistent with Breanna's expressed gender (New York City Department of Education, 2015). Further, it will include a zero-tolerance policy for bullying and harassment (Gay, Lesbian & Straight Education Network, 2015). MHPs can also assist by providing basic training about TGNC-affirmative interactions in the classroom. This type of advocacy can work to address the root of this type of discriminative practice with TGNC children and adolescents.

The Future of Advocacy in Counseling With TGNC Clients and Communities

As the concerns of TGNC people shift and evolve over the changing sociocultural landscape, the role of MHPs in advocating for social justice may also need to shift. We asked a number of MHPs who work with TGNC people to answer the question of what the future of advocacy is in working with TGNC people and communities. The following responses provide some examples of the ways in which MHPs envision the important role of advocacy in TGNC counseling and where TGNC advocacy may evolve in the future for MHPs. Tharyn Grant, LCSW, an MHP and person of color in independent practice in Atlanta, Georgia stated,

> As long as suicide, homelessness, poverty, and discrimination remain a high risk for transgender people, counseling and advocacy cannot be mutually exclusive concepts. I have always alluded to these issues as public health concerns, especially as they continue to affect and further marginalize both communities of color and young people. Overlapping advocacy in counseling with these groups is providing a sound culturally competent service where clients then become empowered to advocate for themselves through treatment. As a social worker, this is the most important service one can provide for clients and families. (T. Grant, personal communication, September 21, 2015)

Scott Leibowitz, a White, cisgender male psychiatrist at Children's Hospital in Chicago, Illinois, reported the following in relation to the future of advocacy in counseling TGNC youth:

My thoughts on the future of advocacy efforts with transgender youth is a challenging task because. . . . There is no one "defined" or "correct" way to live as a transgender person, and when the word is used, society makes automatic assumptions that it defines the essence of the person who identifies in that way. This assumption negates the fact that every single human being has a connection between their gender assigned at birth and their gender identity, which is what I believe needs to be addressed as the root of where all health disparities lie for transgender individuals and youth in particular. . . . Appreciating this concept is not only important for the majority of cisgender individuals in society who are transphobic, but also for the transgender adolescents we serve. . . . I believe that it is [the] healthcare professionals' appreciation that we all have a gender identity, which for some matches [their] body while for others it doesn't—that will give transgender adolescents a fighting start to live as who they are. (S. Leibowitz, personal communication, September 23, 2015)

Stephanie Luz Hernandez, a Latina trans woman MHP intern in Oakland, California, stated,

There is a deep wound between the trans community and the mental health institution that has its roots in Western colonialism. In this country, trans people, and especially trans people of color have had to fight for legitimacy, respect, and fundamental rights and autonomy to make informed decisions that effect [sic] their health and that of their communities. I believe the future of advocacy in counseling with trans folks is helping to move away from a system of over pathologization of trans bodies and identities that has caused institutional trauma to our community, and move toward a model of gender affirming and integrated transgender health and wellness. This trauma-informed model of care focuses on trans individual's resiliency and self-empowerment, and also trusts trans people to be experts on their own lived experience. By using anti-oppressive practices in counseling, clinicians can stop reducing clients to objects of inquiry and make room for more authentic narratives without the fear of gatekeeping and reduced access to medically necessary and life-saving gender affirming procedures. Lastly, how do we get more trans clinicians and clinicians of color providing services that reflect the community that they are serving? There are many institutional barriers that need to be addressed, including lack of resources for access to higher education, the work-for-free culture that surrounds the licensure process, and micro aggressions [sic] from the clinical training environments that make it difficult for marginalized and disenfranchised communities to advance in these positions. (S. Hernandez, personal communication, September 22, 2015)

These first-person perspectives represent the cutting edge of advocacy for TGNC people, and it remains easy to identify that there is still a great deal of work that needs to be done in the area of advocacy and social justice. MHPs are encouraged to understand the ways that their privilege can be used to dismantle the oppression of others.

Chapter Summary

Research has long shown that TGNC people experience extensive discrimination (Grant et al., 2011). MHPs can play a pivotal role in addressing the psychological concerns that result from this discrimination through advocacy. In addition to clinical work, MHPs can play an active role developing and changing policies at local, state, and national levels. Even with the advancements in policy over the past decade, there are still many areas where TGNC people have little to no protection. TGNC people with intersecting or gender nonconforming identities remain at elevated risk for discrimination and violence. The work by MHPs to make this world safer for TGNC people will also help to make the world safer for all people.

References

Agency for Healthcare Research and Quality. (2011). *National healthcare disparities report.* Retrieved from http://archive.ahrq.gov/research/findings/nhqrdr/nhqrdr11/qrdr11.html

American Psychiatric Association. (2000). *Diagnostic and statistical manual of mental disorders* (4th ed., text revision). Arlington, VA: Author.

American Psychiatric Association. (2013). *Diagnostic and statistical manual of mental disorders* (5th ed.). Arlington, VA: Author.

American Psychological Association. (2015). Guidelines for psychological practice with transgender and gender nonconforming people. *American Psychologist, 70,* 832–864. http://dx.doi.org/10.1037/a0039906

Bassichis, D. M. (2007). *"It's war in here": A report on the treatment of transgender and intersex people in New York state men's prisons.* Retrieved from http://srlp.org/wp-content/uploads/2012/08/WarinHere042007.pdf

Baus, J., Williams, R., & Hunt, D. (Directors). (2006). *Cruel & unusual* [Motion picture]. United States: Alluvial Filmworks.

Coleman, E., Bockting, W., Botzer, M., Cohen-Kettenis, P., DeCuypere, G., Feldman, J., . . . Zucker, K. (2012). Standards of care for the health of transsexual, transgender, and gender-nonconforming people, 7th version. *International Journal of Transgenderism, 13,* 165–232. http://dx.doi.org/10.1080/15532739.2011.700873

Cray, A., & Baker, K. (2012). *FAQ: Health insurance needs for transgender Americans.* Retrieved from Center for American Progress website: https://www.americanprogress.org/wp-content/uploads/2012/10/TransgenderHealth.pdf

Deutsch, M. B., & Buchholz, D. (2015). Electronic health records and transgender patients—practical recommendations for the collection of gender identity data. *Journal of General Internal Medicine, 30,* 843–847. http://dx.doi.org/10.1007/s11606-014-3148-7

Fouad, N. A., Gerstein, L. H., & Toporek, R. L. (2006). Social justice and counseling in context. In R. L. Toporek, L. H. Gerstein, N. A. Fouad, G. Roysicar, & T. Israel (Eds.), *Handbook for social justice in counseling psychology* (pp. 1–15). Thousand Oaks, CA: Sage.

Gay, Lesbian & Straight Education Network. (2015). *Model laws & policies.* Retrieved from http://www.glsen.org/article/model-laws-policies

Gender Justice League. (2016). *Transform health project.* Retrieved from http://www.genderjusticeleague.org/transform-health-project/

Glezer, A., McNiel, D. E., & Binder, R. L. (2013). Transgendered and incarcerated: A review of the literature, current policies and laws, and ethics. *Journal of the American Academy of Psychiatry and the Law, 41,* 551–559.

Grant, J. M., Mottet, L. A., Tanis, J., Harrison, J., Herman, J. L., & Keisling, M. (2011). *Injustice at every turn: A report of the national transgender discrimination survey.* Retrieved from http://endtransdiscrimination.org/PDFs/NTDS_Report.pdf

Harrison, J., Grant, J., & Herman, J. L. (2012). A gender not listed here: Genderqueers, gender rebels and otherwise in the National Transgender Discrimination Study. *LGBT Policy Journal at the Harvard Kennedy School, 2,* 13–24. Retrieved from http://www.thetaskforce.org/static_html/downloads/reports/reports/gender_not_listed_here.pdf

Herman, J. L. (2013). Gendered restrooms and minority stress: The public regulation of gender and its impact on transgender people's lives. *Journal of Public Management & Social Policy, 19,* 65–80.

Lambda Legal. (2011). *Glenn v. Brumby et al.* Retrieved from http://www.lambdalegal.org/in-court/cases/glenn-v-brumby-et-al

Lewis, J., Arnold, M., House, R., & Toporek, R. (2003). *Advocacy competencies.* Retrieved from American Counseling Association website: http://www.counseling.org/Publications/

Merksamer, J. (2011). *A place of respect: A guide for group care facilities serving transgender and gender non-conforming youth.* San Francisco, CA: National Center for Lesbian Rights & New York, NY: Sylvia Rivera Law Project.

Mottet, L., & Ohle, J. M. (2003). *Transitioning our shelters.* Washington, DC: National Gay and Lesbian Task Force Policy Institute and National Coalition for the Homeless.

National Center for Transgender Equality. (2016). *Know your rights: Medicare.* Retrieved from http://www.transequality.org/know-your-rights/medicare

National Coalition of Anti-Violence Programs. (2011). *Hate violence against lesbian, gay, bisexual, transgender, queer, and HIV-affected communities in the United States in 2011: A report from the National Coalition of Anti-Violence Programs.* Retrieved from http://avp.org/storage/documents/Reports/2012_NCAVP_2011_HV_Report.pdf

National PREA Resource Center. (2015). *Prison rape elimination act.* Retrieved from http://www.prearesourcecenter.org/about/prison-rape-elimination-act-prea

New York City Department of Education. (2015). *Transgender student guidelines.* Retrieved from http://schools.nyc.gov/RulesPolicies/TransgenderStudentGuidelines/default.htm

Ratts, M., DeKruyf, L., & Chen-Hayes, S. (2007). The ACA advocacy competencies: A social justice advocacy framework for professional school counselors. *Professional School Counseling, 11,* 90–97. http://dx.doi.org/10.5330/PSC.n.2010-11.90

Ratts, M. J., & Hutchins, A. M. (2009). ACA advocacy competencies: Social justice advocacy at the client/student level. *Journal of Counseling & Development, 87,* 269–275. http://dx.doi.org/10.1002/j.1556-6678.2009.tb00106.x

Serano, J. (2013). *Excluded: Making feminist and queer movements more inclusive.* Berkeley, CA: Seal Press.

Transgender Law Center. (2005). *Peeing in peace: A resource guide for transgender activists and allies.* San Francisco, CA: Author. Retrieved from http://transgenderlawcenter.org/issues/public-accomodations/peeing-in-peace

Transgender Law Center. (2016). *Welcoming the all-gender restroom "revolution".* Retrieved from http://transgenderlawcenter.org/archives/12358?utm_source=January+2016+enewsletter+-+1.20.16&utm_campaign=February+2015+Newsletter&utm_medium=email

U.S. Department of Health and Human Services. (n.d.). *Fact sheet: Non-discrimination in health programs and activities proposed rule.* Retrieved from http://www.hhs.gov/ocr/civilrights/understanding/section1557/nprmsummary.html

Vipond, E. (2015). Resisting transnormativity: Challenging the medicalization and regulation of trans bodies. *Theory in Action, 8,* 21–44. http://dx.doi.org/10.3798/tia.1937-0237.15008

World Health Organization. (2016). *ICD-10 Version: 2016: F64 Gender Identity Disorders.* Retrieved from http://apps.who.int/classifications/icd10/browse/2016/en#/F64

Wynn, R., & West-Olatunji, C. (2009). Use of culture-centered counseling theory with ethnically diverse LGBT clients. *Journal of LGBT Issues in Counseling, 3,* 198–214. http://dx.doi.org/10.1080/15538600903317218

Ziegler, K. R., & Rasul, N. (2014). Race, ethnicity, and culture. In L. Erickson-Schroth (Ed.), *Trans bodies, trans selves: A resource for the transgender community* (pp. 24–39). New York, NY: Oxford University.

Index

About the Editors

Anneliese A. Singh, PhD, is an associate professor at The University of Georgia and cofounder of the Georgia Safe Schools Coalition and Trans Resilience Project. Her research, practice, and advocacy have centered on the resilience of transgender and gender nonconforming (TGNC) people, particularly TGNC people of color and youth. She co-led the American Psychological Association Task Force developing psychological practice guidelines with TGNC clients, and she helped develop the American Counseling Association Competencies for Counseling Transgender Clients. Dr. Singh is a multiracial, South Asian, Sikh American. She identifies as gender fluid with cisgender privilege. She passionately works for and believes in justice for all sentient beings.

lore m. dickey, PhD, is an assistant professor in the Department of Psychology and Behavioral Sciences at Louisiana Tech University. He has recently assumed a position as assistant professor and Director of Training in the Department of Educational Psychology at Northern Arizona University. His doctorate is in counseling psychology from the University of North Dakota, and his postdoctoral health policy fellowship was at the Morehouse School of Medicine in the Satcher Health Leadership Institute. His research has focused on understanding the transgender experience including studies on sexual identity development and non-suicidal self-injury. Dr. dickey served as a cochair for the APA Task Force charged with developing *Guidelines for Psychological Practice With Transgender and Gender Nonconforming People*. He identifies as a White trans man with a lesbian history.